Lecture Notes in Information Systems and Organisation

Volume 7

Series editors

Richard Baskerville, Decatur, USA
Marco De Marco, Roma, Italy
Nancy Pouloudi, Athens, Greece
Paolo Spagnoletti, Roma, Italy
Dov Te'eni, Tel Aviv, Israel
Jan vom Brocke, Vaduz, Liechtenstein
Robert Winter, St. Gallen, Switzerland

For further volumes:
http://www.springer.com/series/11237

Leonardo Caporarello · Beniamino Di Martino
Marcello Martinez
Editors

Smart Organizations
and Smart Artifacts

Fostering Interaction Between People,
Technologies and Processes

 Springer

Editors
Leonardo Caporarello
Bocconi University
Milan
Italy

Marcello Martinez
Second University of Naples
Capua
Italy

Beniamino Di Martino
Second University of Naples "Tor Vergata"
Aversa
Italy

ISSN 2195-4968   ISSN 2195-4976 (electronic)
ISBN 978-3-319-07039-1 ISBN 978-3-319-07040-7 (eBook)
DOI 10.1007/978-3-319-07040-7
Springer Cham Heidelberg New York Dordrecht London

Library of Congress Control Number: 2014939048

Printed on acid-free paper

Springer is part of Springer Science+Business Media (www.springer.com)

Contents

Contributors

Tindara Abbate Dipartimento di Scienze Economiche, Aziendali, Ambientali e Metodologie Quantitative, Università degli Studi di Messina, Messina, Italy

Ignacio Aedo Universidad Carlos III de Madrid, Madrid, Spain

Alba Amato Second University of Naples, Caserta, Italy

Carlo Amendola Università degli Studi di Roma La Sapienza, Roma, Italy

Enrico Angioni University of Cagliari, Cagliari, Italy

Barbara Aquilani Dipartimento di Economia e Impresa, Università degli Studi della Tuscia, Viterbo, Italy

Rocco Aversa Second University of Naples, Caserta, Italy

Carlo Batini Università degli Studi di Milano-Bicocca, Milan, Italy

Peter Bednar School of Computing, University of Portsmouth, Portsmouth, UK

Mirjana Kljajić Borštnar Faculty of Organizational Sciences, University of Maribor, Kranj, Slovenia

Alessio Maria Braccini Dipartimento di Economia e Impresa, Università degli Studi della Tuscia, Viterbo, Italy

Francesca Cabiddu University of Cagliari, Cagliari, Italy

Federico Cabitza Università degli Studi di Milano-Bicocca, Milan, Italy

Davide Maria Calandra DIETI, University of Naples, Federico II, Napoli, Italy

Roberto Candiotto Dipartimento di Studi per l'Economia e l'Impresa, Università del Piemonte Orientale, Novara, Italy

Leonardo Caporarello Department of Industrial and Information Engineering, Second University of Naples, Aversa, Italy

Andrea Carugati School of Business and Social Sciences, Aarhus University, Aarhus, Denmark

Tiziana Catarci Dipartimento di Ingegneria Informatica, Automatica e Gestionale "A. Rubert", Sapienza Università di Roma, Rome, Italy

Qian Chen USTC-CityU Joint Advanced Research Center, Suzhou, China

Francesco Crenca Università degli Studi di Roma La Sapienza, Roma, Italy

Giuseppina Cretella Department of Industrial and Information Engineering, Second University of Naples, Aversa, Italy

Francesco Cutugno DIETI, University of Naples Federico II, Napoli, Italy

Beniamino Di Martino Department of Industrial and Information Engineering, Second University of Naples, Aversa, Italy

Tania Di Mascio Università degli Studi dell'Aquila, L'Aquila, Italy

Paloma Díaz Universidad Carlos III de Madrid, Madrid, Spain

Yael Dubinsky IBM Research—Haifa, Haifa, Israel

Carsten Felden Technische Universität Bergakademie, Freiberg, Germany

Daniela Fogli Università degli Studi di Brescia, Brescia, Italy

Bruno Maria Franceschetti University of Macerata, Macerata, Italy

Matteo Gaeta Dipartimento di Ingegneria dell'Informazione, Ingegneria Elettrica e Matematica Applicata, University of Salerno, Fisciano, SA, Italy

Silvia Gandini Dipartimento di Studi per l'Economia e l'Impresa, Università del Piemonte Orientale, Novara, Italy

Rosella Gennari Libera Università di Bolzano, Bolzano, Italy

Antonio Giangreco IESEG School of Management (LEM-CNRS), Lille, France

Svein Hallsteinsen SINTEF ICT, Oslo, Norway

Geir Horn University of Oslo, Oslo, Norway

Shah Rukh Humayoun Computer Graphics and HCI Group, University of Kaiserslautern, Kaiserslautern, Germany

Claudia Koschtial Technische Universität Bergakademie, Freiberg, Germany

Gregor Lenart Faculty of Organizational Sciences, University of Maribor, Kranj, Slovenia

Zhiyong Liu USTC-CityU Joint Advanced Research Center, Suzhou, China

Tianyi Ma Dipartimento di Ingegneria Industriale e della Informazione, University of Pavia, Pavia, Italy

Ana Malešič Faculty of Organizational Sciences, University of Maribor, Kranj, Slovenia

Marcello Martinez Department of Industrial and Information Engineering, Second University of Naples, Aversa, Italy

Alessandra Melonio Libera Università di Bolzano, Bolzano, Italy

Lapo Mola Department of Business Administration, University of Verona, Verona, Italy

Gianmario Motta Dipartimento di Ingegneria Industriale e della Informazione, University of Pavia, Pavia, Italy

Daniele Novi Dipartimento di Informatica, University of Salerno, Fisciano, SA, Italy

Teresa Onorati Universidad Carlos III de Madrid, Madrid, Spain

Antonio Piccinno Università degli Studi di Bari, Bari, Italy

Federico Pigni Grenoble Ecole de Management, Grenoble, France

Rossella Piscopo Dipartimento di Ingegneria dell'Informazione, Ingegneria Elettrica e Matematica Applicata, University of Salerno, Fisciano, SA, Italy

Andreja Pucihar Faculty of Organizational Sciences, University of Maribor, Kranj, Slovenia

Elisabetta Raguseo Politecnico di Torino, Turin, Italy

Luigi Rarità Dipartimento di Ingegneria dell'Informazione, Ingegneria Elettrica e Matematica Applicata, University of Salerno, Fisciano, SA, Italy

Francesca Ricciardi Catholic University of Milan, Milan, Italy

Marco Romano Universidad Carlos III de Madrid, Madrid, Spain

Cecilia Rossignoli State University of Verona, Verona, Italy

Daniele Sacco Dipartimento di Ingegneria Industriale e della Informazione, University of Pavia, Pavia, Italy

Moufida Sadok Higher Institute of Technological Studies in Communications in Tunis, Tunis, Tunisia

Marco Scialdone Second University of Naples, Caserta, Italy

Ada Scupola Department of Communication, Business and Information Technologies, Roskilde University, Roskilde, Denmark

Vasilena Shiderova Technical University of Sofia, Sofia, Bulgaria

Lianlian Song USTC-CityU Joint Advanced Research Center, Suzhou, China

Francesca Spagnoli Università degli Studi di Roma La Sapienza, Roma, Italy

Laura Tarantino Università degli Studi dell'Aquila, L'Aquila, Italy

Luigi Trevisant Dipartimento di Ingegneria dell'Informazione, Ingegneria Elettrica e Matematica Applicata, Centro di Eccellenza su Metodi e Sistemi per Aziende Competitive, University of Salerno, Fisciano, SA, Italy

Geoffrey Tso City University of Hong Kong, Hong Kong, China

Salvatore Venticinque Second University of Naples, Caserta, Italy

Gianluigi Viscusi EPFL-CDM-CSI, Lausanne, Switzerland

Claudio Vitari Grenoble Ecole de Management, Grenoble, France

Linlin You Dipartimento di Ingegneria Industriale e della Informazione, University of Pavia, Pavia, Italy

Alessandro Zardini State University of Verona, Verona, Italy

Composing and Orchestrating the Smart Artifacts: Technological and Organizational Challenges

**Leonardo Caporarello, Beniamino Di Martino
and Marcello Martinez**

The 2013 ItAIS[1] tenth Conference, from which this book is originated, has taken place as pre-event of the ICIS[2] 2013 that was held in Italy for first time. The 2013 ItAIS has attracted contributions far beyond the Italian IS community. In fact, more than 200 authors, from four continents, have contributed to the Conference, whose 100 papers were selected for presentation at the Conference by means of a double-blind review process. Authors do consider ItAIS as a reference annual event where to share and discuss their research-in-progress projects, and their research agenda, and to get very useful feedback based on the different background and perspectives of the Conference participants. The 15 tracks have addressed many aspects of the main Conference theme, that is "Empowering society through digital innovation".

Contributions included in this book have been presented by researchers working in different disciplines, such as: organization, management, human-computer interaction, IS design, and IS development. Moreover, as confirmation of the international standing of the ItAIS Conference and the relevance of the theme, the opening speech—given by Prof. Sambamurthy, an outstanding scholar of the international IS community—has highlighted how digital innovations and technologies are influencing, or determining, the evolution of the socio-economical society.

As a result of the high interest in the Conference, and given the quality of some contributions, it has been decided to organize such contributions in a three-book publication. Each of the three books is focused on a specific sub-theme, and in particular this book is focused on "Smart organizations and Smart artifacts—fostering interaction between people, technology and processes", and collects 23

---

[1] ItAIS is the Italian Chapter of the Association for Information Systems, www.aisnet.org.
[2] ICIS is the International Conference on Information Systems, www.aisnet.org.

L. Caporarello (✉) · B. Di Martino · M. Martinez
Department of Industrial and Information Engineering, Second University of Naples, Aversa, Italy
e-mail: leonardo.caporarello@unibocconi.it

L. Caporarello et al. (eds.), *Smart Organizations and Smart Artifacts*,
Lecture Notes in Information Systems and Organisation 7,
DOI: 10.1007/978-3-319-07040-7_1,
© Springer International Publishing Switzerland 2014

chapters other than this one. This paper is structured in two sections, introduced by this opening paragraph. The Sect. 1, titled as "Smart artifacts in the today environment", intends to give an overview about the relevance of smart artifacts in today organizational environment. The Sect. 2, titled as "The red tape among the all contributions", briefly introduces the papers' contributions.

The book is the result of a teamwork project where many people have actively contributed, and we are grateful to all the Authors, to the Conference Chairs and Committee members, to the members of the Editorial Board, to the Reviewers for their passion and competence.

Finally, we would like to thank all the Series Editors, and in particular Paolo Spagnoletti for his continuous and valuable support.

1 Smart Artifacts in the Today Environment

Nowadays, successful organizations are those able to evolve according to the dynamic and continuously changing of the social and economic environment, which is moreover characterized by the pervasiveness of technology.

In turn, being able to evolve requires flexibility and adaptability. In other words, organizations need to be "smart".

Formally, a smart organization is able to both explore and exploit knowledge in response to opportunities of the digital age [1]. Following this definition, it is possible to highlight two main characteristics of smart organizations: being internetworked, and knowledge-driven. These two characteristics are interconnected.

Moreover, internetwork is, in turn, a facilitator of knowledge creation. In fact, internetworking represents a natural environment for fostering knowledge creation, and innovation, which is fundamental for organizations to succeed.

Following, internetworking not only refers to the interrelations between materials and resources, but also interrelations among people and between organizations [2]. Defining the right set of connections between people and organizations determines the concept of internetworked economy.

The creation and development of knowledge in a internetworked context require the capacity to collaborate in a even more often virtual environment. Thus, collaboration and virtual environment are two enablers of smart organizations.

It is well known as collaborating in a virtual environment—or, in other words, being smart—can allow pursuing several advantages, e.g. resource optimization, exploitation of synergies, increasing the mass of capital investment [3].

Although these mentioned advantages and the long discussion in literature about the necessity for organizations to be a proactive part of the internetworked economy (e.g. [4, 5]), their real capacity to adapt to the environment within which they evolve is still an open issue.

In order to support the understanding of this issue, we could review the role of the environment which smart organizations live in. Given its evolving dynamics, also the environment should be reframed as "smart environment". Consequently, we can state that smart organizations are living in a smart environment [6] where the level and quality of interactions and the behavior of people are essential constituents.

In this context two trends are mainly contributing to the creation of a smart environment.

The first trend is the continuous development of miniaturized technological devices or artifacts that are permeating the environment. The second trend is the increasing request of functionalities of such devices in supporting and enhancing the quality of interaction and behavior.

Thus, also artifacts can be defined as "smart artifacts". A smart artifact can be defined as a combination of Internet and emerging technologies—such as near-field communication, real-time localization, and embedded sensors—that are able to understand and react to their environment [7].

Thus, these artifacts can trace, log, sense, and interpret what's going on in the environment, then are able to act on their own, to intercommunicate with each other, to exchange information with people, and enabling internetworked organizations.

The main characteristics of smart artifacts are:

- To understand events and human activities within and outside their environment;
- To interpret such understanding in order to propose, and in some cases autonomously executing, actions;
- To interact with other artifacts and persons.

A smart artifact aims to enhance the relationships among members of an eventually distributed team, to foster the creation of the social identity, to support collaboration opportunities, and both formal and informal communications [6].

The user involvement also in the design stage of environment-aware systems can make smart artifacts even more successful [8].

There are two types of smart artifacts: systems-oriented, and people-oriented. Both types of systems aim to make the "space" where individuals work able to understand the environment, and consequently to take or suggest actions that can be taken.

In particular, system-oriented artifacts aim to make the "space" able to self-direct actions based on the previous collected information.

A system-oriented artifact is designed to gather and process data and information about persons and their activities (e.g. what they have done) situated within its borders, and actively takes actions without the intervention of human beings. In a smart home, for example, the control system can adjust the heating system or closing windows according to the weather conditions.

A people-oriented artifact is designed to empower and inform users to take responsible actions. So, this type of smart artifacts collects and aggregates data—same as the previous type—and based on that they make suggestions to people about what actions can be performed. In a smart office, for example, the knowledge system can inform members working on same project or knowledge domain about documents can be useful for their job.

From these considerations, it emerges as smart artifacts can extend the awareness about the physical and social environment also through interaction processes between objects and people. Such extended level of awareness can, in turn, foster changes in organizational and people's behaviors.

Moreover, interaction processes are a key success factor for any successful teams [9]. So, as many organizations are increasingly organizing work around teams, smart artifacts can play the role of facilitator of team processes.

This facilitating role is particularly amplified with reference to virtual teams, where the communication and interaction dynamics are even more sensitive for the success of the team [10, 11].

How can smart artifacts support smart organizations to succeed in their smart environment? Let's start formalizing the main three key success factors of smart organizations, that are: those that support organizations to understand its environment; those that allow organizations to properly manage resources; those that foster the organization to achieve its goals [12].

According to the literature, smart organizations do perform better than "not so smart" [12].

What is the contribution of smart artifacts to pursue these three main principles of smart organizations?

Now, based on their capability to gather and analyze data and information, smart artifacts can contribute to each of the three key success factors as follows:

- First factor—understanding the environment: reducing information asymmetry, and consequently mitigating of the risk related to uncertainty, and then facilitating the adoption of a system thinking approach;
- Second factor—managing resources: enhancing the organizational alignment, facilitating the open information flow, and as a consequence informing and increasing the quality and effectiveness of decision making processes;
- Third factor—achieving organizational goals: fostering the creation and dissemination of the organizational culture, helping organizations to be creative and innovative, and supporting continuous learning processes.

2 The Red Tape Among the All Contributions

Technologies are pervasive, and thanks to their capability to process massive data in real-time, new business opportunities emerge. A perspective on these potential opportunities is discussed by Claudio Vitari and Federico Pigni from Grenoble Ecole de Management, in "DDGS Affordances for Value Creation", that analyzes the dynamic interactions between people, organizations, and artifacts.

Andrea Carugati from Aarhus University, Lapo Mola from University of Verona and Antonio Giangreco from Ieseg School of Management also contribute, with their work "The Role of IT in Organizational Networks, Individual Networks, and in Bridging these Two Levels", to the understanding the role of technological artifacts in bridging the individual practices in the context of organizational networks.

A specific focus on the relation between organizations and customers is then provided in "Corporate Customership: the Core Components of the Relationship Between Firm and Customer" by Enrico Angioni and Francesca Cabiddu from University of Cagliari, that clarifies the core components of this relationship.

A particular type of organization-customer relationship is given within the emergency industry where the relationship is between emergency organizations and citizens, and is explored in "EmergenSYS: Mobile Technologies as Support for Emergency Management" by Teresa Onorati, Ignacio Aedo, Marco Romano and Paloma Díaz from Universidad Carlos III de Madrid. In fact, as discussed by, the authors, the analysis and integration of data and information can contribute to increase awareness and share information within citizens' communities about risks related to unexpected events, i.e. natural emergencies, and to support emergency agencies to better respond to these unexpected events.

Moreover, emergency agency, and generally public administrations, can benefit from the use of cloud-based artifacts with the purpose to increase the gathering and distribution of information to citizens' communities. This is phenomenon is referred as "g-Cloud", and it is the topic of "The Economic and Legal Perspectives of Cloud Computing in Italian Public Administration and a Roadmap to the Adoption of g-Cloud in Italy" by Francesca Spagnoli, Carlo Amendola and Francesco Crenca from Università La Sapienza di Roma, with a particular focus on the economic and legal perspective in the Italian context. A different perspective on the same topic is provided by Roberto Candiotto and Silvia Gandini from Università del Piemonte Orientale in "Virtual Organization in the Cloud: the Case of a Web Self-Service Portal", which highlights the main organizational characteristic of a Cloud self-service portal, and its coherence with the main business drivers of Cloud market.

Although the increasing number of adoption of cloud-based solutions in the last few years, by both public and private sectors, it seems several difficult and issues still exist. Giuseppina Cretella and Beniamino Di Martino from the Second University of Naples propose an overview of these applications, analyzing some pros and cons, in "An Overview of Approaches for the Migration of Applications to the Cloud".

So, in this context of real-time and online massive data processing, the organizational capability to measure and evaluate of the value of information is a key factor. Gianluigi Viscusi from École Polytechnique Fédérale De Lausanne and Carlo Batini from Università degli Studi di Milano-Bicocca proposes a multidisciplinary approach to the concept of information value that, according to their paper "Digital Information Asset Evaluation: Characteristics and Dimensions", encompasses information quality, structure, infrastructure and diffusion.

The generation of this value also depends on the active role of the CIO/IT manager. Given the context as described above, they are required to outstand in one particular area, that is the relational capability. A deep discussion about this capability, together with 15 others, is on "Key Capabilities of CIOs and IT Managers for Strategic Competitive Advantage: a Qualitative Field Research" by Cecilia Rossignoli and Alessandro Zardini from University of Verona and Francesca Ricciardi from Catholic University of Milan. Referring to the concept of capabilities, Elisabetta Raguseo from Politecnico di Torino and Claudio Vitari from Grenoble Ecole de Management discuss on how digital data genesis dynamic capability can offer to organizations a higher-level performance in "The Development of the DDG-Capability in Firms: an Evaluation of its Impact on Firm Financial Performance".

Being capable to effectively use smart artifacts does not matter only to CIO/IT managers, but to all the organizational members. As we know, smart artifacts can represent a tool for fostering innovation processes, as discussed by Barbara Aquilani and Alessio Maria Braccini from Università degli Studi della Tuscia and Tindara Abbate from Università degli Studi di Messina. In "Ideas Sharing Through ICT in Innovation Processes: a Design Theory for Open Innovation Platforms" they present in particular some web-based platforms' components necessary to support the open innovation approach.

With this regard, "Delivering Knowledge to the Mobile Enterprise: Implementation Solutions for a Mobile Business Intelligence", by Gianmario Motta, Tianyi Ma, Linlin You and Daniele Sacco from University of Pavia, discusses the implementation of a particular smart artifact, that is a mobile business intelligence system, in a customer care company, and then presents some benefits given by these systems generalized at the SMEs level.

Other papers offer a discussion about the applications of smart artifacts in other domains, such as consumption of energy, and psychological analysis, and financial context. Specifically, as explored by Amato et al. from the Second University of Naples, SINTEF ICT and University of Oslo, in "Software Agents for Collaborating Smart Solar-powered Micro-grids", technology could be applied for gathering and processing real time information on energy consumption for domestic or business use, supporting citizens to use energy when and how necessary only. In "AutoMyDe: a Detector for Pupil Dilation in Cognitive Load Measurement", authors Davide Maria Calandra and Francesco Cutugno from University Federico II of Naples analyze, with also the support of a case study, the application of smart artifacts as a tool for measuring and evaluating the mental effort in human-computer interaction processes.

Smart artifacts can positively contribute for integration of financial information between organizations living in different countries, that may have different legal and financial requirements. Claudia Koschtial and Carsten Felden from Technische Universität Bergakademie and Bruno Maria Franceschetti from University of Macerata present in "Providing a Method for Supporting the Decision Making about a Meaningful XBRL Implementation According to the Specific Situation of an Organization" a methodology to support the decision process for the adoption of a technological standard to support such integration of information.

The designing of successfully smart artifacts require specific competences and expertise, as discussed by Gaeta et al. from University of Salerno in "A Knowledge Management Strategy to Identify an Expert in Enterprise" that presents a structured path to support the search for these expertise, and the effective involvement of the end-user perspective.

Experts and designer of smart artifacts are well aware about the relevance of the end-user perspective as a key success factor for their adoption, where the feedback represents a relevant source of information for the designing stage, as discussed by Shah Rukh Humayoun from University of Kaiserslautern, Yael Dubinsky from IBM Research—Haifa and Tiziana Catarci from Università La Sapienza di Roma in "User Evaluation Support through Development Environment for Agile Software Teams".

With this respect, the paper "Each to His Own: Distinguishing Activities, Roles and Artifacts in EUD Practices", by Federico Cabitza from Università degli Studi di Milano-Bicocca, Daniela Fogli from Università degli Studi di Brescia and Antonio Piccinno from Università degli Studi di Bari, underlines three complementary important notions of end-user development, namely activities, roles, and artifacts, that are useful for enhancing the user involvement into the development process. Moreover, Song et al. from USTC-CityU Joint Advanced Research Center and City University of Hong Kong discuss two metrics in "Understanding User Visiting Behavior and Web Design: Applying Simultaneous Choice Model to Content Arrangement": utility loss and compensating time, that are constructed using the selected utility model to facilitate the designing stage.

Using a socio-technical approach improves the organizational understanding of their job practices and as a consequence, the organizational sustainability, as discussed by Peter Bednar from University of Portsmouth, Moufida Sadok from Higher Institute of Technological Studies in Communications in Tunis, and Vasilena Shiderova from Technical University of Sofia, in "Socio-Technical Toolbox for Business Analysis in practice". Consistently, Ada Scupola from Roskilde University provides in "Guidelines for User Driven Service and E-Service Innovations" a set of guidelines to support the designing of service innovation by involving the user perspective.

Designers of smart artifacts are also facing new challenges related to the generational effect. With respect to these challenges, Di Mascio et al. from Università degli Studi dell'Aquila and Libera Università di Bolzano present in "Engaging "New Users" into Design Activities: the TERENCE Experience with Children" some results of a project aimed at developing a technology enhanced learning system for improving text comprehension in children under 12 years old.

The paper "User-centered Design of a Web-Based Platform for the Sustainable Development of Tourism Services in a Living Lab Context", by Pucihar et al. from University of Maribor, presents some processes and experiences of the user-centered design of a web-based platform in a specific application domain, that is the sustainable development of tourism services.

References

1. Filos, E.: Smart organizations in the digital age. In: Mezgár, I. (ed.) Integration of Information and Communication Technologies in Smart Organizations. Idea Group, Hershey (2006)
2. Levine, R., Locke, C., Searls, D., Weinberger, D.: The Cluetrain Manifesto. The End of Business as Usual. Perseus, Cambridge (2000)
3. Doz, Y.L., Hamel, G.: Alliance Advantage. The Art of Creating Value through Partnering. Harvard Business School Press, Boston (1998)
4. Ticoll, D., Lowy, A., Kalakota, R.: Joined at the bit. The emergence of the e-business community. In: Tapscott, D., Lowy, A., Ticoll, D. (eds.) Blueprint to the Digital Economy. Creating Wealth in the Era of e-business, McGraw Hill, NewYork (1998)
5. Filos, E.: Virtuality and the future of organizations. In: Putnik, G., Cunha, M. (eds.) Virtual Enterprise Integration: Technological And Organizational Perspectives, Idea Group, Hershey
6. Streitz, N.A., Rocker, C., Prante, T., von Alphen, D., Stenzel, R., Magerkurth, C.: Designing smart artifacts for smart environments. IEEE Comput. Soc. **38**(3), 41–49 (2005)
7. Thiesse, F., Michahelles, F.: Smart objects as building blocks for the internet of things. IEEE Internet Comput. **14**(1), 44–51 (2010)
8. Guo, B., Zhang, D., Imai, M.: Toward a cooperative programming framework for context-aware applications. Pers. Ubiquit. Comput. **15**(3), 221–233 (2011)
9. Basaglia, S., Caporarello, L., Magni, M., Pennarola, F.: IT knowledge integration capability and team performance: the role of team climate. Int. J. Inf. Manag. **30**(6), 542–551 (2010)
10. Blake, R., Mouton, J., McCanse, A.: Change by Design. Addison-Wesley, Redding (1989)
11. Malhotra, A., Majchrzak, A., Rosen, B.: Leading virtual teams. Acad. Manag. Perspect. **21**(1), 60–69 (2007)
12. Matheson, D., Matheson, J.E.: Smart organizations perform better. Res. Technol. Manag. **44**(4), 49–54 (2001)

DDGS Affordances for Value Creation

Claudio Vitari and Federico Pigni

Abstract The world is changing, and is changing thanks to the data. New opportunities for business action and service creation are emerging from the massive availability of real-time digital data. We characterize these opportunities proposing a framework rooted in the Technology Affordance theory studying the dynamic interactions between people and organizations, and the technological artifact. This approach provided encouraging results in understanding the dynamic nature of IT based innovation.

Keywords Digital data genesis and streaming · Affordances · Intents · Technological capabilities · Value creation · Service engineering · Service management

1 Research Introduction

The constant interaction of users with devices embedding digital capabilities both voluntary and unconsciously is a reality that has far reaching implications for individuals and human relationships, always and everywhere connected [1]. Volumes of data are born in digital form both as a result of humans' and devices' activities (Digital Data Genesis). Current studies in the Information Systems domain approach the phenomenon from a data management perspective, mainly focusing on the concept of big data. The core reasoning of these studies is that organizations now have the opportunity to collect, process, and store ever-growing

C. Vitari (✉) · F. Pigni
Grenoble Ecole de Management, Grenoble, France
e-mail: claudio.vitari@grenoble-em.com

F. Pigni
e-mail: federico.pigni@grenoble-em.com

L. Caporarello et al. (eds.), *Smart Organizations and Smart Artifacts*,
Lecture Notes in Information Systems and Organisation 7,
DOI: 10.1007/978-3-319-07040-7_2,
© Springer International Publishing Switzerland 2014

and complex datasets to support their decision making processes and strategies. These large and complex databases require specific storage, management, analysis, and visualization technologies to be effectively used, such as: business intelligence and analytics tools to dive and make sense of big data [2, 3]. Very few studies tried to explain the strategic opportunities for extracting value from the real-time streams of digital data that are being created in massive quantities other than through analytics [4]. We think that new forms of value creation emerge from the interplay of real time data streams and a firm's complementary resources [4]. To understand the uses and consequences of real time data streams we adopt a framework rooted in Technology Affordances theory and we consider the dynamic interactions between people and organizations—the social actors—, and the technological artifact. In this paper we will present new conceptual tools to understand and profit from real time digital data streams.

1.1 The Research Perspective: Affordances

Recent research has identified the interplay of social actors' intents and technology capabilities as at the origin of customer value and the consequent success of technological innovations and services [5, 6]. It is from this interplay that uses and customer value emerge—whether planned or serendipitous. Uses and value could be conceived and expected by design or emerge unexpected with use, in either case what emerges are unique capabilities of the bundle that neither the technology nor the social actor alone could exercise [7]. These uses are named Affordances [8]. An Affordance represents the "opportunities for action" as perceived by a social actor in its environment. Moreover, social actors perceive differently the possibilities of an artifact to afford an action. As a possibility for action, rather than the action itself, an Affordance is conceptually separate from a given behavior, and it is the necessary precondition to it. The affordance perspective assumes that a technological artifact has some recognizable functionalities but that their analysis "in-use" has to account for the awareness of social actors' intentions, thus recognizing the object's social nature [8–10]. Thanks to this concept, the materiality of an object and a social actor's perceptions are viewed relationally and jointly in terms of how each favors or shapes actions.

In Information Systems, affordances are the result of the confluence or intertwining of the capabilities provided by information and communication technologies and the actions taken by the social actors using them [11]. In this context, the embedding of digital capabilities in artifacts is indeed seen as a manifestation of the digital materiality of the object itself [1].

We adopted this alternative research perspective because we aim to take a fresh look at the interplay between technology and people, but to do so as in an emerging phenomenon. Affordances allow us to overcome some of limitations of current management theories [12]:

1. That ignore the possibility that humans using technology can enact new practices or outcomes by focusing only on psychological or social behavior;
2. That technology can produce and have unintended uses, thus overcome simplistic or deterministic assumptions about the effects of technology on human and organizational outcomes.

The affordance concept is then promising for gaining a deeper understanding of the possible uses of information technology to engineer and manage services. In so far as we are interested in engineering and managing services we take into consideration affordances that make innovative digital services possible, referring to them as Service Affordances. We consider that the current technological capability to digitally represent and stream actions in real-time (DDG and DDS) provides the opportunity for new service value creation.

2 Research Focus

In this section we focus our attention on the specific category of Service Affordances emerging from Digital Data Genesis and Stream (DDGS). Our main interest is related to the opportunities for servicing customers emerging from organizational intents, technological capabilities, and individuals.

2.1 Defining Digital Data Genesis and Stream

We define Digital Data Genesis as the real-time inception of an informational representation of an event or state of an entity in digital form. The defining characteristic of this phenomenon is that data are born digital: the timing of digital data generation is concurrent with the event that the digital data represent [13, 14]. The fact of a restaurant waiter taking a food order with a palm electronic device as soon as a customer expresses his wishes is a simple example of DDG. The digital data is the information representation of the food order and its creation is concurrent with the customer's order formulation. It's also DDG when the customer her-self passes the order using a touch screen installed at the table. DDG is a different concept from digitalization. Back to the example, DDG would not occur if the order is taken on paper and subsequently input into the electronic cash register. In this case the data existed in another form before becoming digital, data was not born digital but digitalized.

As a consequence, DDG enables information representations of real objects and events, without significant delays (in near real-time). In addition, the digital form of these information representations facilitates their interaction, manipulation and communication in the electronic information space. As previously defined, DDG activity is separated from any consecutive information processing or more sophisticated analytics. Digital Data Streams (DDS) are composed by the flow of data originating from DDG activities and can be intercepted and used by organizations or individuals [4]. Rather than focusing on technical specifications (push vs. pull, RSS vs. messaging), we characterize a DDS pragmatically as a data source that is constantly (or very frequently) changing and evolving. A database that is accessible in real time through an API and is updated as new data becomes available is an instantiation of a digital data stream. Therefore, the defining characteristics of a DDS are timeliness and a continuous flow of DDG events. The prototypical instance of a DDS is one in which DDG events are streamed continuously in real-time. Twitter is an example: each tweet is a DDG event and the tweet-stream, eventually accessible through API, is a DDS. In conclusion, the combination of DDG and DDS makes Digital Data Genesis and Stream (DDGS): the flow of real-time inceptions of informational representations of events or states of entities in digital form that can be intercepted and used by organizations or individuals. For example, a single click on a hyperlink is the digital representation of a person's decision (a DDG event). Activity on a website is a stream of personal decisions, and is aptly called the clickstream.

3 Service Affordances from DDGS

The application of the affordance perspective on DDGS phenomena facilitates the comprehension of the interplay of a social actor's intents with the flow of real-time digital data and the respective technological capabilities that carry it out. The principal social actor's intents contributing to the emergence of service affordances are about the intent to provide value adding services. This intent, stemming from the technological capabilities of DDG and DDS, interacts with the customer's willingness to be serviced. Value is created when the social actor is able to enact the Service Affordances to increase the customer's willingness to pay for its offers or reduce the opportunity cost of the resources it needs to create existing value propositions. The principal technology capabilities contributing to the emergence of Service Affordances from DDGS concern ever more pervasive digital data acquisition, near real-time processing, and telecommunicating systems. In practice, the interplay of these digital capabilities and the above-mentioned social actors' intents results in the Service Affordances. The combination of the multitude of these social actors' intents with the multiplicity of technologies having these capabilities determines infinite Service Affordances: from the waiter's use of palm devices to register and stream food orders to the restaurant kitchen, to worldwide financial high frequency trading round the clock. Hence, we have decided to focus on the affordances that create value in radically new and unique ways. Through an analysis of around 60 different empirical business examples, we identified four of them: Sensing, Mass Sensing, Experimenting, and Coordinating.

3.1 Sensing

We define Sensing as the affordance gained by detecting in real-time the current state of a single given entity (human, object, event…). Examples are the location of a single airplane, the speed of a specific car, or the mood of an individual person. We consider this affordance to be at the base of all the new value creation opportunities offered by DDGS, making it a first-order affordance, as the other DDGS affordances are built on Sensing. Effectively, Web 2.0 and social networks have allowed the creation of new ways for people to express themselves in real time. 4Square, for example, provides Sensing on other people location and "exploration" behavior. Users are uniquely identified and traced through DDG capabilities ("the check-in" and the GPS data). Sensing is an affordance emerging also from machine-to-machine (M2M) data streams as electronic devices have an unprecedented ability to automatically and continuously sense the environment, and automatically react to the incoming flow of data. Examples are the automatic alerting system at an air traffic control center in case of specific flight path deviation or the automatic cruise control of the speed of a car. The technological capabilities that support Sensing affordance include the diffusion of electronic identifiers (RFID chips, flash-tag…) and relative readers (smart phones, RFID readers, cameras…) or those technologies providing the possibility to communicate a status update, and the processing capability to analyze the characteristics of the single entity in near real-time. These characteristics can be brought along by the entity it-self or remotely stored elsewhere and accessed at the moment of the individual identification. The sensing intent is related to the social actors' intention to exceed current bounded perception related to their own sphere of experience. By tapping into a wider characterization of digitally represented entities cognition is extended beyond traditional physical barriers. Well-established examples relate to the Wal*Mart mandate to its suppliers to apply RFID tags to every single product or to all cattle in Canada and Europe.

3.2 Mass Sensing

We define Mass Sensing as the affordance gained by identifying the state of multiple entities in real time, altogether, contextualized by their relationships. Mass Sensing is a second-order affordance based on the Sensing affordance. For example, if real-time sensing makes it possible to locate a single vehicle, it is therefore possible to sense all the cars on a road and traffic congestion could be detected. Both TomTom (http://www.tomtom.com) and Inrix (http://www.inrix.com) are examples of how sensing a mass of vehicles can be used to provide added-value services to drivers in the form of real-time traffic information and more efficient routes. Both companies aggregate information from a multitude of DDS sources, including telecom operators, road sensors, and navigation systems readings. The technological capability that supports Mass Sensing is related to the development of rule-based and filtering functionalities and of complex event processing engines. The joint effect of the capability to filter relevant information and process them provides the opportunity to "sense" and evaluate multiple and meaningful concurrent events. Through these technological capabilities, each entity of the population is uniquely identifiable and distinguishable. The availability online of massive information concerning products, services or user behaviors effectively determines the potential for comparing and choosing based on data available for the entire population. The Sensing intent is related to the social actors' intention to track and trace entire entity populations both in time and space. In business this intent is pursued with the aim of optimizing business processes and streamline activities, and of exerting market power. This intent typically resulted in specific strategic initiatives deployed to increase the control of product and services along supply chains or in retail surfaces or for monitoring resources and capacities (empty seats for airliners, number of passengers, flow of people, products on the shelves, etc.).

3.3 Experimenting

We define Experimenting as the affordance gained by fast cycling data generation and streaming on the entity with actions on this measured entity or its environment. Experimenting is a second-order affordance based on the Sensing affordance. A/B tests on web pages for selecting a layout, or the massive experimentation ongoing in major websites, are examples of this affordance. The Experimenting affordance makes it possible to test and have immediate feedback on business decisions, from the change of a webpage layout to more complex information. New Brands Analytics provides a service that extracts specific feedback from customers' unstructured mentions on social media channels. Firms can then adjust their behaviors in real time, correct any shortcomings, and monitor the outcomes. At the same time, they can experiment with different configurations of the service and fine-tune it on the basis of customers' mentions. The technological capabilities that support this affordance include, in addition to the capabilities required for Sensing affordance (electronic identifiers, readers, processing capability), the actuators (software as well as hardware: thermostats, motors, electro-active polymers...) located in the sensed environment. The social actors' intents that support this affordance are related to the wish to understand the material reality. This wish to understand takes the specific form of the empirical method that arbitrates between competing theories, models and hypotheses through experimental science. The combination of these technological capabilities and human intents allows the emergence of Experimenting.

3.4 Coordinating

We define coordinating as the affordance gained by adjusting a behavior based on fast cycle feedback regarding the current state of other entities. Coordinating is a second-order affordance based on the Sensing one. This affordance is at the base of services such as Foursquare Radar, which enables users to coordinate spontaneously with friends by "sensing" their presence in the area. The technological capabilities that support this affordance include the diffusion of electronic communication devices (mobile phones, computers…) and the telecommunication infrastructure (Internet network, GSM network…) making the information exchange between these devices possible. Moreover, the availability of virtual networks—both social and machine to machine networks—provides the logical infrastructure for the exchange and the digital coordination to emerge. The social actors' intents that support this affordance are related to the willingness to coordinate with the other social actors as well as artifacts. This peer-to-peer approach spreads out together with the principle of human equality and mutual aid in order to achieve objectives beyond the capability of the single individual. The combination of these technological capabilities and human intents allows the emergence of the Coordinating affordance. An example of this affordance comes from the Arab countries where protesters used electronic communication devices (and applications like Twitter and Facebook) to coordinate and rally their supporters without a real or organized coordination [15].

4 Discussion and Conclusions

The affordance perspective facilitates the understanding of the interplay of people or organizational intents and technology capabilities in customer value creation and the consequent success of technological innovations and services. The value of an affordance approach lies clearly in the relational definition of the "affordance" concept linking actors and technology. In a society where an increasing number of activities of public and private organizations are engineered and managed as services, the affordance perspective can be particularly valuable for innovation and competitiveness making managers better "system thinkers" [12]. IT and Information systems are at the core of this transformation. Specifically, the crucial role played by data—through the development of pervasive computing, the spreading of sensors and the increase in the creation, storage, communication and processing of information—incites researchers to study DDGS. In particular, we identify central research questions that could be explored to enhance understanding of the levers for improving service development, engineering and management based on DDGS, through the affordance perspective: What are the levers and barriers in the emergence of DDGS affordances? How do individuals and organizations recognize DDGS affordances? How do individuals and organizations select DDGS affordances for services? To what extent do the organization's capabilities influence service development, engineering and management based on DDGS affordances? We will start answering some of these questions by deepening our knowledge on the around 60 business cases we identified for our four service affordances.

References

1. Yoo, Y., Bol Jr, R.J., Lyytinen, K., Majchrzak, A.: Organizing for innovation in the digitized world. Organ. Sci. **23**, 1398–1408 (2012)
2. Chen, H., Chiang, R., Storey, V.: Business intelligence and analytics: from big data to big impact. Manag. Inf. Syst. Q. **36**, 1165–1188 (2012)
3. Pospiech, M., Felden, C.: Big data—a state-of-the-art. AMCIS 2012 Proceedings (2012)
4. Piccoli, G., Pigni, F.: Harvesting external data: the potential of digital data streams. http://misqe.org/ojs2/index.php/misqe/article/view/475 (2013)
5. Jung, J.H., Schneider, C., Valacich, J.: Enhancing the motivational affordance of information systems: the effects of real-time performance feedback and goal setting in group collaboration environments. Manag. Sci. **56**, 724–742 (2010)
6. Zammuto, R.F., Griffith, T.L., Majchrzak, A., Dougherty, D.J., Faraj, S.: Information technology and the changing fabric of organization. Organ. Sci. **18**, 749–762 (2007)
7. Nevo, S., Wade, M.: The formation and value of IT-enabled resources: antecedents and consequences of synergistic relationships. MIS Q. **34**, 163–183 (2010)
8. Hutchby, I.: Technologies, texts and affordances. Sociology **35**, 441–456 (2001)
9. Fayard, A.-L., Weeks, J.: Photocopiers and water-coolers: the affordances of informal interaction. Organ. Stud. **28**, 605–634 (2007)
10. Montesano, L., Lopes, M., Bernardino, A., Santos-Victor, J.: Learning object affordances: from sensory-motor coordination to imitation. IEEE Trans. Robot. **24**, 15–26 (2008)
11. Majchrzak, A.: Fostering innovation and intellectual capital creation: the paradoxical influence of social media affordances. (2011)
12. Majchrzak A., Markus M. L.: Technology affordances and constraints in management information systems (MIS). In: Kessler, E. (ed.), Encyclopedia of Management Theory, pp. 832–836. SAGE Publications, Inc., Thousand Oaks, doi: http://dx.doi.org/10.4135/9781452276090.n256 (2013)
13. Vitari, C., Piccoli, G., Mola, L., Rossignoli, C.: Antecedents of IT dynamic capabilities in the context of the digital data genesis. ECIS 2012 Proceedings (2012)
14. Raguseo, E., Vitari, C., Piccoli, G.: Gaining competitive advantage from digital data genesis dynamic capability and the moderating role of environmental turbulence. itAIS Conference Proceedings, Rome (2012)
15. Christensen, C.: Twitter revolutions? Addressing social media and dissent. Commun. Rev. **14**, 155–157 (2011)

The Role of IT in Organizational Networks, Individual Networks, and in Bridging These Two Levels

Andrea Carugati, Lapo Mola and Antonio Giangreco

Abstract In this paper, we seek to understand the role of technology at the nexus between the two network levels: as outcome of the decision process at the organizational level and as object of use and performance at the individual level. We aim to capture the role of IT in bridging the individual practices in the context of the larger network system [22]. To do so, we draw on a longitudinal case study of the development and diffusion of a software for the operation and management of nursing homes.

Keywords Social networks · Nursing home · Organizational impacts of IS

1 Introduction

It is widely recognized that the implementation of Enterprise Systems (ES) is a challenging endeavor with both high-risk [1, 2] and potential high rewards. The study of the implementation process [3, 4], and the succeeding stabilization has therefore become a classic topic in IS research. While IS research has essentially looked at the organizational level and the practice level, implementations do not happen in vacuum. Decisions to implement are made by organizations influenced by the network of organizations with whom they have relations [5, 6] or that

A. Carugati
School of Business and Social Sciences, Aarhus University, Aarhus, Denmark
e-mail: andreac@asb.dk

L. Mola (✉)
Department of Business Administration, University of Verona, Verona, Italy
e-mail: lapo.mola@univr.it

A. Giangreco
IESEG School of Management (LEM-CNRS), Lille, France
e-mail: a.giangreco@ieseg.fr

L. Caporarello et al. (eds.), *Smart Organizations and Smart Artifacts*,
Lecture Notes in Information Systems and Organisation 7,
DOI: 10.1007/978-3-319-07040-7_3,
© Springer International Publishing Switzerland 2014

simply are influential in the sector [7]. Decision about usage and adoption are instead made by individuals influenced by their network of colleagues, managers and peers [8–10], and other influential connections [11, 12]. Indeed the networks within which organizations and individuals are embedded have important consequences for the successes and failures of IT initiatives [13] such as ES implementations [5, 11, 14].

Thanks to studies in the organizational theory area, we have learned a great deal about what kinds of networks produce desirable outcomes and what situational characteristics shape how people and organizations construct their social networks [15, 16]. Previous studies have proved few overreaching concepts for drawing the most of one's networks. These results have shown both (i) the characteristic of the networks like bridging ties and filling structural holes [17] and the embeddedness of economic transactions in social networks [18, 19]; and (ii) the characteristics of the actors within the network connected in more or less useful ways [20].

However, from previous literature we can also identify areas that require further study. One of such areas, in the domain of organizational theory, is the nexus between personal networks and larger network systems. According to Ibarra et al. [15], this gap in research was already observed by Boissevain [21], but the organizational literature has grown as two separate camps, with few bridges linking the micro and macro.

The other interesting gap is to be found in IS literature where network studies are almost absent despite the fact that organizational networks—per their definition—include "people, organizational units, behaviors, procedures and technologies" [15], p. 365). In the IS domain, the call for more studies bridging levels of networks has so far being picked up only in few published paper [11]. Today, after much research about the role of networks on the successes of projects and initiatives, we still have much to learn about the role of the technology that makes the network possible and relevant at the same time. The understanding of how individuals and organizations use technology in their internal and external networks is still a question open for debate.

In this paper, we seek to understand the role of technology at the nexus between the two network levels: as outcome of the decision process at the organizational level and as object of use and performance at the individual level. We aim to capture the role of IT in bridging the individual practices in the context of the larger network system [22]. To do so, we draw on a longitudinal case study of the development and diffusion of a software for the operation and management of nursing homes. The software was developed internally and used by one nursing home, and it is now used in 100+ nursing homes, endorsed by the local health authority, and supported by a network of organizations. The story of the success and diffusion of this software is intimately linked to the interaction between the network of individual users reporting positively about the system and the network of organizations supporting its diffusion.

The idea of zooming back and forth between individual and collective phenomena is likely to highlight characteristics of technology as enabler and object of social networks that were previously ignored. This can further be embedded in a

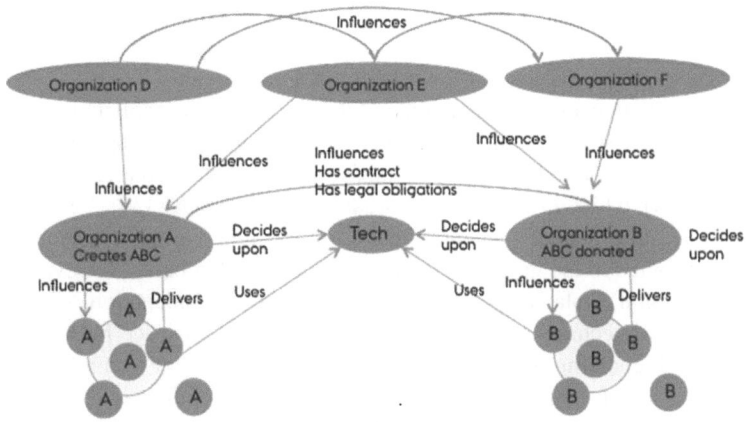

Fig. 1 Basic framework of analysis

discourse of how individuals enact structures of constraint and opportunity within systems of relations explicitly including technology [23, 24]. The basic framework of analysis is showed in Fig. 1. Expanding on this basic component we will build the analysis presented in the next sections.

2 Theoretical Perspectives on IS and Networks

IS literature deals with social networks from two main standpoints: the focus on human capital and the focus on the installed base.

Human capital is related to what people know and their practices. The human capital explanation of success with IT is that an individual will do better with technology if he/she is more capable, more skilled ([25], p. 32). The stream of research on human capital will therefore look at practice to find the explanation of IT uses. Practices and practice lens have become the hallmark of social studies of use and adoption of technology [26, 27]. The main implication of this stream of research is that users need training [9] and socialization with experts [28, 29] to improve their ability to deal with technology.

Installed base is related to how many users a specific technology has, relative to the number of adopters of a competing technology or the number of non-adopters [5]. The installed base explanation of the success of a technology says that success (dominance) depends on the number of adopters of the technology: the more, the better. The most common driver for this success is the appearance of network externalities as the installed base grows [30, 31]: The technology has some characteristics that make it such that every new user adds value to all existing users. Installed base and network externalities consider the users as a homogenous mass: Large numbers of users even out disparities in human capital and varying influences of users in the social network. The main implication of this stream of research is that network externalities have to become apparent so to induce the next person to adopt because of continually increasing value [18, 32, 33].

Both the human capital explanation and the installed base explanation allow for *recursiveness* between IT and its effects. Increasing human capital (skills and practices) leads to higher interpretive flexibility and better configurations of the technology [34], which in turn leads to organizational changes [35]. The size of the installed base may lead to technological success, but the technological performance contributes to the growth or demise of the installed base. However, both in the human capital explanation and in the installed base explanation of the *recursiveness* between technology and organizations, there is no space for the structure of the network enabling and constraining the use of a certain technology.

The other set of studies dealing with technology evolution is to be found in network literature. Here the main idea is that players in the network are nodes connected by ties of various types [14, 36]. An actor within this network can be found central or peripheral [11] and at various network levels like group, organization, or industry [15, 37]. When discussing the diffusion of technology at multiple network levels, it is necessary to focus on two main diffusion processes: (1) diffusion of ideas because ideas participate in decision making of management when deciding upon technology implementation; and (2) diffusion of practice because users will decide upon use, adoption, and workarounds with technology depending on how this caters to their daily practice. The salient network characteristic in relation to diffusion of ideas and practices is the network *density* [20, 38].

Networks that are *dense*, i.e. populated by similar actors with aligned interests, will tend to diffuse new practices relatively fast because interests are aligned and language and trust to mobilize these interests are readily available [39]. Conversely, dense networks will tend to resist new ideas because of the uniformity of information circulating in the network [18, 39].

Networks that instead are *sparse* include multiple players from diverse fields and present abundance of structural holes [38]. Many different actors are more likely to contribute to the creation new ideas because boundary spanners [26] are likely to emerge and fill the structural holes and identify new opportunities [17, 25]. On the other side, sparse networks will not be conducive of new practices because of the many structural holes impeding common practices to be understood, valued, trusted, and adopted [40].

Dense and sparse networks are therefore respectively conducive of and resisting to new practices and new ideas. With respect to the processes of diffusion of technology (ideas) and practices, network studies would therefore suggest that dense networks, at group level, and sparse networks, at managerial level, would be conducive of the best condition for technology to diffuse and be adopted.

Network theory addresses the issue of network persistence and evolution over time with the concept of *residual* network [14]. Information is the mechanism that makes it possible to consider networks as stable entities: "In theory the network residue of yesterday would be irrelevant to the market behavior of tomorrow ... Continuity would be a by-product of buyers and sellers seeking one another out as a function of supply and demand ... selecting requires that I have information ... Information can be expected to spread across people in a market" ([25], pp. 33–34).

Thanks to studies from the network theory area, we can learn a great deal about what kinds of networks produce certain outcomes and what behavioral characteristics shape how people and organizations construct their social networks [15]. However, extant network literature does not address in depth the specificity of technology either as a product of the network or as an antecedent and enabler of it. Furthermore, the link between personal (ego) networks and larger (organizational) network systems, the nexus where ideas become decisions and actions become practices, is mostly absent from network theories [10, 15, 37]. In IS literature, the call for more studies of network's structures has so far being picked up only in few studies [11]. However, these few studies have focused on the impact of network structures on systems success and have not yet addressed the impact of technology on network success, its density or sparsity, the persistence or decrease of structural holes, the diffusion of actions and ideas. Today, after much research on the role of networks on the successes of projects and initiatives, we still have much to learn about the opposite dynamic: The role of the technology in making the network possible and successful at the same time.

3 Research Design and Context

To answer the research question, we studied the network dynamics around the design and diffusion of an ES for the management of nursing homes. The software was initially developed in an Italian nursing home, Fondazione Santa Clelia (FSC), where the manager felt the need to reorganize the work in a professional and modern manner. The system—called ABC—was used by the manager as a battling ram to do away with old habits (and employees) and pave the way for operations based on objective measures and standardized processes. On the basis of its effective implementation at FSC, the ABC software has diffused to other nursing homes; it has been handed over to a software house that follows its development professionally; and it has been named as best practice by the local health care authority. The software and it has now spread to more than 100 nursing homes in the region and beyond in a network that includes hospitals, banks, consultants, public officials, medical doctors, physiotherapists, psychologists, and more.

4 Data Collection and Analysis

The data collection at began with informal talks with FSC in 2005, though the data used in this article were collected formally in four field trips.

The first field trip (October 2008) aimed at understanding the dynamics of the network at the beginning of the ABC history. We interviewed five people: the general manager, the software developer, the administrative assistant, and two nurses. We used semi-structured interviews to understand how the software was developed and implemented from the original idea to the current use.

After analyzing the first set of data, we updated the interview guide for the second round of interviews (September 2009). We focused the second round of interviews on the individual network inside FSC. We investigated the individual uses and organizational consequences of ABC and how the changes were fed back to the programmer and included into the software. We interviewed 14 people: 10 employees, 2 guests, the general manager, and the developer. Moreover, one of the researchers observed a nurse during her shift to understand how the software was used and the impact of this IT tool on the way people worked and interacted.

The third field trip (October 2012) aimed at understanding the structure of the larger network system. We interviewed a manager of the local health authority responsible for the control and financing of the nursing homes of the region. We also interviewed the owner of the software house. Both interviews investigated the modality of diffusion of ABC: from the policy point of view for the local health authority, and from the commercial point of view for the software house. In this occasion we also gathered the contacts for the other nursing homes using the ABC system.

The fourth field trip (November 2012) focused on ABC as connecting element between the larger network and the individual networks of four nursing homes. We interviewed the directors of the nursing homes that had the contact with the local health authority and the software house and we interviewed the personnel—nurses and health technicians—regarding their use of ABC and their relation to the larger network system.

4.1 Data Analysis: From a Development Idea to a Regional Revolution

Our analysis of the evolution of ABC and of the networks around it shows five states of the networks that can be connected to five stages of maturity of the technology in use.

Phase 1. The first phase was started by an idea of the newly arrived general manager. The general manager had a business education and felt that he needed numbers to run the structure properly. As he admitted "IT was the only way I knew that we could use. But there was nothing on the market and I just did not know if we had the skills to do it". He met however a retired software developer that volunteered his work for the development of ABC. The adventure of FSC with IT thus began in 1999. The initial network was essentially only internal at FSC. The network was selective in relation to the participants and was designed to be

Fig. 2 FSC develops the
ABC software

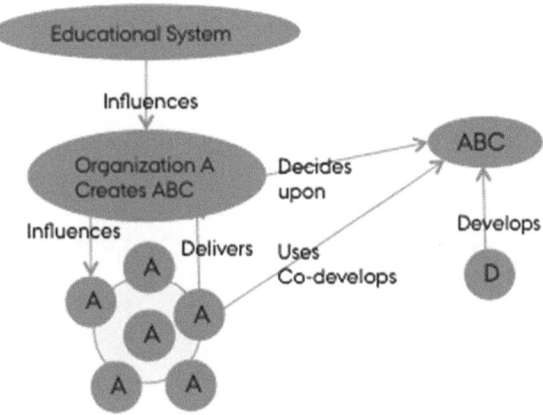

such because the purpose of the software was to create an elite group that would shape the future organization. This group was connected to the external developer to help FSC with their idea. In this phase IT attracted only internal actors (Fig. 2). The users (A) quickly understood the network characteristics of ABC using peer to peer sanctioning to assure the complete use of the system. They also interacted often with the developer (D) to gradually add elements to ABC according to emergent needs.

Phase 2. As the software became more performing and the users demanded more advanced features.

A manager talked about these features with colleagues from other nursing homes. The need for better management was felt in many nursing homes and a new generation of managers was stepping in. It did not take long for other managers of nursing homes to manifest their interest in installing the software (Fig. 3). In this second phase the performance of IT and the convincing arguments of the manager began to attract new actors to the organizational network while ABC is also influenced by the existing external network (e.g. the hospital).

Phase 3. More and more nursing homes began to get interested in using the system, but the engineer that was helping FSC realized that he could not follow additional implementations of the software and therefore the director on FSC made an agreement with a software house to further develop and commercialize the ABC. The software helps again in extending the external network and changes the function of the developer that assumes a more consulting role (Fig. 4). However, we also observed that, while in FSC the medical doctors were regular users of the system, in the other organizations this was not happening.

Phase 4. The main event in phase 4 is the active entrance in the network of the Local Health Care System (AUSL). Typically the role of the AUSL was that of control by manually going through paper records, and then digitize them. ABC gave the AUSL the possibility to receive data directly in electronic form decreasing costs while having more data, more often, and more precise. The AUSL established therefore a public interface for data transfer (Fig. 5).

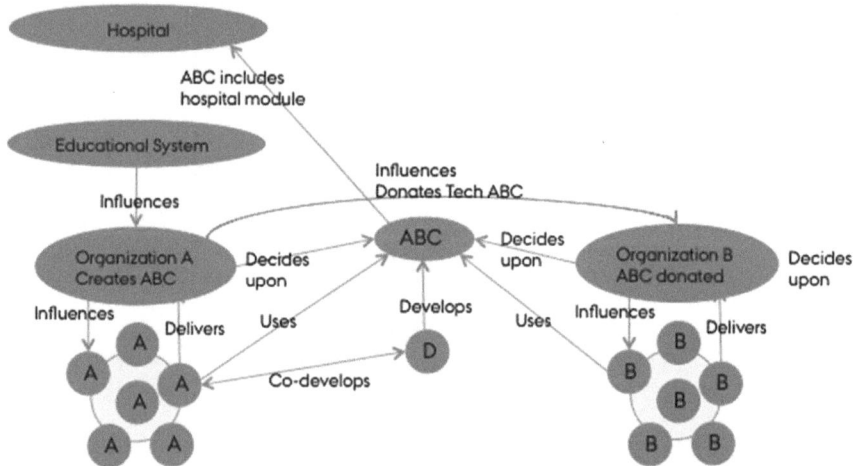

Fig. 3 ABC requested by other nursing homes (org *B* with users *B* as example)

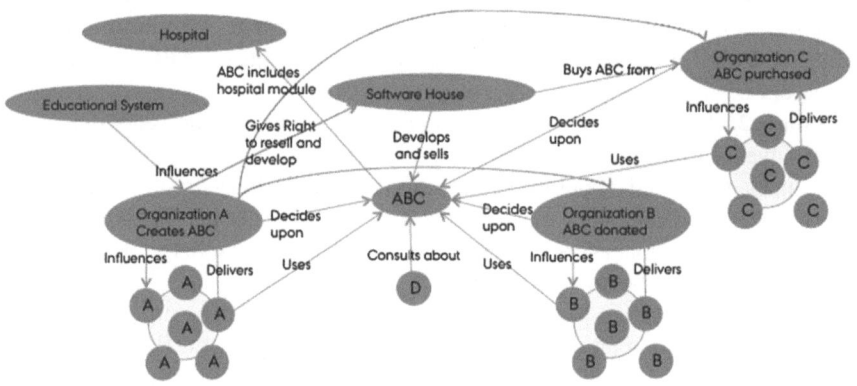

Fig. 4 ABC commercialized by software house and sold to other nursing homes

Phase 5. In the last phase identified so far, the AUSL has decided to declare ABC the software of choice for all the nursing homes in the county (about 60 organizations). To do so without stretching too much the budget of the nursing homes, the AUSL entered an agreement with the foundation of a local bank that would finance the cost (approximately 800 k €) of hardware and software ant the without costs for the adopting organizations. This allowed the diffusion time to be very short and already now all nursing homes in the county have adopted ABC.

Our preliminary interviews with this last group of organizations (Org. D in Fig. 6) shows a similar pattern as before with acceptance among nurses and technicians leading to high satisfaction with the system and non-acceptance among medical doctors.

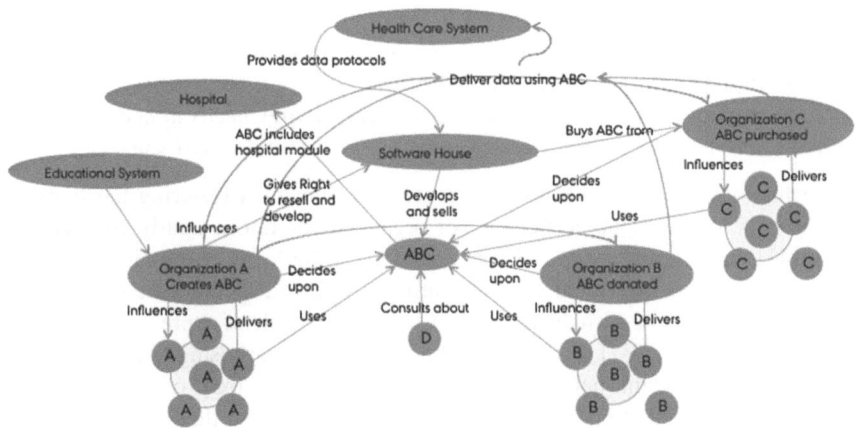

Fig. 5 ABC used to deliver data to the regional health care system

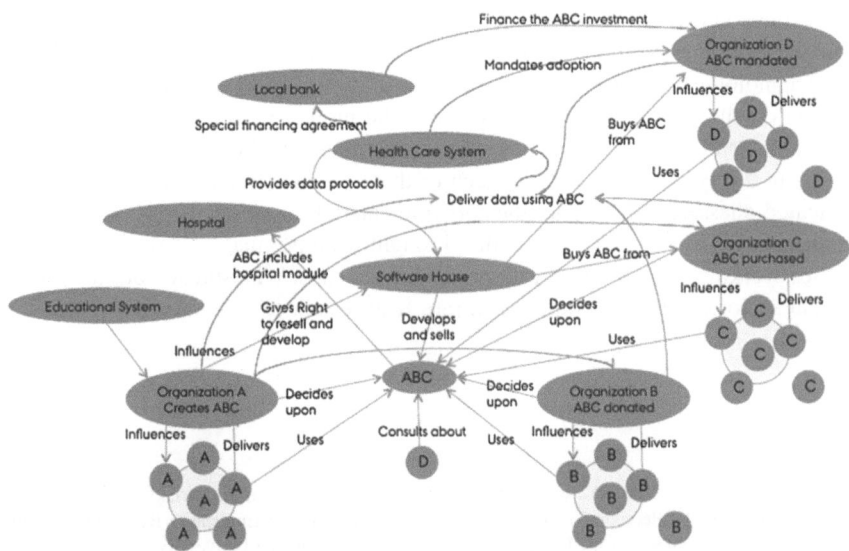

Fig. 6 ABC becomes the mandated solution from the regional health authority

5 Preliminary Contributions

The multi level analysis shows the diversity of emergent network elements and the—mostly unintended—entanglement of technology and networks. Over time we observe 3 main results:

- *Technology evolution is pivotal for network evolution*
- *Actors in the network and network levels are not organized hierarchically: They are emergent, dynamic, and included ad hoc*
- *Network structures do not replicate easily: Technology needs to account for the detail and network studies need to open the box or individual use.*

Technology plays a central role the network dynamics fostering the transformation of a loosely coupled network of organizations into a tightly coupled network [41]. The formation of the network, both at the level of the larger network system and at the individual level, is intimately linked to the state of the technology and emergent ad hoc rather than being the result of a pre-existent multi-level decomposition [37]. When the technology was at early stages and delivering small local results, the network was likewise small and only of closely related actors. In accordance to previous results (e.g. [11]), we find that the autonomy of the development team was instrumental for the initial system success. As the technology began to mature and produce bigger results, the network also began to grow beyond the borders of the initiator. At this stage, the technology played a double role: at the individual level within the organizations it had to be flexible enough to adapt to local needs (e.g. medical doctors refusing to use it or refusing to share their notes), while at the level of the larger network system it had to be standardized enough to be selected by the local health authority and hospitals as the technology of choice for data transfer. The impact of the degree of centralization on success in our analysis seems to be more connected to the fit with the individual and organizational network rather than on the characteristics of the actors in the system [11]. Albeit much of these design choices were the results of educated guesses, the fact that the software catered to the needs of both networks contributed to the positive cycle that brought a home made software created by nurses working from a morgue to be one of the most widespread solutions in the Italian sector of nursing homes … a rare feature indeed!

References

1. Grabski, S.V., Leech, S.A., Lu, B.: Enterprise system implementation risks and controls. In: Seddon, P.B., Willcocks, L., Shanks, G. (eds.) Second-Wave Enterprise Resource Planning Systems: Implementing for Effectiveness, pp. 1–19, Cambridge University Press, Cmabridge (2003)
2. Caporarello, L., Viachka, A.: Individual readiness for change in the con-text of enterprise resource planning systems implementation. Paper presented at the 16th Americas conference on information systems 2010, AMCIS 2010, 2 827–2 836
3. Sumner, M.R.: How alignment strategies influence ERP project success. Enterp. Info. Syst. 3(4), 425–448 (2009)
4. Wenrich, K.I., Ahmad, N.: Lessons learned during a decade of ERP experience: a case study. Int. J. Enterp. Inf. Syst. 5(1), 55–73 (2009)
5. Suarez, F.F.: Network effects revisited: the role of strong ties in technology selection. Acad. Manag. J. 48(4), 710–720 (2005)

6. Powell, W.W., White, D.R., Koput, K.W., Owen-Smith, J.: Network dynamics and field evolution: the growth of interorganizational collaboration in the life sciences. Am. J. Sociol. **110**(4), 1132–1205 (2005)
7. Currie, W.: Contextualising the IT artefact: towards a wider research agenda for IS using institutional theory. Info. Technol. people **22**(1), 63–77 (2009)
8. Northcraft, G.B., Polzer, J.T., Neale, M.A., Kramer, M.R.: Diversity, social identity and performance: emergent social dynamics in cross-functional teams. In: Jackson, S.E., Ruderman, M.N. (eds.) Diversity in Work Teams: Research Paradigms for a Changing Workplace, pp. 69–96. APA, Washington, D.C. (1995)
9. Orlikowski, W.: Knowing in practice: enacting a collective capability in distributed organizing. Organ. Sci. **13**(3), 249–273 (2002)
10. Rossignoli, C.: The contribution of transaction cost theory and other network-oriented techniques to digital markets. IseB **7**(1), 57–79 (2009)
11. Sasidharan, S., Santhanam, R., Brass, D.J., Sambamurthy, V.: The effects of social network structure on enterprise systems success: a longitudinal multilevel analysis. Info. Syst. Res. **23**(3), 658–678 (2012). doi:10.1287/isre.1110.0388
12. Tichy, N.M.: Networks in organizations. In: Nystrom, P.C., Starbuck, W.H. (eds.) Handbook of Organizational Design, pp. 225–249. Oxford University Press, New York (1981)
13. Depaoli, P., Za, S.: Towards the Redesign of e-business Maturity Models for SMEs. In: Baskerville, R., De Marco, M., Spagnoletti, P. (eds.) Designing Organizational Systems. Lecture Notes in Information System and Organization LNISO, vol. 1. Springer, Heidelberg
14. Brass, D.J., Galaskiewicz, J., Greve, H.R., Tsai, W.: Taking stock of networks and organizations: a multilevel perspective. Acad. Manag. Rev. **47**(6), 795–817 (2004)
15. Ibarra, H., Kilduff, M., Wenpin, T.: Zooming in and out: connecting individuals and collectivities at the frontiers of organizational network research. Organ. Sci. **16**(4), 359–371 (2005). doi:10.1287/orsc.1050.0129
16. Magni, M., Pennarola, F.: Stand by me: the quality of interorganizational relationships as antecedent of IT adoption. Proceedings of the 13th European Conference on Information Systems, Information Systems in a Rapidly Changing Economy, ECIS 2005 (2005)
17. Burt, R.S.: Structural Holes: The Social Structure of Competition. Harvard University Press, Cambridge (1992)
18. Granovetter, M.S.: Economic action and social structure: the problem of embeddedness. Am. J. Sociol. **91**, 481–510 (1985)
19. Uzzi, B.: The sources and consequences of embeddedness for the economic performance of organizations: the network effect. Am. Sociol. Rev. **61**, 674–698 (1996)
20. Burt, R.S.: The contingent value of social capital. Adm. Sci. Q. **42**, 339–365 (1997)
21. Boissevain, J.: Friends of Friends: Networks, Manipulators and Coalitions. Basil Blackwell, London (1974)
22. Casalino, N., Buonocore, F., Rossignoli, C., Ricciardi, F.: Transparency, openness and knowledge sharing for rebuilding and strengthening government institutions (2013) IASTED Multiconferences—Proceedings of the IASTED International Conference on Web- Based Education, WBE 2013, pp. 866–871
23. Sorrentino, M.: Taking care of invisible technology. Eur. J. Info. Syst. **14**, 507–509 (2005)
24. Magni, M., Provera, B., Proserpio, L.: Individual attitude toward improvisation in information systems development. Behav. Info. Technol. **29**(3), 245–255 (2010)
25. Burt, R.S.: Structural holes versus network closure as social capital. In: Lin, N., Cook, K., Burt, R.S. (eds.) Social Capital: Theory and Research. Sociology and Economics: Controversy and Integration Series. Aldine de Gruyter, New York, pp 31–56 (2001)
26. Levina, N., Vaast, E.: The emergence of boundary spanning competence in practice: implications for implementation and use of information systems. MIS Q. **29**(2), 335–363 (2005)
27. Carlile, P.R.: Transferring, translating, and transforming: an integrative framework for managing knowledge across boundaries. Organ. Sci. **15**(5), 555–568 (2004)

28. Lave, J., Wenger, E.: Situated Learning: Legitimate Peripheral Participation. Cambridge University Press, Cambridge (1991)
29. Suchman, L.: Making a case: knowledge and routine work in document production. Workplace Studies: Recovering Work Practice and Informing System Design, pp. 29–45. Cambridge University Press, Cambridge (2000)
30. Brynjolfsson, E., Kemerer, C.F.: Network externalities in microcomputer software: An econometric analysis of the spreadsheet market. Manag. Sci. **42**(12), 1627–1647 (1996)
31. Burt, R.S.: Structural Holes: The Social Structure of Competition. Harvard University Press, Cambridge (1992)
32. Pontiggia, A., Virili, F.: Network effects in technology acceptance: laboratory evidence, (2008). ICIS 2008 Proceedings. Paper 130. http://aisel.aisnet.org/icis2008/130 (2008)
33. Cordella, A., Mola, L., Rossignoli, C.: Software market configuration: a socio-technical explanation. ICIS 2009 Proceedings, 154 (2009)
34. Tyre, M.J., Orlikowski, W.J.: Windows of opportunity: temporal patterns of technological adaptation in organizations. Organ. Sci. **5**(1), 98–118 (1994)
35. Orlikowski, W., Hoffman, D.: An imporvisational model for change managment: the case of groupware technologies. Inventing the Organizations of the 21st Century, pp. 265–282. MIT, Boston (1997)
36. Marzo F., Za S., Spagnoletti P.: Modeling Dependence Networks for Agent Based Simulation of Online and Offline Communities, Lecture Notes in Computer Science, vol. 7879, Springer, Heidelberg (2013)
37. Moliterno T.P., Mahony D.M.: Network theory of organization: a multilevel approach. J. Manag. **2** (37), 443–467 (2011)
38. Obstfeld, D.: Social networks, the Tertius Lungens orientation and involvement in innovation. Adm. Sci. Q. **50**(2005), 100–130 (2005)
39. Granovetter, M.: The impact of social structure on economic outcomes. J. Econ. Perspect. **19**, 33–50 (2005)
40. Krackhardt, D., Hanson, J.R.: Informal networks: the company behind the chart. Harv. Bus. Rev. OnPoint, Spring **2011**, 30–37 (2011)
41. D'Urso, P., De Giovanni, L., Spagnoletti, P.: A fuzzy taxonomy for e-Health projects, Int. J. Mach. Learn. Cybernet. **4**(6), xx, (2012). doi:10.1007/s13042-012-0118-4

Corporate Customership: The Core Components of the Relationship Between Firm and Customer

Enrico Angioni and Francesca Cabiddu

Abstract Past research developed a new theoretical framework, named Corporate Customership, that specifies the link between three fields most concerned with innovation: corporate entrepreneurship (CE), IT value-co-creation and user-centered innovation (DI). At the goal of this article is to clarify the core components of the relationship between firm and customer and deepen the basic dimensions of this new theoretical framework, in order to build up the defining aspects and boundaries of Corporate Customership, its context and form, and identifying possible developments for further research.

Keywords Relationship · Entrepreneur · Customer · Co-creation · Active role · Information technology

1 Introduction

The evolution of the relationship between firms and customers has brought us to consider a new theoretical framework, Corporate Customership; and a new driver of innovation, the customer [1].

Firms can exploit their customers in search of efficiencies, risk sharing and value creation, and build up long-lasting relationships that can be helpful in creating higher value that will be mutually beneficial [2, 3].

Nowadays, firms need to find specific values that can be included from the start of a relationship with business customers to collaborate with them [4, 5]. Focusing

E. Angioni (✉) · F. Cabiddu
University of Cagliari, V.le S. Ignazio 17, 09123 Cagliari, Italy
e-mail: enricoangioni83@gmail.com

F. Cabiddu
e-mail: fcabiddu@unica.it

L. Caporarello et al. (eds.), *Smart Organizations and Smart Artifacts*,
Lecture Notes in Information Systems and Organisation 7,
DOI: 10.1007/978-3-319-07040-7_4,
© Springer International Publishing Switzerland 2014

on the processes and development of these activities may represent the next frontier in the advantage seeking behaviour of firms [4, 6]; especially in the B2B (Business-to-business) environment [4]. These activities and the exploitation of these resources are necessary to better understand the customers and their needs.

In this paper, the previous research about Corporate Customership [1] will be expanded, in order to find and build up the boundaries which localise this theoretical approach. This is accomplished, thanks to the development of a model that encloses the base elements for these kinds of interactions between firms and customers.

2 The Corporate Customership

Corporate Customership [1] has been described as a new theoretical framework in order to show how firms' innovations are shaped by the relationship between organizations and customers and how information technology can enhance this process. We suggest below that there is a need for a new and expanded theory of innovation development that better explain the role of customer on this process. The latter is considered to be a figure that plays an active role and shares its contribution and its capacity to innovate by the exploitation of essential means, such as information technology [1].

This kind of relationship finds its nature on three different theories: Corporate Entrepreneurship, approach aimed to the development of the internal processes through unilateral contribution of the entrepreneur [7]; Value Co-creation, theory based on the interactions and the contribution of the customer in order to develop a beneficial value [8]; User centered innovation, theory that implies a strong centrality of the customer and the development of the firm are build around its needs [9]. They show different gaps and dimensions that have been the starting point in order to find a complementarity, which allows the development of the basic dimensions for the approach mentioned above.

Thanks to this integration we have found the elements to lay the basis for a new theoretical framework based on a new relationship between firm and customer, the Corporate Customership [1].

3 Why Corporate Customership?

First of all, it is very important to justify the motivation behind what has delivered this new kind of approach.

Firstly, the role of the customer must be defined in this relationship. This figure, in Corporate Customership, is an essential dimension who is considered and exploited by the firm as a resource [1, 9–11], in order to exploit the innovative capacity that the customer has developed; thanks to the development of information technology [9].

Thus, beginning with these assumptions, the customer starts as a collaborator, and as a partner that the firm wants and needs to exploit, in order to develop the internal processes that the firm needs to shape its activity and cope with the dynamism of the environment; and obviously, understand and satisfy the customers' needs.

Thus, Corporate Customership starts with the assumption of creating a new kind of relationship between firms and customers, with the aim of enclosing the latter in the development of the internal processes.

Therefore, we set out to extend this prior theory and research by first identifying the core components of the relationship between firm and customers. Next, we examine how they operate as determinants that influence the internal innovation process.

4 Which Perspective?

There are various implications that stem from this kind of approach, and mainly from the elements that are enclosed within them. We argue that this approach is mainly focused on the relationship and interactions, than the development of processes. As a consequence, the Corporate Customership is mainly due to the link between the Value Co-creation and the User Cantered Innovation that highlight the important role of the services [12] and the customer as an essential partner and resource for these kinds of developments. Furthermore, focusing on the approach above all on these two theories means a central role for technology, first of all for an independence growth capability of the customer, and secondly to build up and develop the collaboration between the actors by a means specific IT approach.

The Corporate Customership, as stated, is an approach that is based on a firm's perspective that must exploit the innovation supplied by the user [13, 14], who is considered as a driver for the innovation [1].

5 Overview of the Model's Core Components

Consider the development of the internal innovation processes from the perspective of the firm's means, learn more about the continuous dialogue between firms and customers [1]. Through continuous dialogue, firms can relate their efforts to individual customers, reduce uncertainty in capital commitments and even spot and eliminate sources of environmental risk and dynamism [15].

Thus, it is important to understand the basis of these interactions and find the elements that are enclosed in this kind of relationship, which are focused on the collaboration, the context and the means. The key building blocks of the interactions on the Corporate Customership approach must be defined based on the characteristics of this approach, it can be argued that the relationship is based on key elements or building blocks: Transparency, Access information, Competences, Collaboration and Open data.

- Transparency: is considered to be the base of the interactions, and it gives the capacity to offer a complete visibility and traceability of the process. In the past, firms benefited from information asymmetry, but nowadays this asymmetry is defaulted [15]. As a consequence, information about firms' activities is now more accessible, which offers a new level of transparency that allows the customer to get more information than in the past.
- Access information: is the possibility for the customer to get tools and obviously information, in order to gain new market possibilities, or in other words, new opportunities in emerging markets. The customer can become the manager of the value creation process [16].
- Competences: this element is directly linked with the context. It can be argued that Corporate Customership [1] is a kind of approach that must to be focused on a kind of relationship that needs to express competences and skills from both parts of the relationship; skills that are typical of the B2B context.
- Collaboration: is a dimension closely linked with the first two elements, and obviously linked with dialogue. Collaboration is considered to be a process by which two or more parts adopt a high level of cooperation to maintain a trading relationship over time [17]. Having a relationship means having a bilateral contribution, and that both parties have the power to shape its nature and future direction over time [17].
- Open data: to provide effective support for the functioning of the logistics channel, a company's information system should support both proprietary and shared data; since they are needed to manage the company. The shared data should be available through appropriate information interfaces to customers, logistics suppliers or any other stakeholder [18, 19].

The elements mentioned above are the components of the TACCO Model, and they represent the dimensions that are the basis for the interactions between the firm and the customer on the basis of a Corporate Customership framework.

It is possible for an individual customer to get access to as much information as they need from the firm. Both access and transparency are critical to having a meaningful dialogue, which is one of the most important elements of the interaction because it shows that nowadays, the logic of the market can be viewed as a set of conversations between firms and customers [20]. It is not easy to build up dialogue in an interaction between two unequal partners [21]; although the Corporate Customership is based on the firm's perspective, the customer must be considered as an equal partner to build dialogue through the exploitation of transparency, access to information and tools.

Competence represents the elements that are closely linked with the context. Corporate Customership is an approach that is focused on the B2B context (business-to-business). This assumption is due to the fact that "competencies designate how specific competitive capabilities are acquired and leveraged; they constitute the realisation of a complex pattern of strategic choices" ([22], p. 1722). Synthesising the B2B competences represents a bundle of tangible and intangible assets and resources that work together to create competitive capabilities [23, 24]. The Corporate Customership is based on a collaborative relationship that aims to improve the internal processes through the help of the customer, this kind of work does not fit on the competences and needs of a simple final user, typical of the B2C (business-to-consumer) context. Therefore, in the B2B context skills such as technical skills, market acuity and knowledge channels can be found [25], which are very helpful for the typical relationship of Corporate Customership and at the same time are the main differences from the B2C context and from its typical customer.

Collaboration is essential as well because through this kind of relationship, the various actors in the value chain ensure that they benefit from the relationship. Both partners enhance the value of the network and, at the same time, profit from being involved in the relationship [26]. The common core element of such networks is cooperation among distinct, but related firms that allow these firms to share mutual benefits and gain a competitive advantage over their competitors outside of the network [27]. The competitive advantage and the value added depend on the ability of a firm to build up with stakeholders, as well as within them [28].

Finally, an open data approach implies that data sharing between parties in the supply chain is of fundamental interest, and that the flow of information is essential for carrying out an effective and efficient development of the processes. The exploitation of technology is essential in order to reach different aspects that are very important for the firm. Establishing electronic links with customers enables companies to transmit and receive information in order to develop activities based on crowdsourcing models, for example. By using more advanced technology and data sharing, one can increase the resource utilisation, and thus reduce costs [29]. Development in information and communication technology has made it possible to integrate the supply chain so that the links between firms and customers are easier to establish. The elementary factor in making these links feasible is that the companies must develop the information systems in accordance with standards and communication technology that the other parties can agree upon [30].

These elements or building blocks, that establish the TACCO Model, are the dimensions from which the firm needs to start in order to build up the interactions to prepare for collaboration with the customer. The building blocks do not necessarily combine with each other in a particular way; however, they are the elements around which the firm needs to refer to in order to establish a relationship. They are necessary in order to guarantee access and transparency within the dialogue and establish collaboration; furthermore, they have to supply the weapons to the customer through an open data approach in order to guarantee an equal position and role.

6 Conclusion and Future Directions

The components mentioned above, are aimed to find the boundaries and in order to focus a possible case study. We focused the Corporate Customership mainly linking the Value Co-creation and User Centered Innovation, in order to highlight the collaborative relationship between firm and customer. On the other hand, through the TACCO Model we pointed out the dimensions of the relationship typical of the Corporate Customership, based on competences and skills, typical of the B2B context, and an Open data approach therefore a strong exploitation of technology.

The next step will be to find these items in the policy of a firm in order to develop a case study and understand the true applicability of the Corporate Customership.

References

1. Angioni, E., Cabiddu, F.: Beyond entrepreneurial and user innovation: toward a theory of customership. In: EGOS 2013, 29th EGOS Colloquium, Bridging Continents, Cultures & Worldviews, HEC University, Montreal, 4–6 July 2013
2. Barry, J., Terry, T.S.: Empirical study of relationship value in industrial services. J. Bus. Ind. Mark. **23**(4), 228–241 (2008)
3. Gil-Saura, I., Frasquet-Deltoro, M., Cervera-Taulet, A.S.: The value of B2B relationships. Ind. Manag. Data Syst. **109**(5), 593–609 (2009)
4. O'Cass, A., Ngo, L.V.S.: Examining the firm's value creation process: a managerial perspective of the firm's value offering strategy and performance. Br. J. Manag. **22**(4), 646–671 (2011)
5. Prahalad, C.K., Ramaswamy, V.C.: Co-opting customer competence. Harv. Bus. Rev. **78**(1), 79–90 (2000)
6. Bendapudi, N., Leone, R.P.S.: Psychological implications of customer participation in co-production. J. Mark. **67**(1), 14–28 (2003)
7. Zahra, S. A.: Predictors and financial outcomes of corporate entrepreneurship: an exploratory study. J. Bus. Ventur. **6**(4), 259–285 (1991)
8. Kohli, R., Grover, V.S.: Business value of IT: an essay on expanding research directions to keep up with the times. J Assoc. Info. Syst. **9**(1), 23–39 (2008)
9. Von Hippel, E.C.: Democratizing Innovation. MIT Press, Cambridge (2005)
10. Angioni, E., Cabiddu, F.T.: The dynamics of innovation: linking corporate entrepreneurship and IT-enabled value co-creation. Organizational Change and Information Systems. pp. 293–300. Springer, Berlin (2013)
11. Payne, A.F., Storbacka, K., Frow, P.: Managing the co-creation of value. J. Acad. Mark. Sci. **36**(1), 83–96 (2008)
12. Vargo, S.L., Lusch, R.F.S.: The four service marketing myths: remnants of a goods-based, manufacturing model. J. Serv. Res. **6**(4), 324–335 (2004)
13. Sawhney, M., Verona, G., Prandelli, E.: Collaborating to create: the internet as a platform for customer engagement in product innovation. J. Interact. Mark. **19**, 4–17 (2005)
14. Priem, R.L.: A consumer perspective on value creation. Acad. Manag. Rev. **32**(1), 219–235 (2007)

15. Prahalad, C.K., Ramaswamy, V.: Co-creating unique value with customers. Strategy Leadersh. **32**(3), 4–9 (2004a)
16. Prahalad, C.K., Ramaswamy, V.C.: The Future of Competition: Co-creating Unique Value with Customers. Harvard Business School Press, Boston (2004)
17. Sullivan, T.J.T.: Collaboration. In: Friedman, A.M., Kaplan, H.I., Sadock, B.J. (eds.). McGraw-Hill (1998)
18. Coyle, J., Bardi, E.J., Langley, C.J.C.: The Management of Business Logistics, 6th edn. West Publishing, St. Paul (1996)
19. Stefansson, G.S.: Business-to-business data sharing: a source for integration of supply chains. Int. J. Prod. Econ. **75**(1), 135–146 (2002)
20. Levine, R., Locke, C., Searls, D., Weinberger, D.C.: The Cluetrain Manifesto: The End of Business as Usual. Perseus Publishing, Cambridge (2001)
21. Prahalad, C.K., Ramaswamy, V.S.: Co-creation experiences: the next practice in value creation. J. Interact. Mark. **18**(3), 5–14 (2004)
22. Roth, A.V., Jackson, W.: Strategic determinants of service quality and performance: evidence from the banking industry. Manag. Sci. **41** (11), 1720–1733 (1995)
23. Barua, A., Konana, P., Whinston, A., Yin, F.: An empirical investigation of net-enabled business value. MIS Q. **28** (4), 585–620 (2004)
24. Leonard-Barton, D.S.: Core capabilities and core rigidities: a paradox in managing new product development. Strateg. Manag. J. **13**(S1), 111–125 (1992)
25. Rosenzweig, E.D., Roth, A.V.: B2B seller competence: construct development and measurement using a supply chain strategy lens. J. Oper. Manag. **25**(6), 1311–1331 (2007)
26. Kothandaraman, P., Wilson, D.T.: The future of competition: value-creating networks. Ind. Mark. Manag. **30**(4), 379–389 (2001)
27. Jarillo, J.C.S.: On strategic networks. Strateg. Manag. J. **9**(1), 31–41 (1988)
28. Kandampully, J.S.: B2B relationships and networks in the internet age. Manag. Decis. **41**(5), 443–451 (2003)
29. Martin, A.: Infopartnering: The Ultimate Strategy for Achieving Efficient Consumer Response. Oliver Wight Publications (eds.), Essex Junction (1995)
30. Copal, C., Cypress, H.: Integrated Distribution Management. Irwin Publishing, Homewood (1995)

EmergenSYS: Mobile Technologies as Support for Emergency Management

Teresa Onorati, Ignacio Aedo, Marco Romano and Paloma Díaz

Abstract Emergency response is a critical phase of the Emergency Management (EM) process. EM operators have to deal with several difficulties such as easily communicating with victims and witness and retrieving information as accurate as possible. The emergency response can be defined as the result of the negotiation between common citizens and EM operators. Information technologies and particularly the web 2.0 open up new possibilities for integrating citizens' knowledge in the EM process. This approach not only can improve the capacity of local agencies to respond to unexpected events but also will contribute to build resilient communities aware of risks and able to mobilize their social capital to cope with disasters. In this paper we present a set of mobile tools designed to support the negotiation between common citizens and EM operators. Such tools can guide citizens in gathering effective information and keeping them informed with personalized information about the emergency.

Keywords Emergency management · Mobile computing · Augmented reality · Collaboration support · Interaction design

T. Onorati (✉) · I. Aedo · M. Romano · P. Díaz
Universidad Carlos III de Madrid, Madrid, Spain
e-mail: tonorati@inf.uc3m.es

I. Aedo
e-mail: aedo@ia.uc3m.es

M. Romano
e-mail: mromano@inf.uc3m.es

P. Díaz
e-mail: pdp@inf.uc3m.es

L. Caporarello et al. (eds.), *Smart Organizations and Smart Artifacts,*
Lecture Notes in Information Systems and Organisation 7,
DOI: 10.1007/978-3-319-07040-7_5,
© Springer International Publishing Switzerland 2014

1 Introduction

When an emergency occurs, governmental and no governmental agencies aim to solve the situation quickly. Within this scope, the management of updated information is a crucial activity in order to save as many people as possible. In particular, thanks to the fast growing of Web 2.0 technologies common citizens are taking a more active role in each phase of the Emergency Management (EM) process, namely preparedness, response, mitigation and recovery. With the support of effective Information and Communication Technology (ICT) tools, they become intelligent agents capable of contributing to reach a better solution for the crisis situation. Indeed, citizens can track alerts and the evolution of hazards, coordinate and collaborate in the local response, support community preparation or provide information and knowledge on how to recover from a disaster [1]. Moreover, citizens can be engaged in more activities, as it has been done in some local community response grids [2]. For instance, tools like Google Spreadsheets or Forms offer a very simple, quick, cheap and accessible mechanism that was used to coordinate the two thousand people who volunteered to help 60 min after the Boston Marathon bombing [3]. More advanced tools to visualize geo-referenced information in crisis maps [4] or grassroots online [5] like Sahana and Ushaidi might contribute to support a more active participation from citizens providing them with technological platforms to react to disasters.

Nowadays, the increasing usage of intelligent technologies as smartphones or tab-lets has prompted users to be active witness of any event happing around them. Photos, videos or audio recordings about common or exceptional circumstances are usually uploaded and shared within social platforms (e.g. Instagram). This practice could be particularly useful in case of emergencies in order to promote the participation of citizens as active agents and, in this way, contribute to generate resilient communities that have their own capacities and resources to deal with hazards and disasters [6].

The usage of mobile technologies in emergency situations has been already illustrated in [7]. Here the authors illustrate as these kinds of technologies can support EM operators during the management of a crisis directly in situ. This is because they allow operators to move easily from a place to another one bringing with them light and powerful instrumentation. Moreover, the authors highlight the importance to use advanced visualization modalities to allow the reading of a big amount of relevant data on small sized screens.

In classical approach, during the preparedness phase of the EM process, the governmental agencies are in charge of designing plans and training first responders to be ready to act in case of a critical event. Giving to citizens a more participative role, it is also crucial to manage social structures and communication channels to make the cooperation between EM workers and citizens easier [2]. In this way, the citizens can be prepared to be less vulnerable, helping not only themselves but also the response activities of the EM workers.

In other words, a crisis response can be defined as a negotiation between citizens and emergency agents. Indeed, as more accurate information citizens can

provide as more adequate can be the agents' response. For this proactive participation to be possible and effective, communities of citizens need to be empowered
to contribute successfully. In this context, even if citizens already have a powerful
means to communicate with emergency agents, which is the European 112
emergency number, they do not always exploit it.

From an initial survey we conducted involving EM operators and common
citizens, indeed, we state that often citizens avoid calling the emergency number if
they are not directly involved into the emergency. Sometimes they just think to be
not able to describe the event or they merely think that other people will call
instead of them. On the other hands even the emergency workers report the lack of
collaboration and accurate coming by the side of the citizens.

In the last decade, some alternatives to the traditional 112 calls have been
proposed exploiting the capabilities of modern mobile technologies. A relevant
example is SafetyGPS [8] that is experimenting in Spain. It allows people to send
messages about critical events to the Twitter account of a particular emergency
operation center.

Microsoft HelpBridge [9] supports citizens in connecting with organizations
involved in disaster response, allowing them to donate or offer themselves as
volunteers. This kind of applications presents some limitations that we want to
overcome in the present research.

The research group that is developing this project has a long proven experience
in developing software solutions aimed at supporting emergency operations during
different kinds of situations. A significant example of the work done so far has
been presented in [10]. SEMA4A is a knowledge base for making alert notifications about emergencies and evacuation procedures accessible for everybody in
any situation and in spite of any physical impairment. Based on this solution,
iNERES has been developed as a mobile application for receiving emergency
alerts [11]. In addition to SEMA4A, it exploits advanced mobile visualizations to
guide citizens in evacuating an in-door environment during a crisis situation. Such
advanced visualizations are based on emergent technologies such as augmented
reality techniques, which are usable and effective for involving users.

Based on our previous experience, in this paper we are going to introduce the
EmergensSYS project. This project aims at improving the communication and
cooperation between citizens and EM workers and consequently to improve the
efficiency of the response phase. Citizens are provided with different software tools
running on two of the main mobile platforms, Android and iOS. Mainly, we
distinguish between two different kinds of tools. Through the first one, users can
notify the EM organization about an incident as witness or victim. Through the
second one, users can receive alerts about current crisis that could affect them
directly. Moreover, these tools can be considered as collaborative actions for
sharing information between citizens and operators. The tools have been designed
exploiting a user-centered approach, involving a group of citizens and emergency
experts of the Valencia police. Moreover the scientific literature and existing
industrial solutions have been considered during the requirements extractions.

The next section is divided into two subsections that describe through scenarios the usages and the features of developed EmergenSYS prototypes. In the last section, some considerations and conclusions are given.

2 EmergenSYS Tools

The emergency response can be defined as the result of the negotiation between common citizens and EM operators. In such negotiation, common citizens offer information to receive adequate help.

The tools described in this section are part of the EmergensSYS project aimed at improving the communication between citizens and EM workers to enhance the negotiation and therefore the response. Citizens are provided with different software tools running on two of the main mobile platforms, Android and iOS, and their information is integrated in the systems used by the EM organizations.

In order to better describe the functionalities of the tools we present two emergency scenarios in which we show their potentialities. Each one of them is introduced focusing on three main factors: the *context* in which the tool is applied, the *system* description, and the *usage* by common citizens.

2.1 Scenario 1: Bomb Removal

Context. The Civil Protection of Madrid localized in a populated urban area an unexploded bomb of the civil war. The main objectives of the civil protection are to keep citizens involved into the crisis informed about the emergency, facilitating evacuation procedures and avoiding other citizens reaching the affected area. This would allow the emergency workers to remove the bomb and make safe the whole area without human obstacles.

System. The prototype developed to support the response of such emergency follows the architecture shown in Fig. 1a. The system retrieves the geographical position from the users' devices to determine if they are in the crisis area. If they are, they receive instructions for the evacuation. Otherwise, they receive general information about the situation. The evacuation route can be showed in different ways depending on the kind of the emergency and the users' abilities as proposed in [11]. There are two advanced visualization modes (see Fig. 1b): bi-dimensional maps and augmented reality views that overlap information on the images coming from the phone camera. Textual and audio descriptions can also be sent to users with visual impairment exploiting the design described in [12]. The system establishes the most appropriate visualization modality for each user on the basis of their profile, though they can always switch to the one they prefer.

The emergency response is strictly related to the negotiation between citizens and emergency agents. On one hand, citizens cooperate sending data about their

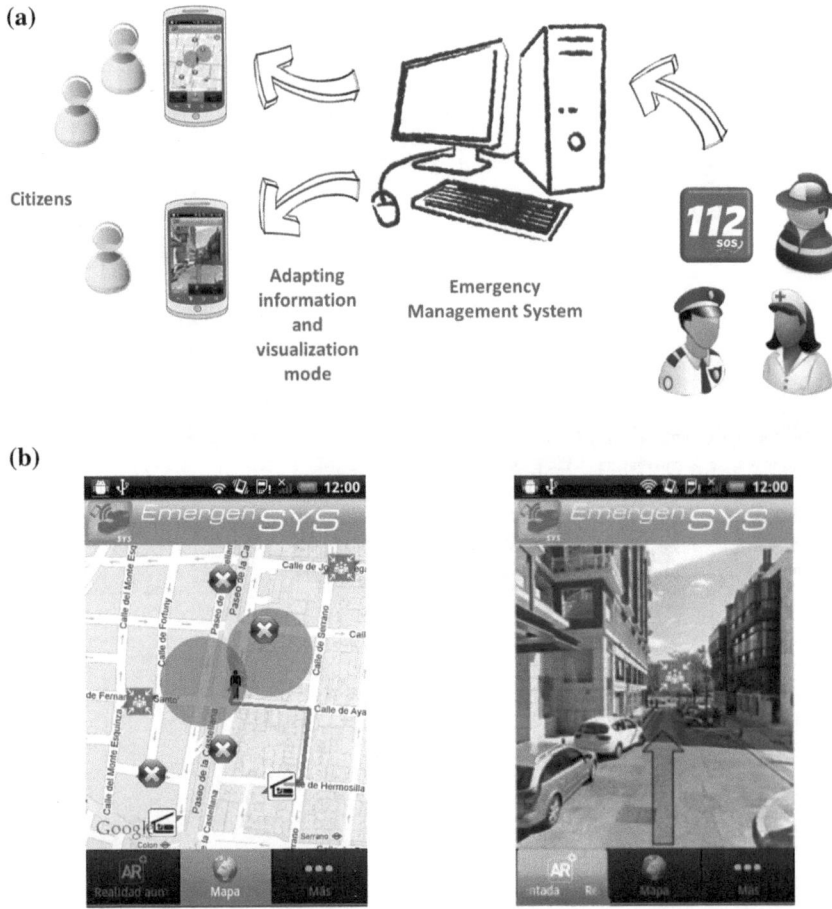

Fig. 1 Receiving alerts and evacuation plans from emergency agents **a** System architecture **b** Visualization modes in the interface

position and their profile to the command center. On the other hand, agents offer better services dealing more efficiently with the emergency response knowing the number of people involved and their situation. Then they send instructions personalized on the users' necessities.

Usage. The emergency response starts during the first hours of a working day; therefore, agents find out that the majority of the people are already far away from the affected area. However, they need to evacuate the remaining population and prevent that people got access to the area and to some streets that the artificers can use to carry the bomb. If people are still inside the critical area they receive a personalized evacuation route and all the information that can be useful. Figure 1b shows the crisis area depicted thorough red circles, the denied streets and the evacuation route. If people are outside the crisis area, they receive only information about the denied areas.

Fig. 2 Collecting data from human sensors **a** System architecture **b** Crisis selector **c** Multimedia manager **d** Map position

2.2 Scenario 2: Car Accident

Context. A car accident, involving a silver Mercedes, happened in a street beside a university campus of Madrid. The car impacted against a guardrail and only the car driver has been involved. The driver gets down the car and then falls down unconscious. A witness wants to alert the local police. The accuracy level of the information provided to the EM workers can make the emergency response adequate or not.

System. Figure 2a shows the architecture of the tool aimed to support this scenario. Through the mobile application, the witness can select the kind of emergency (see Fig. 2b). Successively, he can also send videos and pictures and/or a textual or audio description of the current situation (see Fig. 2c), and share his location. Texts or voice messages are less useful as many citizens do not provide

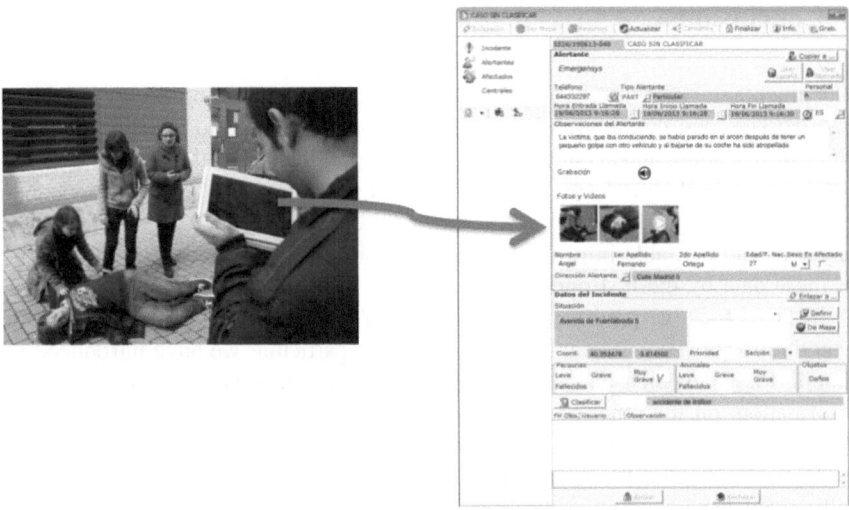

Fig. 3 Sending a report of an accident (simulated) and integrating it in the 112 EM system

relevant information to evaluate the situation. In fact, one of the main requirements to collaborate is to speak the same language, and normal citizens lack technical knowledge on risks [13].

Personal details, that are part of the user profile, are automatically extracted from the user's phone. The message is delivered to the EM center that, first of all, analyses and filters the contained information and then redirects it to the most appropriate emergency department. If citizens are not able to describe the emergency they can press a panic button and the application will try to automatically retrieve information to infer what happened (current user position, the user positions in the last hours, user profile, names of the people that the authority may contact, etc....).

Usage. The witness uses the mobile tool to alert the emergency operators. Through the application he takes three pictures of the current situation. The first two pictures have as subject the victim and the details of the abrasions. The last picture shows the involved car blocking the traffic. Moreover he describes recording directly his voice the evolution of the accident and point out the car position on the map (see Fig. 2d). Thereafter he sends the information to the command center. An emergency operator visualizes the message and thanks to the pictures carries out the conditions of the victim and of the traffic situation. He organizes the action involving an ambulance with adequate instrumentations and a tow car to remove the roadblock and reactivate the normal road safety. Figure 3 shows how a tester sends a report in a simulated accident and how this information is directly integrated in the interface that EM operators are using.

3 Conclusions

The emergency response can be considered as the result of a negotiation between EM workers and common citizens. Common citizens have to provide EM operators with as more and accurate information as possible about the emergency, their conditions and the grade of their engagement, in order to get the most adequate response. A successful solution for the crisis depends on the speed of gathering effective and trustable information about the situation and a proper interpretation of these data by the EM operators.

In this paper we presented the EmergenSYS project aimed at supporting the negotiation between citizens and EM agents. In particular we have introduced the mobile tools designed on one hand to guide people in easily gathering effective information, on the other hand to keep them informed about the crisis with personalized information to get safe areas or to stand by the affected ones.

The usability and the utility of the tools described in this paper were successfully evaluated in a pilot experience whose results are not detailed in this paper since the focus is on technical aspects of the applications and their usage. Further work will focus on other phases of the EM process. Particularly, we speak about those that could help to establish a continuous relationship with citizen to guarantee they will be able to use the tools when a crisis happens.

Acknowledgement This work is supported by the project emerCien grant funded by the Spanish Ministry of Economy and Competitivity (TIN2012-09687). EmergenSyS is a funded project by Spanish Ministry of Economy and Competitivity under INNPACTO programme. We also thank the collaboration of our industry partners Planet Media and Collaborative S.A.

References

1. White, C.M.: Social Media, Crisis, Communication, and Emergency Management: Leveraging Web 2.0 Technologies. CRC Press, Boca Raton (2012)
2. Jaeger, P.T., Shneiderman, B., Fleischmann, K.R., Preece, J., Qu, Y., Wu, F.P.: Community response grids: E-government, social networks, and effective emergency response. Telecommun. Policy 31(2007), 592–604 (2007)
3. Meier. P.: Self-organized crisis response to #BostonMarathon attack. http://irevolution.net/2013/04/16/bostonmarathon-attack/ (2013). Accessed Sept 2013
4. Oreilly, T.: What is Web 2.0: design patterns and business models for the next generation of software. Commun. Strateg. **17** (1) (2007)
5. Palen, L., Anderson, K. M., Mark, G., Martin, J., Sicker, D., Palmer, M., Grunwald, D.: A vision for technology-mediated support for public participation and assistance in mass emergencies and disasters. Proceedings of the 2010 ACM-BCS Visions of Computer Science Conference (ACM-BCS '10). British Computer Society, Swinton, 8-12 (2010)
6. Murphy, B.: Locating social capital in resilient community-level emergency management. Nat. Hazards **41**(2), 297–315 (2007)
7. Paolino, L., Romano, M., Sebillo, M., Vitiello, G.: Supporting the on-site emergency management through a visualization technique for mobile devices. J. Locat. Based Serv. **4**(3&4), 222–239 (2010)

8. www.safetygps.com. Accessed 11 Dec 2013
9. www.microsoft.com/about/corporatecitizenship/en-us/nonprofits/HelpBridge.aspx. Accessed 11 Dec 2013
10. Malizia, A., Onorati, T., Diaz, P., Aedo, I., Astorga-Paliza, F.: SEMA4A: an ontology for emergency notification systems accessibility. Expert Syst. Appl. **37** (4), 3380–3391 (2010)
11. Aedo, I., Yu, S., Díaz, P., Acuña, P., Onorati, T.: Personalized alert notifications and evacuation routes in indoor environments. Sensors **12**(6), 7804–7827 (2012)
12. Di Chiara, G., Paolino, L., Romano, M., Sebillo, M., Tortora, G., Vitiello, A.: Ginige: the Framy user interface for visually-impaired users. ICDIM **2011**, 36–41 (2011)
13. Waugh, W.L., Streib, G.: Collaboration and leadership for effective emergency management. Public Adm. Rev. **66**(s1), 131–140 (2006)

The Economic and Legal Perspectives of Cloud Computing in Italian Public Administration and a Roadmap to the Adoption of g-Cloud in Italy

Francesca Spagnoli, Carlo Amendola and Francesco Crenca

Abstract Cloud computing has reached a high level of adoption worldwide. In Italy, the adoption of Cloud Computing for the Public Administration is still far from the European and American best practices due to infrastructural, economic, legal and organisational culture reasons. The Italian Public Administration is facing enormous challenges in order to build a long term strategy capable of delivering the benefits required from the government and citizens, evaluating and reducing the potential regulatory, economic and environmental risks. The new emerging paradigm of the Public Administration, that many authors called as "g-Cloud", should be implemented and managed through a common and coherent strategy. Starting from a comparative analysis of the g-Cloud state of the art in Europe and in America, the objective of the paper is to provide a roadmap showing the future steps needed for the adoption of g-Cloud in Italy, by analyzing the main economic and legal perspectives of Cloud Computing for the Italian Government and Public Administration.

Keywords Cloud computing · Public administration · g-Cloud · Economic perspectives · Legal perspectives · SWOT analysis · Roadmap

1 Economic Perspectives of g-Cloud

Cloud Computing is not a new concept; it is a combination of older technologies which have been developed in different contexts, such as Grid Computing, web 2.0, Application Service Provider and others. The success of Cloud infrastructures

F. Spagnoli (✉) · C. Amendola · F. Crenca
Università degli Studi di Roma La Sapienza, Roma, Italy
e-mail: francesca.spagnoli@uniroma1.it

C. Amendola
e-mail: carlo.amendola@uniroma1.it

F. Crenca
e-mail: francescocrenca@libero.it

L. Caporarello et al. (eds.), *Smart Organizations and Smart Artifacts*,
Lecture Notes in Information Systems and Organisation 7,
DOI: 10.1007/978-3-319-07040-7_6,
© Springer International Publishing Switzerland 2014

stems from the huge economic benefits that the platform generates, such as: easier access, faster cycle times, ease of deployment, optimised utilisation, greater utilization rates, enhanced business continuity and refocusing IT on business value, best-in challenge technology adoption, reuse and share of resources, greater efficiency of provision due mainly to the scalability of services, flexibility, allowing to create new computing resource to experiment with, more rapid and increased ROI or time to value with lower upfront investments, reduced development, delivery and operation costs, support and maintenance, agility, reducing time to market. The pure technological benefits of Cloud technologies, such as flexibility, scalability, easy use, greater utilization rates and efficiency of provision, have higher impact on g-Cloud because they allow to eliminate CAPEX, increase OPEX and improve ROI, which are attractive propositions for Public Administrations. In the current economic scenario, these capabilities allows public companies to construct new systems without the need of huge capital investments in new IT infrastructure and further to grow the new systems to meet ever-changing business requirements at a rapid pace, which undoubtedly is a drift for innovation. Another relevant benefit of g-Cloud is the development of virtual ownership resources and user-friendly interfaces, which improve Identity and Federation management mechanisms for large g-Cloud communities.

Moreover, according to OECD [1], Cloud Computing technologies can contribute to handle the economic crisis with high-speed internet, green ICTs and smart applications, increasing ICT specialists employment. The Cloud Computing profitability is based on economies of scale which, as a result, leads to better optimized rates. The main benefit of Cloud infrastructures are also related to the reduction of production costs. In addition to investment costs, the operation of infrastructures and the use of the services, we need to consider also the cost that does not emerge from transaction, for instance the opportunity cost needed to carry out activities as software update, learning and implementation of new regulations, or to enable the decision making process for the purchase, installation and the creation of new infrastructures to meet the continuously evolving needs of the market. Cloud Computing infrastructures allow companies and institutions to reduce investment fixed costs in IT (hardware and software) of the initial phase of business (when typically a company produces less quantity of products), transforming them into an operating cost for the company or the institution [2]. The services purchased by the cloud providers are variable costs that can increase or decrease as a function of demand and of the production.

The reduction of the fixed IT cost and of the total fixed costs, and the consequent increasing of the IT variable cost and of the total variable costs is determined by the Cloud Computing pay-as-you-go model reducing the total cost. Cloud Computing allows companies and institutions to reach the break-even point earlier and thus reduce the losses [3].

From the economic perspective, the most relevant weakness of Cloud infrastructures is the lack of a validated and widely accepted business model concerning pricing, ROI, cost structure, TCO versus outsourcing comparison and predictions about eventual costs of service interruption or disruption, especially in the Public Administration context. Furthermore, another considerable issue is related to marginal costs: indeed, depending on the volume of data and compute, operating on a Cloud provider's infrastructure may become more expensive than providing the necessary IT infrastructure in-house. A mixed-use strategy, in which some of the applications and services are delivered in-house and others continue to be hosted in the Cloud, should be considered by the Public Administration in order to allow a slow but safe migration of the data to the Cloud. The Cloud Computing weaknesses can have a negative impact on the Government because they can affect the reputation, trust and confidence due to data loss, account phishing and fraud, and cause even more economic damages for the institution and national and local level. To date, there are no developed models to quantify the economic and social cost played up by these losses. Furthermore, at the economic level, an exact forecast method to predict economic performances of Cloud technologies has not yet been developed. This issue makes the economic evaluation process of g-Cloud strategies even more cumbersome. However, the most outstanding problem for a fast adoption of g-Cloud in the Government environment is the loss of data control due to the Cloud abstractions. The success of performance management issues for g-Cloud applications will depend on what minimal abstractions can be exposed to users, in order to enable the needed performance behaviours and be adequately controlled.

2 Legal Perspectives of g-Cloud

Currently, there are no specific National or European rules which govern contracts for the Cloud Computing. Contracts offered by Cloud providers belong to the category of so-called "for adhesion" contracts, in which the clauses are not negotiable, and often do not define some sensitive issues, such as accountability, service levels, applicable laws. These contracts may therefore not be consistent with the regulations governing in Italy the public contracts [4]. Ernesto Belisario [5] believes that, with reference to the SaaS contract, which is concluded between the parties, it should be considered within the category of public services, governed by articles. 1655 and subsequent, as it is required by the Public Procurement Code [6]. Stefano Bendani [7] states that a Cloud Computing service, having the characteristics of a provision of one or more software supplied by an organization with resources and their own management by means of a payment of a fee, it may be inserted in the configuration of "service contracts". The Public Administration, which wants to make use of Cloud Computing, has to follow the procedures for awarding according to the rules of public evidence. The Cloud contract has its cause in the providing of the required service, respecting the minimum agreed Service Level Agreements (SLA) [8]. First, the service supplier must ensure the presence, on the Italian territory or within the EU, of the infrastructure used specifying that, to the contract, the Italian law has to be applied. The service provider has to ensure an adequate monitoring system to check the activities and the services provided by the supplier and contractual penalties for the violation of any agreed standard of quality. Then, it will be necessary to define the obligations for the service supplier, the commitments to be assumed at startup, execution and conclusion of the contract, the continuity degree in service delivery, checks to verify that the proper service performances are provided, the definition of appropriate systems which are activated in case of unforeseen events or malfunction of the instruments, in order to avoid or limit any interruption of the service, the preparation of systems for data security supporting the recovery mode and the storage in case of malfunctions. The Public Administration, which wants to acquire Cloud products and services must therefore follow all the procedures needed for the identification of the economic contractor and must sign with this subject a public contract according to the Legislative Decree n. 163/2006 [6] and its implementing regulation, approved by Presidential Decree. 207/2010 [9].

The article. 13 of Legislative Decree no. 39/1993 [10] provides that the conclusion by the Public Administration of contracts for the construction of automated information systems (such as certain major contracts under art. 9–17) has to be preceded by the execution of feasibility studies aimed to the definition of organizational and functional targets of the administration. Unlike to other countries, where Cloud Service suppliers are subjected to a certification, in Italy, due to the absence of specific qualification procedures for a Cloud Service provider, it will be required a high quality standard of the qualification system of the provider (Articles 41 and 42 of the Code). The criterion to be used to identify the best contractor should be related to the most favorable economic offer (Art. 83 of the Code).

2.1 Security and Privacy in g-Cloud

The Cloud infrastructure for the PA must comply with Italian art. 19 of the Privacy Code co. 3 for what is related to the communication of common data to private entities, and these have to be admitted just when them are provided for by a rule of law. Specific care should be made also with regard to the territorial area involved in the data transfer, because while for the European Union it must be considered a protection model suitable to EU standards, it does not happen the same thing for their transfer to non-European areas. There are, however, specific tools to make possible the transfer, like as: (1) the individual's approval, (2) the Model Clause, approved by the European Commission, (3) the Binding Corporate Rules (BCR), and in case of data importer belongs to the United States of America, (4) the Safe Harbor.

In choosing, therefore, a particular procurement model of IT services it must be well to consider all opportunities for effective and efficient mechanisms for managing the security offered by the Cloud Service Provider (CSP). The Cloud

Service Consumer (CSC) should consider the reputation of the CSP, the laws and legal compliance, allocations of roles and responsibilities between the CSP and the CSC, the right to control, the third-party access to sensitive and confidential information, data segregation between customers (in particular in the public Cloud type), the accessibility, the portability and the data interoperability, and the secure data deletion at the appointed time. In addition, the CSC must demand from CSP guarantees of transparency, guarantees of privacy, focus on the management of cross-border flow of information, assurance of conformity (the customer can carry out audits on compliance with laws and industry standards, affecting the data transferred in the Cloud) certifications provided by third parties on the proper execution of the services in the Cloud, a contract, which, among other things, must contemplate the case in which are necessary adaptations of compliance (e.g. new regulations of Privacy or of sector) in a non-punitive manner for the customer and the right to the Audit. Waiting, therefore, for the reform of the Directive 95/46/EC [11] on the protection of individuals with regard to the processing of personal data and their freedom of movement, should be kept, today, to the utmost account the official positions of the Italian Guarantor and, at European level, those of the Working Group art. 29 [12], which have addressed some aspects of the regulation of cloud computing. It is important that personal information may be modified or canceled with effect on all copies in the system. This issue is addressed, today, only on a technical level, lacking even a law in this regard. Another problem to be solved is related to the minimization of the data and of the treatments (data minimization), as the Cloud, by its nature, works on the opposite principle, that of the redundancy information. The Legislative Decree 196/2003 [13]—Code regarding the protection of personal data (Privacy) provides data backup (especially those sensitive and judicial), which is a form of information redundancy, as a minimum measure of security. Even the Legislative Decree 82/2005 [14] and Legislative Decree 235/2010 [15], containing rules aimed at business continuity and disaster recovery assume forms of data redundancy.

Digit PA [16], in its guidelines, aims to ensure the continuity of the functioning of public organizations. It must be not forgot that in the Privacy Code, art. 22, co. 3 and 5, the principle of data minimization has a mandatory meaning in the public context and respects certain types of data (sensitive and judicial). As regards the protection of personal data one of the most delicate aspects is the role allocation. Given that the Public Administration, which acquires Cloud services, it is indeed, considered the data controller, the problem arises for the Cloud provider, which could be considered autonomous owner of treatment or manager. The current legislation on the protection of personal data, for a number of reasons stated by the Italian Institute for privacy [17] considers it as an independent data controller, as opposed to what you defers in the practice of the agreements, which defines it, instead, head outside. The apical position of the holder, moreover, corresponds to the legal responsibility that led him to exercise control and report on the claim of responsibility (pursuant to art. 29 Privacy Code). Since the transmission of data to another data controller goes to integrate a communication operation, if the recipient is a private entity and provided data are common data, it is needed the support of a specific provision of the law (Article 19 co. 3 Privacy Code). The same applies to judicial data, according to the general rule of art. 21 Privacy Code [13], which for the lawfulness of the processing requires the express provision of the law of the Data Protection Authority. It will be important, therefore, for what concerns the beneficiary administration to enforce the rule of art. Co. 6 22 of the Privacy Code [13] on the use of encryption techniques, which make the data unintelligible, whether the cloud provider is responsible or autonomous owner of treatment. The principle of separation from other personal data is important (art. 22, co. 7 Privacy Code) [13].

3 SWOT Analysis of g-Cloud

3.1 Strengths

The main strengths of Cloud infrastructures for the PA are related to the fact that through the Cloud, the PA is able to implement synergies based on the standardization and sharing of resources. It enables the rationalization of the public infrastructure, by reducing unnecessary expenses and increases economies of scale for the PA. Cloud encourages the introduction of technologies and services useful for implementing fast innovation processes. This kind of efficiency in the P.A. will delete the duplication of functions and management activities, the under-utilization of computing resources, energy consumption, fragmentation of contracts with suppliers. Data portability allows the client to stop the service without incurring in inconveniences that are difficult to predict (Table 1).

3.2 Weaknesses

Before choosing a Cloud infrastructure, the client should consider that, relying on a remote supplier, it may lose the complete and direct control over their data. It is important that the P.A. defines with the Cloud provider a contingency plan. Latency issues can appear through Cloud. If the application requires a large amount of data to be transferred, the Cloud is not the best choice to be adopted, as the benefits brought by a large computational capacity would be largely obscured. Moreover, currently there are no international or national widely accepted contracts/legislations about Cloud Computing. Nowadays, Cloud contracts mostly belong to the category of the so called "Membership" contracts, in which the terms are not negotiable and often do not define sensitive aspects (e.g. responsibilities, level of services, applicable legislation).

Table 1 SWOT analysis of g-Cloud

Strengths	*Weaknesses*
• Economic and organisational impact	• Loss of direct control on data
• Shared infrastructures	• Connectivity issues
• Portability and interoperability	• Latency issues
• Maintenance and simplified updates	• Limitations of the regulation
• Reliability	
Opportunities	*Threats*
• No capital expenditures	• Migration of data and service availability
• Elasticity	• Data security issues
• Sharing of information and control	• Privacy issues
• Economic benefits	• Potential problems of security during the deletion of data
• Reduction of complexity	
• Self-service provisioning	
• Utilities	

3.3 Opportunities

Cloud computing will significantly reduce the risk factor of the projects, allowing to develop a greater experimentation. Start-up costs will be reduced, as well as the costs of errors or closure. Furthermore, Cloud Computing infrastructures allow to facilitates access to data and programs remotely, anytime, from any computer connected to the Internet, including portable devices. As regards the control, Cloud Computing allows clients to install new features more quickly and integrate them with existing ones. This allows to reduce the time for planning, decision-making and deployment. Updating and monitoring of IT centralized tools are more controllable. Self-service provisioning through a simple web portal, rather than through an IT process, can reduce losses in the pattern of consumption, allowing provisioning and rapid integration of new services.

3.4 Risks

In case of accidents or technical failures it could be difficult for the user to migrate data from one system to another Cloud, or to exchange information with entities that use Cloud services of different vendors, producing portability or interoperability of data risks. Data security issues can be relevant in g-Cloud. The data controller must ensure that technical and organizational measures are designed to minimize the risks of destruction or loss of data, even if accidental or in case of an unauthorized access, that treatment is not in accordance with the purposes of data collection, data editing as a result of unauthorized or non-compliant. The owner of the processing of personal data, which transfers the treatment on the Cloud, must designate Cloud provider as controller. The Privacy regulation provides that the holder exercises a power control in relation to the controller, ensuring the correct execution of instructions in relation to personal data processed. The regulation also sets out precise rules for the transfer of personal data outside the EU, which does not provide an adequate level of protection.

4 Roadmap to the Adoption of g-Cloud in Italy

The current Italian Public Administration is constituted by a very fragmented infrastructure, often inefficiently managed. The central P.A. has 1,033 data centers, and the local P.A. is constituted by other 3,000 data centers with high costs [4]. The IT spending of the Italian P.A. is huge and related to hidden costs of ownership (about 1 billion per year), when, optimizing human resources and energy expenditures, the P.A. could spend no more than 270–300 million [4]. The Cloud would enable the Italian P.A. to reduce costs, system inefficiencies and delays. A well-defined process of transformation for the correct adoption of g-Cloud in Italy is necessary and to this end we suggest the following roadmap in order to provide the basis for optimizing the efficiency of the Italian Public Administration:

- to rationalize the IT infrastructure, currently consisting of about 20,000 people working on the management of data centers and requiring 140 billion a year for expenditure of servers
- to adopt energy saving policies through the implementation of a Cloud infrastructure
- to initiate a dematerialization process, reducing and possibly eliminating the need to maintain data in a paper form. In this way, in addition to costs, Clouds would also reduce the time required to manage and dispatch information, improving the efficiency of the employees of the central and local P.A.
- to standardize the IT platforms, by using a single central infrastructure, which will be connected to different private clouds for local Public Administrations requiring an higher level of protection of personal data
- to develop a single contract for the central platform and specific other personalized contract for the private Clouds, carefully evaluating the Service Level Agreements (SLA) that should be adopted
- to provide targeted training to the employees that will use the new IT infrastructures, in order to provide also information about the new organizational culture
- to initiate sharing process of standardized procedures and common applications, improving services for citizens. This process will allow the P.A. to refocus local resources toward the most relevant activities and ensure a more effective execution of common activities.

5 Conclusions

The previous economic and legal perspectives analysis of g-Cloud in Italy provides a short overview of the current situation and several consideration about Cloud Computing for the Public Administration sector. By taking into account the huge delay of the Italian Public Administration in using Cloud platforms and in completing the data dematerialisation process, we consider that it will take at least 10 years for a full adoption of these infrastructures. The Public Administration will start to use a private Cloud infrastructure, but only by implementing an hybrid model, allowing to provide a homogeneous set of applications anywhere, anytime and from any device, the Italian P.A. will completely benefit from the advantages of Cloud solutions. To achieve this goal, the Italian P.A. has to change the organisational culture and to understand what are the potential risks related to Cloud infrastructures, in order to manage them effectively, since the signing of the contract with the provider, through the required Service Level Agreements.

References

1. OECD.: Network Developments in Support of Innovation and User Needs. DSTI/ICCP/CISP(2009)2/FINAL, OECD, Paris (2009)
2. Pierre Audoin Consultants: Economic and social impact of software & software-based services. http://cordis.europa.eu/fp7/ict/ssai/docs/study-sw-report-final.pdf (2010)
3. The Open Group: Cloud computing for business: the open group guide. http://www.wiki.opengroup.org (2010)
4. DigitPA: Raccomandazioni e proposte sull'utilizzo del cloud computing nella pubblica amministrazione, version 2.0 of June 28, 2012. http://www.digitpa.gov.it/sites/default/files/notizie/Raccomandazioni%20Cloud%20e%20PA%20-%202.0_0.pdf (2012)
5. Belisario, E.: Cloud computing in legal informatics, No. 17 eBook Lawyer Media (2011)
6. Dlgs 12 aprile 2006, n. 163, Codice dei contratti pubblici relativi a lavori, servizi e forniture in attuazione delle direttive 2004/17/CE e 2004/18/CE, in Gazzetta Ufficiale n. 100 del 2 maggio 2006—Supplemento Ordinario n. 107. http://www.camera.it/parlam/leggi/deleghe/06163dl.htm (2006)
7. Bendani, S.: Software as a service: legal aspects and negotiation. Altalex.it (2008)
8. Bellini, F., D'Ascenzo, F., Ghi, A., Spagnoli, F., Traversi, V.: Legal Issues and Requirements for Cloud Computing in e-Science. The New Springer Series: Lecture Notes in Information Systems and Organisation (LNISO), vol. 2 (2012)
9. Dlgs 5 ottobre 2010, n. 207, Regolamento di esecuzione e attuazione del decreto legislativo 12 Aprile 2006, n.163 recante "Codice dei contratti pubblici relativi a lavori, servizi e forniture in attuazione delle Direttive 2004/17/CE e 2004/18/CE, in Gazzetta Ufficiale n.288 del 10/12/2010—Supplemento Ordinario n. 270. http://www.regolamentoappalti.it/ (2010)
10. Dlgs 12 febbraio 1993, n. 39, Norme in materia di sistemi informativi automatizzati delle amministrazioni pubbliche, a norma dell'art. 2, comma 1, lettera mm), della legge 23 ottobre 1992, n. 421, in Gazzetta Ufficiale n.42 del 20/02/1993. http://www.normattiva.it/uri-res/N2Ls?urn:nir:stato:decreto.legislativo:1993-02-12;39 (1993)

11. The European Parliament and the Council: Directive 95/46/EC of the European Parliament and of the Council of 24 October 1995 on the protection of individuals with regard to the processing of personal data and on the free movement of such data, in Official Journal L 281, 23/11/1995 P. 0031—0050. http://eurlex.europa.eu/LexUriServ/LexUriServ.do?uri=CEL EX:31995L0046:en:HTML (1995)
12. The European Parliament, Article 29 Data Protection Working Party: Opinion 1/2010 on the concepts of "controller" and "processor". Article 29 Data protection working party, data protection and data security issues related to cloud computing in the EU 11. http://ec.europa. eu/justice_home/fsj/privacy/docs/wpdocs/2010/wp169_en.pdf (2010)
13. Dlgs 30 giugno 2003, n. 196, Codice in materia di protezione dei dati personali, in Gazzetta Ufficiale n. 174 del 29 luglio 2003—Supplemento Ordinario n. 123. http://www.camera.it/ parlam/leggi/deleghe/03196dl.htm (2003)
14. Dlgs 7 marzo 2005, n. 82, Codice dell'amministrazione digitale, pubblicato nella Gazzetta Ufficiale n. 112 del 16 maggio 2005—Supplemento Ordinario n. 93. http://www.camera.it/ parlam/leggi/deleghe/05082dl.htm (2005)
15. Dlgs 30 dicembre 2010, n. 235, Modifiche ed integrazioni al decreto legislativo 7 marzo 2005, n. 82, recante Codice dell'amministrazione digitale, a norma dell'articolo 33 della legge 18 giugno 2009, n. 69, in Gazzetta Ufficiale n.6 del 10-1-2011—Suppl. Ordinario n. 8. http://www.normattiva.it/uri-res/N2Ls?urn:nir:stato:decreto.legislativo:2010-12-30;235!vig= (2010)
16. Digit PA: Guidelines for disaster recovery of public administration. http://www.digitpa.gov. it/sites/default/files/linee%20guida%20per%20il%20disaster%20recovery%20delle%20pa_ 0.pdf (2011)
17. The Italian Institute for privacy: Cloud computing and data protection in Italy: a challenge as an example for Europe. In: Law and Economics Information Technology and the Privacy Act (2011)

Virtual Organization in the Cloud: The Case of a Web Self-Service Portal

Roberto Candiotto and Silvia Gandini

Abstract The interpretation of organizations like dynamic entities imposes some fundamental challenges for today managers. Firms have not derived value simply by linking IT to their business processes: they have learned how to benefit from IT by developing a competency in creating and evolving an enterprise in IT architecture, able to identify and implement the organization's strategic objectives. Some providers that operate in the Cloud market have faced this challenge by developing their infrastructure as a virtual platform, which are useful to reach economies of scale and to support innovation at the same time. This work, through the analysis of a successful case, is aimed to point out the organizational characteristic of a Cloud self-service portal, and its coherence with the main business drivers of Cloud market.

Keywords Service management · Service strategy · Service lifecycle · Virtual organization · Cloud computing · Platform as a service · ITIL V3

Although this work is the result of a common will, every paragraph has been written by a single author; particularly:
1st and 4th sections by Roberto Candiotto;
2nd and 3rd sections by Silvia Gandini.

R. Candiotto · S. Gandini (✉)
Dipartimento di Studi per l'Economia e l'Impresa, Università del Piemonte Orientale,
Novara, Italy
e-mail: silvia.gandini@eco.unipmn.it

R. Candiotto
e-mail: roberto.candiotto@eco.unipmn.it

L. Caporarello et al. (eds.), *Smart Organizations and Smart Artifacts*,
Lecture Notes in Information Systems and Organisation 7,
DOI: 10.1007/978-3-319-07040-7_7,
© Springer International Publishing Switzerland 2014

1 Introduction

The concept of Service Lifecycle is central to the discipline of IT Service Management, performed by the IT Service Provider through people, process and Information Technology. This discipline can be seen as an enabler of IT governance objectives, because it is not concerned with the details of how to use a particular vendor's product, or necessarily with the technical details of the systems under management. Instead, it focuses upon providing a framework to structure IT-related activities and the interactions of IT technical personnel with business customers and users. According to this perspective, it is vital that services are seen in their entirety from strategic conception to retirement and that they are reviewed and improved throughout their life; the business model for Service Management is a great platform to build excellent services that contribute to economic recovery and business improvement. This is why IT Service Management is often equates with the Information Technology Infrastructure Library (ITIL), the official publication of the Cabinet Office in the United Kingdom.[1]

The vision of computing like a service focuses on the linkage between business processes and IT services so that the first can be seamlessly automated using the second; Service Computing has led to develop software for millions to consume, rather than to run on their individual computers [1]. To deliver this vision, many computing paradigms have been proposed over the last few years,[2] but Cloud Computing represents an extension of them wherein the capabilities of business applications are exposed as sophisticated services that can be accessed over a network.[3]

Many researchers focused their attention on this phenomenon, focusing on its potential to transform large parts of the IT industry [2, 3], and identifying its most relevant features such as the prevalence of economic variables and of organizational implications and goals [4, 5] over purely technological aspects. But very few works have concretely analyzed what potentialities can emerge from the combination of the global availability of Cloud Computing infrastructure at a low cost and innovative Cloud services, in order to realize virtual platform for

---

[1] ITIL is the most widely adopted approach for IT Service Management in the world. It provides a practical, no-nonsense framework for identifying, planning, delivering and supporting IT services to the business. *Source* http://www.itil-officialsite.com/qualifications/creditprofiler.aspx.

[2] Here are some paradigms promising to deliver IT as a service: Web, Data Centers, Service-Oriented Architecture, Grid Computing, P2P Computing, Market-Oriented Computing.

[3] In our previous work (*Organizations and new IT paradigms: processes and organizational implications related to Cloud Computing projects*, ItAIS Conference 2012) Cloud Computing was defined as a set of technologies, typically in the shape of a service offered to a client by a provider, which enable to store, to file away and to process data items, thanks to the use of hardware and software resources, distributed and shared in a virtual platform on line.

service-oriented strategies.[4] Providers able to build process-driven applications in the Cloud, can assemble and orchestrate them in a customer oriented Self-Service Portal, to fully deliver useful business advantages and efficient solutions. The portal framework is strongly inspired by the concept of Virtual Organization, defined as the organizational model that uses technology to dynamically link people, assets and ideas.

In the light of previous considerations, and through the analysis of the success case of Kelyan Integrated Self-Service Portal,[5] this paper's objective is to answer the following research questions:

1. According to the Cloud paradigm:

   - What are the most recent trends in the market of Cloud platforms?
   - What are the top benefits IT providers should assure final users?

2. According to the organization of a Self-Service Portal:

   - What kind of resources Cloud providers need, to structure the portal like a Virtual Organization?
   - How the Service Lifecycle approach can influence the phases through which the portal is developed?
   - What are the main activities of each of the phase?

2 The Market of Cloud Platforms

Companies currently employ Cloud services in order to improve their business scalability and to deal with fluctuations in resource demands. However, at present, a large part of Cloud providers have inflexible pricing, generally limited to flat rates or tariffs based on usage thresholds, and consumers are restricted to offers from a single provider at a time. Moreover, many providers have proprietary interfaces to their services thus restricting the ability of consumers to swap one provider for another. Since user requirements for Cloud services are varied, providers should be able to ensure that they can be flexible in their service delivery while keeping final users isolated from the underlying infrastructure.

Cloud Computing can be divided in two main areas: (a) *Cloud services and applications* and (b) *Cloud infrastructure*. The first one delivers business driven

---

[4] Literature analysis has been realized on the abstracts of 733 paper, from January 2009 to June 2013, of these publications: *European Journal of Information Systems, Information Systems Journal, Information Systems Research, Journal of AIS, Journal of MIS, MIS Quarterly* [first six excellence journal and review according to the ranking of Association for Information Systems (AIS)]. The analysis has shown that only two paper are related to the design, the use, and the implications of virtual processes for Service Strategy in the Cloud sector.

[5] http://www.kelyan.it

value, with a subscription model based on "Pay as you Use"; applications are virtualized, and customers can access and use without having them physically implemented in their IT environment. The infrastructure area delivers computing capacity, network capacity, and storage capacity as needed, in a usage model based on "Pay as you Grow".

This is the key concept of Public Cloud, based on a customized platform to suit the needs of end-users, where providers can sell applications, or provide access them-selves as a service. Virtualized platforms possess the capability to strongly support the association of dynamically composable services with Web Service interfaces, and the creation of third party value added services, by building service shop-windows on the Cloud.

According to Forrester Research, the Platform as a Service (PaaS) will become a $15 billion market in the USA by 2016 and is now starting to expand, leading many Information Systems vendors to make their old product suitable for the Cloud. Not all of them will be able to do this with their own resources; actually in fact the Cloud market is characterized by the presence of the following categories of provider:

- *Utility provider* Generally equipped with relevant infrastructures and economic capabilities, they can be provider of applications, conceived as Cloud services, or provider of functions for the elaboration of data and for basic business processes.
- *Niche provider* Generally skilled in services for the support of specific functional activities, they use their specialization to offer personalized services and organizational behaviors closer to IT outsourcing logics.

Hence, it's reasonable to think that: (1) the collaboration of both on a virtual platform could lead Cloud to generate additional revenue streams for customers by enhancing, extending, and inventing new value propositions; (2) Cloud is being used to improve, transform, and create new organizational value chains, on condition that providers can assure the following top benefits[6]:

1. *Cost flexibility* It is a key reason many companies consider Cloud adoption in the first place. A major challenge for Cloud providers is finding ways to reduce capacity quickly, particularly where some parts of customers' businesses are in trouble and no longer have money or budget to fund the IT services. Cloud services can in fact help an organization reduce fixed IT costs (software licenses, servers and net-working equipment) by enabling a shift from capital expenses to operational expenses.
2. *Business scalability* By allowing for rapid provisioning of resources without scale limitations, Cloud enables a company to benefit from economies of scale without the high costs in time and finance. To impact on customers' businesses

---

[6] The described benefits have been identified through the collaboration with IBM (direct interviews in the period May–June 2013).

it is important for Cloud providers to define their IT services in terms that final users understand, describing them in a Service Catalogue.

3. *Market adaptability* By enabling businesses to rapidly adjust processes, products, and services to meet the changing needs of the market, Cloud in turn facilitates rapid prototyping and innovation and helps speed time to market. To do this, Cloud providers must project a Service Portfolio, in order to represent the commitments and investments made across all their customers and market spaces. The portfolio enables providers to optimize their investments and develop service offerings that will maximize value to the business.

4. *Masked complexity* Cloud provides a way for organizations to hide some of the intricacies of their operations from final users, helping them to attract a broader range of consumers. Because complexity is veiled from the end user, a company can expand its product and service sophistication without also increasing the level of user knowledge necessary to utilize or maintain the product or service.

5. *Ecosystem connectivity* Cloud facilitates external collaboration with partners and customers, which can lead to improvements in productivity and increased innovation. Through the development of Cloud platforms providers can bring together disparate groups of people who can collaborate and share resources, information, and processes.

3 The Organization of a Virtualized Self-Service Portal

Cloud Computing is "a model for enabling ubiquitous, convenient, on-demand network access to a shared pool of configurable computing resources (networks, servers, storage, applications, and services) that can be rapidly provisioned and re-leased with minimal management effort or service provider interaction".[7] The concept of "interaction" between different resources in a virtual space is based on the idea of an organization that uses networks of communication as a framework, and technology as a tool and enabler for innovation. When Cloud Computing is conceived as a public service, it can be interpreted as a Virtual Organization, where the infrastructure is provisioned for an open use by the general public, resources are shared, and dynamically allocated, according to customers' real needs.

The analysis of a top provider in the PaaS market has enabled us to identify some guidelines, that characterize the planning, the development, and the organization of an Integrated Self-Service Portal (Fig. 1).

---

[7] *Source* http://www.nist.gov/.

Fig. 1 The organization of
Kelyan integrated self-service
portal

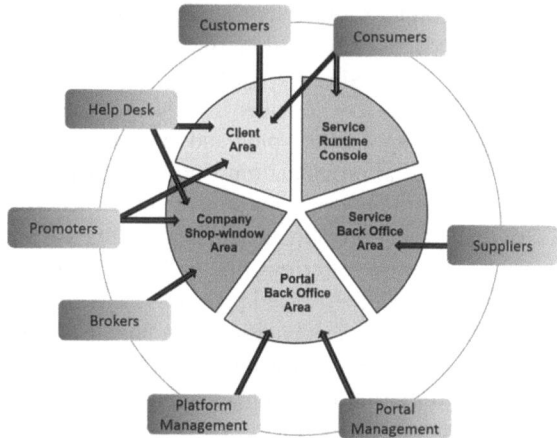

Analyzed company Kelyan[8]
Research methodology success case study
Goals

- identification and description of the main roles involved in the Virtual Organization of the portal;
- influence of the Service Lifecycle approach over the portal design, development, and operation;
- resources interaction in virtual processes.

Based on the idea that the portal is a service itself, the first step of the analysis has been focused on the main roles involved in the whole supply chain, from the back office to final customers.

The portal is conceived as a platform on the Internet, suitable for actions of different actors to converge; operation is managed exclusively through web interfaces, thus respecting and implementing the Cloud paradigm. In order to describe the organization of the portal, it is so important to detail the main typologies of actor, that is the role that persons or external systems take on the portal. Hence, it is possible to distinguish between:

- *Consumer* the person, or the Information System, that uses applications for every single service, so consuming the resources offered by the portal.
- *Customer* the person that asks and pays for the service. The awarding of this role implies that a client's organization gives one identified person the responsibility of requiring services for a group of consumers.

[8] We thank Kelyan's manager Andrea Bouchard and Luca Ferraris (Nash), that have allowed the realization of this work with their willingness, professionalism, attention, and sensitivity. The case has been analyzed through direct interviews in the period February–June 2013.

- *Help Desk* it has the responsibility to solve problems, or to give assistance to final users, at a first (on line) or a second (on remote) level.
- *Promoter* the team of Customer Relationships Management, that points out service opportunities, and supports the selling process. The portal web structure gives the promoter the possibility to publish on the Internet services description, promotional e-mails, and specific service conditions.
- *Broker* the person, or the organization, that buys and resells services through its own virtual shop. This role is autonomous in the choice of the products to sold, and in the formulation of pricing strategies for the services.
- *Supplier* the organization that produces single services offered on the portal, with a total responsibility of their services quality.
- *Platform Management* the team that must support the portal service, by developing, and then maintaining and evolving, the Cloud platform. This role doesn't take directly part to the portal operation, but it is fundamental in order to assure service continuity.
- *Portal Management* the team that is responsible for the services delivery.

In the second step of the analysis, the portal planning and development has been related to the Service Lifecycle theory, and to the main guidelines of ITIL® V3. The comparison has allowed to articulate the portal creation in the following phases:

1. *Definition of the Service Strategy* The main goal of this phase is the definition of a Service Portfolio, useful to identify services ready to be offered, and services still to be studied and developed. This is fundamental for a provider non only to achieve and maintain a competitive advantage, but also to be aware of business opportunities and of its own quickness in serving final customers.

   Consequently, the Back Office Management has focused its attention on value creation for final users, in order to answer the following questions:

   - what is the most suitable set of services to reach strategic goals?
   - what are the informational needs necessary to satisfy customers' requirements?

   Answers have been found through a correct definition of the final market, and the identification of necessary strategic objectives, like distinctive capabilities, IT infrastructures, organizational figures, and financial resources. Hence, it has been important to project and improve the coordination and control systems, and to prepare the future execution, also with the support of simulation activities.

   The main constraints of this phase can come from the evaluation process of the risks related to possible changes in the Service Strategy, and from the choice of an effective set of Key Performance Indicators to measure the services offered by the portal.

2. *Service Design and Transition* The mail goals of this phase are the design of the offered services and the management of the related processes, systems, and functions required to realize, test, and implement them. It's important for the Back Office Management to adopt a planning-oriented approach, in order to realize quality services, respecting at the same time estimated costs. The

transition is in fact efficient and effective when it can realize business requirements, within the bounds of costs and necessary resources, as established during the design activities.

From a technical point of view every service is composed of a set of single elements; service elements are designed to be independent, as there are no bonds of relation between them. This condition allows providers and clients to realize different combinations of final services, to better satisfy final users' requirements, but keeping at the same time standardized procedures, as recommended by the Cloud paradigm.

During this phase, the Back Office Management has been responsible for the identification of a common part of data and functionalities in the services to be presented on the portal. With reference to this common part, a standard interface has been realized by a Service Design Team, in order to define:

- the *Service Element Describer*, that contains menus for the connection to the portal server and for the delivery process (for instance, the chosen consumption objectives purchased in units for each element);
- the *Service Element Model*, that represents a rule for the definition of service con-tracts and comprehends all attributes to manage different contractual typologies.

Afterwards, a Service Transition Team has prepared the real deployment of the portal, through specific test activities and the implementation of pilot services.

The main constraints of this phase can come from the availability of time and economic resources for the services planning activities.

3. *Service Operation* This phase requires the execution and the coordination of necessary activities to deliver and manage the portal services. The involvement of the whole portal organization allows the creation of a virtual supply chain, whose actors interacts through web interfaces and, within well-defined procedures, are quite autonomous in their activities.

The concept of "self-service" is fundamental to the portal framework. No direct contact is necessary between the Portal Back Office Area and the administrators of each individual client, that operate on the Service Runtime Console. Moreover, the portal enables delegation of administrative responsibilities from the PaaS provider to the client itself, by providing clients with complete control over the provisioning aspects of the platform. In summary:

- administrators have a self-service dashboard where they can manage users and roles, manage subscriptions to applications for the client, view metering data and inspect provisioning problems;
- final users (suppliers, brokers, promoters, customers, and consumers) have a self-service dashboard where they can manage their profile as well as their application subscriptions.

The delivery process is articulated as follows:

- Suppliers must activate dedicated servers for the service delivery, register service elements on the portal, and pay a periodic rent to sell them. The services registration is bound by standardized procedures, as said in the phase of Service Design and Transition, so imposing, by one side, the configuration of technical characteristics (through the Describer), on the other side, the definition of the model for each presented element.
- Brokers buy single service elements by suppliers, compose them into specific services, in coherence with their business requirements. The service element approach allows them to combine "pieces" from different suppliers, to create their own service offer, to be exposed on a web shop-window. They can also avail of a support by promoters, to give multiple services a major visibility.
- Customers buy single service elements from suppliers or complete services from brokers, and activate delivery contracts. Each contract is associate to a "state", for the control of consumption and contractual variables. The consumption meters are configured for each customer and for all the consumers he represents, giving the portal system the possibility to automatically pro-duce periodic payments.

During this phase, a team of the Portal Back Office Area, the Service Level Management team, is dedicated to monitoring activities, in order to determine the value of each delivered service, and to assure a continual service improvement. Measurements used can regard technology (performance and availability of components and applications), processes (performance of Service Management activities), or final performance of services.

4 Conclusions

The comparison between market characteristics, as defined in Sect. 2, and those empirically verified through the case study, has allowed us to deduce that the real challenge for providers consists in the capability to project their own services in the most coherent way with regard to the more relevant market business drivers, and then to provide those services with standardized procedures. This reflection implies that each provider must avail itself to infrastructures able to support both single applications and Cloud platform, to facilitate clients in reaching their specific goals, but leaving them autonomous in the configuration/integration of their business processes.

Moreover, providers that have the economic and technical capabilities to structure a self-service portal can support innovation under different perspectives:

- they can impact on market growth giving final users access to new solutions at lower cost (this is possible when the same application is shared by several clients);

- they can reduce entry costs in new markets, giving niche providers the opportunity to compete in the Cloud sector with their own specialized solutions.

Finally, future steps in the research will be focused on a deeper analysis of the customer perspective, to understand if it is possible to identify different categories of final users, in relation to their own business goals, and if there are more successful Cloud services for each market segments.

References

1. Buyya, R., et al.: Cloud computing and emerging IT platforms: vision, hype, and reality for delivering computing as the 5th utility, Future Generation Comput. Syst. **25**, 599–616 (2009)
2. Leavitt, N.: Is cloud computing really ready for prime time? Computer **42**(1), 15–20 (2009)
3. Armbrust, M., et al.: A view of cloud computing—clearing the clouds away from the true potential and obstacles posed by this computing capabilities. Commun. ACM **53**(4), 50–58 (2010)
4. Aymerich, F., Fenu, G., Surcis, S.: An approach to a cloud computing network. In: Proceedings of the 1st International Conference on the Applications of Digital Information and Web Technologies (2008)
5. Ahronovitz, M., et al.: A white paper produced by the cloud computing use case discussion group. Cloud Computing Use Cases, vol. 10 (2010)

An Overview of Approaches for the Migration of Applications to the Cloud

Giuseppina Cretella and Beniamino Di Martino

Abstract Cloud computing represents one of the most promising paradigms for software development nowadays. Many companies consider moving entire applications or parts of them to the cloud. As customers transition their applications and data to the cloud, it is important that the level of service provided in the cloud environment be equal to or better than the service provided by their traditional IT environment. The transition to cloud computing, however, still implies difficult and cumbersome efforts. Recently a lot of initiatives, defining approach to support the migration of application to the cloud, have emerged. In this paper we propose an overview of these approaches taking into account advantages and disadvantages of adopting them.

Keywords Cloud computing · Porting to the cloud · Migration to the cloud · Model driven engineering · Cloud patterns

1 Introduction

Cloud computing has become increasingly popular with the industry due to the clear advantage of scalability and elasticity via dynamic on-demand provisioning of resources that enable the users to quickly scale up or scale down according to their needs and cost reduction thanks to its pay-per-use model. Today, many companies consider moving entire applications or parts of them to the cloud, since

G. Cretella (✉) · B. Di Martino
Department of Industrial and Information Engineering, Second University
of Naples, Aversa, Italy
e-mail: giuseppina.cretella@unina2.it

B. Di Martino
e-mail: beniamino.dimartino@unina.it

L. Caporarello et al. (eds.), *Smart Organizations and Smart Artifacts*,
Lecture Notes in Information Systems and Organisation 7,
DOI: 10.1007/978-3-319-07040-7_8,
© Springer International Publishing Switzerland 2014

cloud computing is transforming the competitive markets, offering new ways to create and deliver additional value to companies (and private). Any organization, also with small computing infrastructure, can benefit from the cloud. Cloud services allow the company to continue to deliver their application as usual but turn away from the organization all the costs and issues of maintaining servers and devices.

In the current cloud scenario there are so many alternative definitions of solution from different vendors, thus it can be difficult to describe or decide what the cloud can be used for in the context of a specific application.

Due to the growing number of provider offers and the lack of a standard representation of services, the choice of the cloud provider is a very hard task for a cloud user and the transition to cloud computing is still difficult and cumbersome effort. For these reason we need to overcome many challenges to promote the adoption of cloud computing paradigm.

We need to address two different aspects: the modernization of legacy software to exploit current cloud-based technologies and portability and interoperability among different cloud platforms.

Managing software modernization is still a significant challenge in general and even more ambitious when a change of the software delivery paradigm needs to be addressed such as in the case of cloud computing. Additionally, porting an application developed for a cloud solution to another one requires the analysis of the application programming interface each solution offered from the cloud providers.

The above mentioned challenges lead to the need for developers to be able to design their software systems for multiple Clouds and for operators to be able to deploy and re-deploy these systems on various Clouds depending on the convenience.

The introduction of a new layer of abstraction improves the portability and re-usability of cloud related concerns among several clouds. Indeed, even if the system is designed for a specific platform including framework, middleware, or cloud services, these entities often rely on similar concepts, which can be abstracted from the specificities of each cloud provider. Typically, the topology of the system in the cloud as well as the minimum hardware resources required to run it can be defined in a cloud-agnostic way. Thanks to this new abstraction layer, one can map a platform specific model to one or more cloud providers.

Recently a lot of initiatives, defining approaches to support the migration of application to the cloud, have emerged. Some of them, such as the initiatives that rely on Model Driven Engineering and semantic approach, adopt the cloud-agnostic abstraction methodology as key point.

In this paper we propose an overview of approaches based on Cloud Pattern, Model Driven Engineering and semantic modeling. In particular, Sect. 2 clarifies the role of Cloud Patterns in the migration of applications to cloud computing process. Sections 3 and 4 provide an overview of projects and efforts based on MDE methodology and semantic as modeling approach. Finally Sect. 5 provides a comparison of the above mentioned approaches.

2 Approaches for the Migration Based on Cloud Patterns

In the current cloud scenario, where many alternative solutions are offered from different vendors, the developers could gain advantage of a technique to identify the most viable architectural solution for their porting activity. This need fits well with the definition of *Cloud Patterns*, i.e., sets of prepackaged and preconfigured architectural solutions, exposed by using the concepts and mechanism of the software engineering design patterns.

Patterns describe common aspects of cloud computing environments and of application design for cloud computing. Some patterns can be useful in understanding the appropriate organization of the software stacks on which applications depend. Patterns can also be useful in understanding what changes may be necessary to the application code for successful migration to the cloud computing environment.

A number of Cloud Patterns catalogues are emerging, proposed both from academia, such as [1] and commercial cloud providers such as Amazon [2] and Windows Azure [3] and IBM [4]. These initiatives aim to provide Cloud Pattern catalogues containing descriptions of solutions to recurrent problems in cloud architectures definitions.

The different catalogues offer their contents with different abstraction and detail levels, and due to their background they have different purposes.

Some of them are closer to a specific cloud platform, thus they present patterns more detailed in terms of cloud components to use to implement the pattern and propose also specific platform dependent cloud services to use during the development and deployment of the application. Instead, vendor independent catalogues are more general and don't expose specific solutions to implement but rather propose an architectural model as a solution to given categories of problems. Thus Cloud Patterns can enable a vendor independent and agnostic migration activity to the cloud.

Anyway, most of the current, vendor independent, pattern catalogues lack in defining a clear mapping between pattern components and real, specific services offered by cloud vendors. Nevertheless it will be possible to establish the mapping to real cloud solutions to overcome the gap between the agnostic design and the real implementation.

Following a specific Cloud Pattern or a composition of Cloud Patterns to perform the migration and porting of application to cloud represents a best practice: the patterns themselves represent a support for the redesign and deployment of application on the cloud and furthermore the solutions provided by design patterns are proven, so their consistent application tends to naturally improve the quality of system designs.

3 Model-Driven Engineering for Cloud Computing

The OMG Model-Driven Architecture (MDA) [5] is a model-based approach for the development of software systems. The MDA relies on three types of models for three layers of abstractions: the *Computational Independent Model* (CIM), the *Platform Independent Model* (PIM) and the *Platform Specific Model* (PSM). The first model describes what the system is expected to do but hides all the technical details related to the implementation of the system. The Platform Independent Model describes views of the systems in a platform independent manner so that it can be mapped to several platforms at the PSM levels. The Platform Specific Model refines the PIM with technical details required for specifying how the system can use a specific platform.

The main feature and benefits of MDA from the cloud prospective are the facilitation of portability, interoperability and reusability of parts of the system which can be easily moved from one platform to another, as well as the mainte-nance of the system through human readable and reusable specifications at various levels of abstraction. In the context of cloud computing the Model-Driven Development can be helpful to allow developers to design software system in a cloud and-agnostic way and to be supported by model transformation techniques into the process of instantiating the system into specific and multiple clouds. This approach, which is commonly summarized as "model once, generate anywhere", is particularly relevant when it comes to design and management of applications across multiple clouds, as well as migrating them from one cloud to another.

For this reason combining Model Driven application engineering and the cloud computing domain is currently the focus of several research groups and projects, such as MODACLOUDS [6] DEVAs [7] ARTIST [8].

The MODACLOUDS project proposes a Model Driven approach aims at supporting system developers and operators in exploiting multiple Clouds for the same system and in migrating part of their systems from cloud to cloud as needed.

The MODACloudML platform relies on a Domain-Specific Language for the design and execution of applications on multiple clouds. The Model-Driven Engineering approach adopted by the MODACloudML platform allows the developers to build the system at various levels of abstraction. The three envi-sioned levels are: the *Cloud-enabled Computation Independent Model* (CCIM) to describe an application and its data, the *Cloud-Provider Independent Model* (CPIM) to describe cloud concerns related to the application in a cloud-agnostic way, and the *Cloud-Provider Specific Model* (CPSM) to describe the cloud con-cerns needed to deploy and provision the application on a specific cloud.

Each layer of the architecture contains various models that can be manipulated within the MODACloudML environment.

For the Cloud-enabled Computation Independent layer the models are: the *Requirements Model* that completes and formalizes the service functional description; the *Service Definition Model* that describes the software to be developed as a set of components or services; the *Data Model* that describes the main data structures associated with the software to be; the *Usage Model* that specifies the way users are expected to exploit the functionality of the software to be; the *Service Orchestration Model* that describes the behavior of the glue between components and services.

For the Cloud-Provider Independent layer the models are: the *Design Alternative and Deployment Model* that describe the assignment of application components to underlying resources and the design alternatives and constraints that will drive the search of optimal solutions performed by design time exploration tools; the *Data Model* that describes data model in terms of logical models as flat model, hierarchical model and relational model.

For the Cloud-Provider Specific layer the models are: the *Design Alternative and Deployment Model* that describes the assignment of application components to underlying resources and the design alternatives and constraints that will drive the search of optimal solutions performed by design time exploration tools that depend on the characteristics of the cloud resources of a specific cloud provider; the *Data Model* that describes the data model based on the specific data structures implemented by the cloud providers.

The approach presented in [7] utilize the MDE methodology as modeling approach that simplifies cloud architecture design, as well as to achieve platform independence from IaaS providers. By designing DEVAs (distributed ensembles of virtual appliances) non-expert users can easily architect interdependent virtual appliances on Infrastructure as a Service clouds. DEVA models include quality of service (QoS) constraints, which can account for the non-functional requirements of the modeled architecture. The approach propose two DEVA metamodels with the main difference being that one allows the instantiation of resource-independent (RI-DEVA) models, and the other allows resource-dependent (RD-DEVA) models.

The distinction between resource dependent and independent models enables to separates the concern of modeling a DEVA and the concern of modeling the resources needed to run such DEVA. Through the definition of resource independent model a user can let DEVA framework allocate the required resources based on the specified high-level policies and constraints. This can be achieved by transforming an RI-DEVA to a RD-DEVA using model to model (M2M) transformations.

The transformation between these models can be done in various ways. The task is to translate quantifiable constraints and policies to available resources in an IaaS cloud.

ARTIST proposes a software modernization approach covering business and technical aspects. In particular, ARTIST employs Model-Driven Engineering techniques to automate the reverse engineering of legacy software and forward engineering of cloud-based software in a way that modernized software truly benefits from targeted cloud environments.

ARTIST proposes a model-based software modernization process that consists of a pre-migration, migration, and post-migration phase.

Before the migration is performed, the Legacy Software is analyzed in the pre-migration phase concerning technical and non-technical consequences of possible migration strategies. This analysis results in well-defined Migration Goals constituting the input for the decision-making on how the migration should be performed in the subsequent phases. In a first step of the migration phase, models are reverse-engineered from the legacy software. These Legacy Platform-Specific Models comprise all specifics imposed by the platform the legacy software is built on. To enable the coverage of a wide range of current and future modernization scenarios and the reuse of reoccurring platform-independent migration patterns across several modernization scenarios, the legacy PSM is transformed into a higher-level representation, named PIM (Platform-Independent Model). The PIM abstracts from platform-specifics, such as software runtime environments and data management capabilities. These platform-specifics need to be adapted to the offerings of cloud providers, as their cloud environments are typically unique and operate on different virtualization layers, i.e., from infrastructure to platform to software as a service.

PIMs are then subjected to model transformations, which are selected based on the migration goals defined in the pre-migration phase. These transformations realize the actual migration by applying optimization patterns and integrating cloud-specific modernization opportunities. As a result, model-based representations of the migrated software that comprise platform-specifics compatible with the selected cloud environment are produced. Such a "Cloudified" PSM is transformed into the executable migrated software hosted in a cloud environment. In the post-migration phase, the model-based representations of legacy software and migrated software are employed to derive Equivalence Tests. They aim at verifying that the migrated software behaves as expected. Furthermore, non-functional properties are evaluated to certify if the migration goals are fulfilled. This is achieved by analyzing the execution of migrated software to obtain quality Measures which are checked against defined migration goals.

4 Semantic Modeling for Cloud Computing

The development of applications for the cloud requires programming skills and knowledge about the several programming models, APIs and underlying infrastructures, which are provided by cloud vendors. This is due to the differences in the semantic of the resources offered because the providers use proper terms and semantics and no uniform representations of resources are offered. As stated in [9], semantic models are helpful in three aspects of cloud computing. The first is functional and nonfunctional definitions. The ability to define application functionality and quality-of-service details in a platform-agnostic manner can immensely benefit the cloud community. This is particularly important for porting application code horizontally. The second aspect is data modeling. A crucial difficulty developers face is porting data horizontally across clouds. The third aspect is service description enhancement. Clouds expose their operations via Web services, but these service interfaces differ between vendors. The operations' semantics, however, are similar. Metadata added through annotations pointing to generic operational models would play a key role in consolidating these APIs and enable interoperability among the heterogeneous cloud environments.

Two of these three aspects are addressed by the mOSAIC project [10], in particular in two components of the mOSAIC framework, the Semantic Engine [11] and the Dynamic Discovery and Mapping system [12].

The Semantic Engine and associated ontologies, a knowledge base have been developed to support the cloud application developer in the tasks of discovering the needed functionalities and resources for application development through vendor independent representations of such application components, and representation of generic programming concepts and patterns, including application domain related ones.

The Semantic Engine introduces a high level of abstraction over the cloud APIs and cloud resources, by providing semantic based (in particular by using ontologies) representation of abstract functionalities and resources, related by properties and constraints, and Application domain level concepts and application patterns. Inference rules representing developer experts' knowledge and reasoners are also used. In particular the Semantic Engine enables the mOSAIC API developer to semantically describe and annotate developed APIs and components, at abstract functional level, to specify inference rules, and the user (the cloud application developer) to specify application domain related concepts and application patterns, possibly utilizing concepts and ontologies from the application domain under consideration, and likewise upper ontologies.

The Semantic Engine overcomes syntactical differences representing the API semantically, independently from the programming model. It offers a catalog of functionalities related to cloud domain and patterns related to design and specific application domains, representing services and resources in agnostic way.

From the view point of the developer the application is designed (by using the associated GUI) starting from the application domain concepts, which are not related to cloud computing.

The Semantic Engine guides the developer from suitable application and design patterns to Cloud Patterns. In such a way, the developer can reach a suitable design for the cloud application. Following this, the developer can use the Semantic Engine to obtain the actual application descriptors needed by the mOSAIC platform to successfully deploy the application on a selected IaaS provider.

The growing number of cloud providers that deploy their offers led to increase more and more the need to automate some discovery mechanisms and alignment facilities.

A possible solution to this problem is proposed through the application of semantic and matchmaking technologies. In particular the Dynamic Discovery and Mapping system provides the discovery of new cloud services (dynamically) deployed by providers already included within the mOSAIC framework, or by new cloud providers not yet included.

The Discovery and Mapping Service' target is to discover cloud providers' functionalities and resources, compare and align to the mOSAIC API, thus supporting agnostic and interoperable access to cloud providers' offers.

This module of the mOSAIC framework is mainly based and supports already existing languages for the semantic description of Web Services and it is proposed to use both node level and structural level matching to discover the mapping between cloud providers' services and mOSAIC APIs.

It includes a reasoner, which analyses a semantic description of a given new cloud service and infers information about how it can be integrated within the mOSAIC framework.

The matchmaking technique consists in selecting different types of matching algorithm at node level and structural level that can be applied and allows different levels of precision and recall.

A semantic matchmaking between the mOSAIC cloud ontology and the service description will be performed to identify: the kind of cloud resource that is provided, the compliance with the available mOSAIC APIs, the compliance with the existing mOSAIC connectors and Provider agents, the service binding information.

If the service is fully supported by the mOSAIC framework as it is, the new provider will be registered as a new available one and it will be considered in the next negotiation. On the other hand, if the new discovered service cannot be automatically integrated within the mOSAIC framework, or even only partially, the developer will be alerted about the limitations regarding its use and/or the missing information or technological extensions necessary to integrate it.

5 Conclusion

The transition to cloud computing requires a certain effort since the development of applications for the cloud requires programming skills and knowledge about the several programming models, APIs provided by cloud vendors and cloud patterns to fit the cloud environment. Due to the lack of sharing programming model and interface also the porting of application among clouds requires in most case the rewriting of the whole application according to the new provider interface and programming model. This paper present an overview of existing approach for porting application to the cloud such as approach based on Cloud Patterns, Model Driven Engineering or semantic modeling.

The analysis of the above described methodologies has highlighted advantages and limitations of different approaches. In particular the first common limitation of some approaches based on MDE (such as MODACLOUD and DEVA) is that the metamodels relies only on the IaaS layer, even if PaaS is a more complex and interesting scenario. Another issue of all the MDE approach analyzed is the feasibility and the difficult to produce and maintain the various models. In DEVA the translation consists in the mapping among quantifiable QoS constraints and subjective performance metrics provided by current IaaS providers, however, in some case, it isn't so clear how the model transformation engine works and how much this process is automatic.

Artist seems to be a promising project with ambitious goals. The defined methodology, even if at an early stage, provides a complex and comprehensive scenario which includes several aspects. However it is not yet possible to assess the results of the project and the actual usability of the approach.

References

1. Mietzner, R., Schupeck, W., Fehling, C., Leymann, F.: A collection of patterns for cloud types, cloud service models, and cloud-based application architectures (2011). http://www. cloud-council.org/ConvergenceofCloudSocialMobileFinal.pdf
2. Aws cloud design patterns (2013). http://en.clouddesignpattern.org/
3. Windows azure application patterns (2013). http://www.windowsazure.com/enus/develop/ net/architecture/
4. Chen, Z.X.: IBM workload deployer: pattern-based application and middleware deployments in a private cloud. IBM, International Technical Support Organization, Poughkeepsie (2012)
5. Soley, R.: OMG: model driven architecture. Object Management Group (2000)
6. Ardagna, D., Di Nitto, E., Mohagheghi, P., Mosser, S., Ballagny, C., D'Andria, F., Casale, G., Matthews, P., Nechifor, C.-S., Petcu, D. et al.: Modaclouds: a modeldriven approach for the design and execution of applications on multiple clouds. In: 2012 ICSE Workshop on Modeling in Software Engineering (MISE), pp. 50–56. IEEE (2012)
7. Collazo-Mojica, X.J., Sadjadi, S.M.: A metamodel for distributed ensembles of virtual appliances. In: SEKE, pp. 560–565 (2011)
8. Bergmayr, A., Bruneliere, H., Izquierdo, J.L.C., Gorronogoitia, J., Kousiouris, G., Kyriazis, D., Langer, P., Menychtas, A., Orue-Echevarria, L., Pezuela, C. et al.: Migrating legacy software to the cloud with artist. In: 2013 17th European Conference on Software Maintenance and Reengineering (CSMR), pp. 465–468. IEEE (2013)
9. Sheth, A., Ranabahu, A.: Semantic modeling for cloud computing, part 2. IEEE Internet Computing 14(4), 81–84 (2010)
10. Di Martino, B., Petcu, D., Cossu, R., Goncalves, P., Máhr, T., Loichate, M.: Building a mosaic of clouds. In: Euro-Par 2010 Parallel Processing Workshops, pp. 571–578. Springer (2011)
11. Cretella, G., Di Martino, B.: Towards a semantic engine for cloud applications development. In: 2012 Sixth International Conference on Complex, Intelligent and Software Intensive Systems (CISIS), pp. 198–203. IEEE (2012)
12. Cretella, G., Di Martino, B.: Semantic and matchmaking technologies for discovering, mapping and aligning cloud providers's services. In: Proceedings of the 15th International Conference on Information Integration and Web-based Applications and Services (IIWAS2013) (2013)

Digital Information Asset Evaluation: Characteristics and Dimensions

Gianluigi Viscusi and Carlo Batini

Abstract Information growth makes the understanding of the value of digital information assets a key issue to information systems management. To this end, the paper discusses the results of the reconstruction of a multidisciplinary literature, addressing information value or some of the related concepts or drivers. The analysis allows identifying characteristics and dimensions relevant to digital information asset evaluation. In particular, information capacity results as a core characteristic of information value, encompassing information quality, information structure, information infrastructure, and information diffusion.

Keywords Information value · Digital information asset · Information capacity · Information quality · Information utility

1 Introduction

The increasing volume and variety of available information [1, 2] makes the understanding of its value a key issue to information systems management, both in private and public sector [3], raising new questions on institutional implications on formal organisations, work practices, and the production of meaning at societal level [4, 5]. Indeed, information value has provided evidence of its relevance to evaluate the benefits of collecting information to reduce uncertainty in specific decision-making contexts such as healthcare [6, 7], and to directly inform policy

G. Viscusi (✉)
EPFL-CDM-CSI, Odyssea Station 5, 1015 Lausanne, Switzerland
e-mail: gianluigi.viscusi@epfl.ch

C. Batini
Università degli Studi di Milano-Bicocca, Viale Sarca 336, U14 20126 Milan, Italy
e-mail: batini@disco.unimib.it

L. Caporarello et al. (eds.), *Smart Organizations and Smart Artifacts*,
Lecture Notes in Information Systems and Organisation 7,
DOI: 10.1007/978-3-319-07040-7_9,
© Springer International Publishing Switzerland 2014

decisions about, e.g., research priorities at national level [8]. In the above scenario, information industry market share is continuously expanding, encompassing media such as newspapers and televisions, credit rating agencies, market research firms, financial analysts, social media such as Youtube, Facebook, Linkedin, and Twitter, but also small companies and individual experts, e.g., in finance, law, engineering, medicine [9]. Likewise, information industry focus is actually on selling information products, that is products that can be codified and "digitized", used in decision making, and paid by decision makers [9, 10]. Thus, digital information actually represents an asset for organizations.

Taking these issues into account, we analyze the literature on information value to identify characteristics and dimensions suitable to be considered for the evaluation of digital information assets. It is our point that information value and the problems considered in this paper have actually practical relevance for business in strategic initiatives and operations such as, e.g., mergers and acquisitions of organizations, having an information asset characterized by very large and heterogeneous data bases. The paper is organized as follows. First we provide a literature review, subsequently resuming it in order to identify information value characteristics and dimensions. Conclusion and future work conclude the paper.

2 Literature Review

Notwithstanding information growth has achieved inedited dimensions with the diffusion of social networks and Web 2.0 technologies, there is no generally accepted approach for the measurement of the information value, nor comprehensive studies replicating for information value what has been carried out for measuring information systems success by DeLone and McLean [11, 12]. As pointed out in Moody and Walsh [13] *while hardware and (rarely) software assets are capitalized, the valuation of information has been largely ignored, even though this is a much more valuable asset from a business viewpoint.* However, the academic interest in information value has evolved in terms of focus across different disciplines.

Early studies in information value have been carried out in the area of information economics [14], where a recognized starting point is the work of Blackwell on the comparison of experiments for describing which one is more informative for a decision problem [15]. Economists have investigated information value mainly focusing on problems of asymmetric information and game theory for quantifying the benefits of additional information under uncertainty [16, 17]. Nonetheless, the growing relevance and adoption of enterprise systems and the consequent role of the information technology (IT) in business shifted the attention towards the information value associated with value chain issues [18]. Furthermore, the growing of the investments in information and communication technology poses IT business value as a central research question, mainly in the information systems field [19–23]. In an accurate survey, Melville et al. [19]

shown how IT business value extent and dimensions are dependent upon internal and external factors (complementary organizational resources of the firm, partners, competitive and macro environment). Thus, the above perspectives allow to identify *information utility* as a first characteristics of information value. Information utility refers to a vast literature [17], and can be determined in terms of its financial value, pertinence, and transaction costs [17–19, 24–27], thus strictly related to the usage and the perspectives of the decision maker on value, e.g., cost-benefit or else capability oriented [28].

As for the change of focus from information value to information systems evaluation, we consider one of the earlier comprehensive surveys on assessing information value carried out by Niv Ahituv [29], which provides as "interim" conclusions to the problem that (i) *the information value and the value of the information system cannot be separated*, (ii) *the quantity of information is not likely to serve as an argument in the information value function*; (iii) *the information value function is a multiple attribute function. Its arguments are characteristics of an information system; its results* (i.e. *dependent variables*) *relate to benefits* [29].

Besides these conclusions, it should also be noted that Ahituv [30] formerly provided a first set of characteristics of information value: *timeliness* (dimensions: *recency, response time,* and *frequency*), *contents* (dimensions: *accuracy, relevance, level of aggregation* and *exhaustiveness*), *format* (dimensions: *media, color, structure, presentation,* etc.), and *cost*. As for these characteristics, Ahituv [30] points out several issues related to the identification of specific variables, their measurement and tradeoffs, the functional relationship between variables, and finally how to formulate a joint value function. At the state of the art these issues are still open and as pointed out by Moody and Walsh [13] "there currently exists no consensus on how to measure the information value. In practice, information has a *notional* value only: people think it is valuable but they can't put a number on it".

Notwithstanding the assessment of information value apart from information systems economic performance [23] or IT business value [19] is actually an issue scarcely considered both in research and practice, it is worth noting that the emerging focus on information systems as information infrastructures [31, 32] can be related to a change in the needs and availability of information, renewing the research interest on the information value, likewise. Considering *information infrastructure* as "installed base" [33], organizations tend to create, e.g., databases of interest through a series of projects and realizations that result in a database architecture often characterized by anomalous behaviors. Such behaviors concern the redundancy of representations, the misalignment of data among different databases, the incoherence in business rules related to the same objects in different databases, and errors in data that result in the heterogeneous representation of records pertaining to the same real world object. As a consequence, in the last few years, both industry and academia have investigated data integration solutions both from theoretical and practical perspectives [34].

Furthermore, the adoption of information and communication technologies in organizations and, in particular, of enterprise systems [35] has led scholars in information systems and knowledge management fields to investigate frameworks for the management of information at organizational level [13, 36, 37]. Among the others, we point out the I-Space conceptual framework, proposed by Max Boisot [25, 26], which considers the degree of *structure* of a knowledge asset as dependent by the two basic strategies for extracting information from data, and their *diffusion* in a given population: *codification* ("creating categories to make clear and reliable distinctions between state of the world that one can act upon", [38]) and *abstraction* (reducing the number of categories used for classifying phenomena). As for diffusion, it is worth noting that the increasing relevance of social networks at global level and open government initiatives in the public sector has promoted a set of studies investigating the value of information not merely from a cost-benefit or else market oriented perspective, but for understanding and critically evaluating the political, social, and public value of a given digital information asset [39–41].

Taking these issues into account, we point out a first association of information value to *information quality*. Indeed, information is increasingly being recognized as a key economic resource and the basis for achieving competitive advantage [13]. However, the information value decreases if information contains errors, inconsistencies or out-of-date values. Therefore, high information quality levels can be considered an initial guarantee for the potential usefulness of information [42]. Data and information quality literature provides a thorough classification of quality dimensions [43]. Analyzing the most relevant contributions, it is possible to define a common basic set of quality dimensions including accuracy, completeness, currency, consistency [44].

The correlation between information value and information quality has been further analysed in literature on information systems and information science [13, 42, 43, 45, 46]: considering, e.g., accuracy, the higher the accuracy of information, the higher its usefulness and value. Low accuracy levels can be very costly since they can cause both operational errors and incorrect decision making. Furthermore, information value also depends on the age of the information [13], its validity decreasing over time. With the advent of the web, the current diffusion of social networks and availability of "big data", new dimensions have been investigated for characterizing the quality of an information source in terms of *credibility* [47]; an example is the relevance of judgment topic in information retrieval or, e.g. *believability*, that considers whether a certain source provides data that can be regarded as true, real and credible, and *reputation* or *trustworthiness* that consider how trustable is the information source. Finally, the above phenomena related to information growth impact also on studies considering the information life cycle management as source of information value, currently focused on risk analysis dimensions [48].

3 Characteristics and Dimensions: A Classification

In Table 1 a first classification of the main characteristics of information value is provided, together with a set of related dimensions, emerging from state of the art analysis. Besides information *utility*, it is worth noting that Table 1 introduces *information capacity* as a complex characteristic made up of *information quality, structure, infrastructure,* and *diffusion.* In the following, we further detail this choice by discussing the relationships between capacity and these information value characteristics.

Francalanci et al. [49] and Ardagna et al. [50] consider the information processing capacity of an organization as the effort required to produce the quantity of information that a set of cooperative processes within a network can process in a time unit. In Miller et al. [51] the information capacity of a given schema corresponds to its set of instances, and the information capacity preservation is investigated when integration transformations are performed on a set of schemas. In [52] the concept of information capacity is investigated within data integration architectures, seen as the increment in the number of queries that can be expressed over a set of integrated databases, and that could not be performed querying databases locally.

It is worth noting that the above contributions refer to information capacity as related to information structure and infrastructure. However, considering the information infrastructure dimension, the concept of capacity may be also related to IT capability as *the possibility and/or right of the user or a user community to perform a set of actions on a computational object or process* [56]. Therefore, information capacity may be considered as well as the set of investments and capabilities influencing a firm performance [57]. Besides these characteristics, information quality can also be considered actually a relevant dimension of information capacity, for being recognized as related to the capacity to access, maintain and actually use data by individuals and organization [59, 60]. In conclusion, we may consider capacity a complex characteristic of a digital information asset determined by its information quality, information structure, and legacy information infrastructure. Thus, considering the definition of information system provided by [58], we point out information capacity refers to the current stock of *understandings* informed by a given installed base.

Taking these issues into account, information capacity represents the potential of a digital information asset that can be defined and evaluated independently from the usage, on the one hand, determining the economic utility of a digital information asset; on the other hand, enabling capabilities providing a social or else public value perspective [28, 39] on the digital information asset. Accordingly, information value evokes a complex property too, but more properly depends on several factors, such as the context (private or public) and the usage or the process that uses data, and the perspectives of the decision maker on value, e.g., cost-benefit or else capability oriented [61].

Table 1 Information value characteristics and dimensions from the literature review

Characteristics		Dimensions	Citations
Information Capacity	Information quality	Accuracy, accessibility, completeness, currency, reliability, timeliness, usability, credibility, believability, reputation, trustworthiness	[13, 36, 37, 47, 48, 53]
	Information structure	Abstraction, codification, derivation, integration	[13, 16, 25, 26]
	Information diffusion	Scarcity, sharing	[13, 25, 26]
	Information infrastructure	Abstraction, embeddedness, evolving (timeliness), flexibility, openness, sharing, standardization (codification)	[33, 54–56]
Information utility		Financial value, pertinence, transaction costs	[17–19, 24–27]

Figure 1 shows the model we propose for digital information asset evaluation, where information value is related to the multiple factors considered in Table 2: namely *information capacity, information quality, information structure, information infrastructure, information diffusion*, and *information utility*. The main hypothesis underlying the proposed model is that information value has to be interpreted either in terms of *information utility* of the *IT capabilities* enabled by a digital information asset (e.g., a cost-benefit analysis of the queries enabled by a digital information asset having a given information capacity), or else in terms of the *overall capabilities* the digital information asset may enable in a given social or public initiative (costs are considered, but are not determinants). It is worth noting that information diffusion is a direct driver of information utility, being information flow and exchanges enabled by selected business processes using the different queries that extract information relevant to them.

Taking these issues into account, we point out that the overall *information capacity* is considered at the basis of the evaluation of the digital information assets. Accordingly, it is worth noting the relevance we attribute to information capacity, being influenced by:

(1) *information quality*: in particular, the model considers the accuracy, completeness, accessibility, relevance, and timeliness of the overall data currently available for user queries;

(2) *information structure*: as the degree of integration of the data structure considered, in terms of actual databases, virtual integrated databases, and extended databases;

(3) *information infrastructure*; as the "shared, evolving, open, standardized, and heterogeneous installed base" ([62], p. 60), in the model it is instantiated in terms of actual Data Base Management Systems (DBMS), Enterprise Systems (ERP, CRM, SCM, etc.), Data Integration technologies, Information and Communication technologies (Barcode, RFID, etc.).

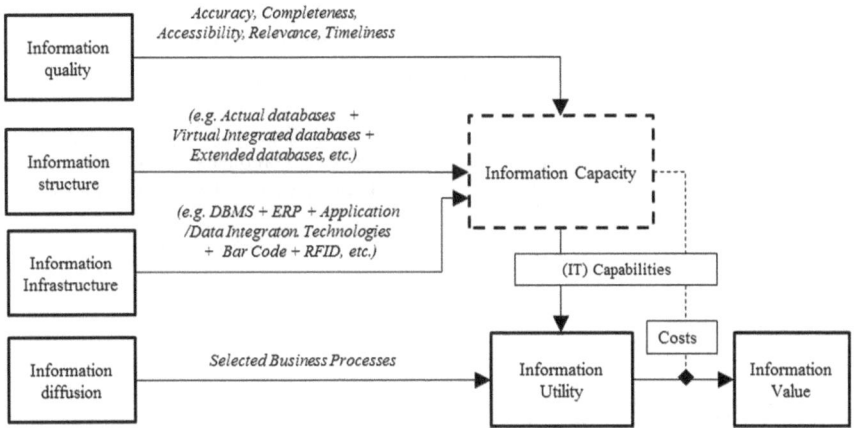

Fig. 1 The proposed model for digital information asset evaluation

Finally, we observe that information value is also influenced by the costs related to the design and maintenance of a given level of information capacity.

4 Conclusion and Future Work

In this paper we have discussed characteristics and dimensions for digital information asset evaluation, resulting from a reconstruction of the multidisciplinary literature that addressed information value or some of the related concepts or drivers. The search has been carried out on leading databases for different research areas (information systems, information science, computer science, economics, sociology, among others), such as EBSCO, ISIWeb of Knowledge, IEEE Explore, ACM Digital Library, Informs, AIS Electronic Library (AISeL), and JSTOR. As for the keywords, we have used the following preliminary set: information value, information AND value, information AND perceived value, information AND realistic value, information AND normative value, information value AND economics, information value AND social, information value AND public, information value AND quality, information capacity, information AND capacity, information value AND capacity, information AND evaluation. The analysis on the cited papers (out of 140 considered) allows to identify, besides information utility, information capacity as a core component of information value, made up of concepts such as information quality, information structure, information infrastructure, and information diffusion.

Nevertheless, we acknowledge the limitations of the above state of the art analysis, due the complex and multidisciplinary nature of information value. Accordingly, we are going to develop a further systematic survey for a detailed literature review [63]. The goal is to provide a comprehensive perspective and a classification of available dimensions and constructs for information value supporting further research in digital information asset evaluation.

Acknowledgments The work presented in this paper has been partially supported by the FutureEnterprise FP7 Project Grant agreement no: 611948 for Coordination and Support action, and by the Italian PON project PON01_00861 SMART (Services and Meta-services for SMART eGovernment).

References

1. The Economist: Data, data everywhere (2010)
2. Pospiech, M., Felden, C.: Big data: a state-of-the-art. AMCIS 2012 (2012)
3. McAfee, A., Brynjolfsson, E.: Big data: the management revolution. Harv. Bus. Rev. **90**(10), 61–68 (2012)
4. Kallinikos, J.: Governing Through Technology. Palgrave Macmillan, Basingstoke (2011)
5. Kallinikos, J.: The Consequences of Information: Institutional Implications of Technological Change. Edward Elgar, Cheltenham (2006)
6. Yokota, F., Thompson, K.M.: Value of information literature analysis: a review of applications in health risk management. Med. Decis. Mak. Int. J. Soc Med. Decis. Mak. **24**, 287–298 (2004)
7. Claxton, K., Neumann, P.J., Araki, S., Weinstein, M.C.: Bayesian value-of-information analysis: an application to a policy model of Alzheimer's disease. Int. J. Technol. Assess. Health Care **17**, 38–55 (2001)
8. Claxton, K.P., Sculpher, M.J.: Using value of information analysis to prioritise health research: some lessons from recent UK experience. Pharmacoeconomics **24**, 1055–1068 (2006)
9. Sarvary, M.: Gurus and Oracles: the Marketing of Information. The MIT Press, Cambridge (2012)
10. Shapiro, C., Varian, H.R.: Information Rules: A Strategic Guide to the Network Economy. Harvard Business School Press, Boston (1999)
11. DeLone, W.H., McLean, E.R.: Information system success: the quest for the dependent variable. Inf. Syst. Res. **3**, 60–95 (1992)
12. Petter, S., DeLone, W., McLean, E.: Measuring information systems success: models, dimensions, measures, and interrelationships. Eur. J. Inf. Syst. **17**, 236–263 (2008)
13. Moody, D., Walsh, P.: Measuring the value of information: an asset valuation approach. ECIS 1999 (1999)
14. Arrow, K.J.: The economics of information: an exposition. Empirica **23**, 119–128 (1996)
15. Blackwell, D.: Equivalent comparison of experiments. Ann. Math. Stat. **24**, 265–272 (1953)
16. Gilboa, I., Lehrer, E.: The value of information: an axiomatic approach. J. Math. Econ. **20**, 443–459 (1991)
17. Keisler, J., Collier, Z., Chu, E., Sinatra, N., Linkov, I.: Value of information analysis: the state of application. Environ. Syst. Decis. **34**, 1–21 (2013)
18. Glazer, R.: Measuring the value of information: the information-intensive organization. IBM Syst. J. **32**, 99–110 (1993)
19. Melville, N., Kraemer, K., Gurbaxani, V.: Review: information technology and organizational performance: an integrative model of IT business value. MIS Q. **28**, 283–322 (2004)
20. Willcocks, L.P., Lester, S.: Beyond the IT productivity paradox. Wiley, Chichester (1999)

21. Brynjolfsson, E., Yang, S.: Information technology and productivity: a review of the literature. Adv. Comput. **43**, 179–214 (1996)
22. Hitt, L.M., Brynjolfsson, E.: Productivity, business profitability, and consumer surplus: three different measures of information technology value. MIS Q. **20**, 121 (1996)
23. Dedrick, J., Gurbaxani, V., Kraemer, K.L.: Information technology and economic performance : a critical review of the empirical evidence. ACM Comput. Surv. **35**, 1–28 (2003)
24. Blanton, J.E., Watson, H.J., Moody, J.: Toward a better understanding of information technology organization: a comparative case-study. MISQ Q. **16**, 531–555 (1992)
25. Boisot, M.: Knowledge assets: securing competitive advantage in the information economy. Oxford University Press, New York (1998)
26. Boisot, M.: Information space: a framework for learning in organizations, institutions, and culture. Routledge, London (1995)
27. Sajko, M., Rabuzin, K., Bača, M.: How to calculate information value for effective security risk assessment. J. Inf. Organ. Sci. **30**, 263–278 (2006)
28. Zheng, Y.: Different spaces for e-development: what can we learn from the capability approach? Inf. Technol. Dev. **15**, 66–82 (2009)
29. Ahituv, N.: Assessing the value of information: problems and approaches. In: DeGross, J.I., Henderson, J.C., Konsynski, B.R. (eds.) International Conference on Information Systems (ICIS 1989). pp. 315–325. Boston, Massachusetts (1989)
30. Ahituv, N.: A systematic approach towards assessing the value of an information system. MIS Q. **4**, 61–75 (1980)
31. Ciborra, C., Braa, K., Cordella, A., Dahlbom, B., Failla, A., Hanseth, O., Hepso, V., Ljungberg, J., Monteiro, E., Simon, K.A.: From Control to Drift: the Dynamics of Corporate Information Infrastructures. Oxford University Press, Oxford (2000)
32. Remenyi, D., Money, A., Sherwood-Smith, M., Irani, Z.: The Effective Measurement and Management of IT Costs and Benefits. Butterworth Heinemann, Oxford (2000)
33. Monteiro, E., Pollock, N., Hanseth, O., Williams, R.: From artefacts to infrastructures. Computer Supported Cooperative Work (2012)
34. Bernstein, P.A., Haas, L.M.: Information integration in the enterprise. Commun. ACM **51**, 72 (2008)
35. Markus, M.L., Tanis, C., van Fenema, P.C.: Enterprise resource planning: multisite ERP implementations. Commun. ACM **43**, 42–46 (2000)
36. Simpson, C.W., Prusak, L.: Troubles with information overload—moving from quantity to quality in information provision. Int. J. Inf. Manage. **15**, 413–425 (1995)
37. Skyrme, D.: Ten ways to add value to your business. Manag. Inf. **1**, 20–25 (1994)
38. Boisot, M., Li, Y.: Organizational versus market knowledge: from concrete embodiment to abstract representation. J. Bioeconomics. **8**, 219–251 (2006)
39. Cordella, A., Bonina, C.M.: A public value perspective for ICT enabled public sector reforms: a theoretical reflection. Gov. Inf. Q. **29**, 512–520 (2012)
40. Harrison, T.M., Guerrero, S., Burke, G.B., Cook, M., Cresswell, A., Helbig, N., Hrdinova, J., Pardo, T., Hrdinová, J.: Open government and e-government: democratic challenges from a public value perspective. Information Polity: The International Journal of Government & Democracy in the Information Age, pp. 83–97. ACM, College Park, MD, USA (2011)
41. Wijnhoven, F.: The Hegelian inquiring system and a critical triangulation tool for the Internet information slave: a design science study. J. Am. Soc. Inf. Sci. Technol. **63**, 1168–1182 (2012)
42. Wang, R.Y., Strong, D.M.: Beyond accuracy: what data quality means to data consumers. J. Manage. Inf. Syst. **12**, 5–33 (1996)
43. Madnick, S.E., Wang, R.Y., Lee, Y.W., Zhu, H.: Overview and framework for data and information quality research. J. Data Inf. Qual. **1**, 1–22 (2009)
44. Batini, C., Scannapieco, M.: Data Quality: Concepts, Methodologies and Techniques. Springer, Berlin (2006)

45. Fallis, D.: On verifying the accuracy of information: philosophical perspectives. Libr. Trends. **52**, 463–487 (2004)
46. Eppler, M., Helfert, M.: A Framework for the Classification of Data Quality Costs and an Analysis of Their Progression. IQ 2004, pp. 311–325., MIT Sloan School of Management, Cambridge, MA, USA (2004)
47. Rieh, S.Y., Danielson, D.R.: Credibility: a multidisciplinary framework. Annu. Rev. Inf. Sci. Technol. **41**, 307–364 (2007)
48. Tallon, B.P.P., Scannell, R.: Information life cycle. Commun. ACM **50**, 65–69 (2007)
49. Francalanci, C., Piuri, V.: Designing information technology architectures: a cost-oriented methodology. J. Inf. Technol. **14**, 181–192 (1999)
50. Ardagna, D., Francalanci, C., Piuri, V.: Designing and rightsizing the information system architecture. Inf. Syst. Front. **6**, 229–245 (2004)
51. Miller, R.J., Yoannidis, Y., Ramakrishnan, R.: The use of information capacity in schema integration and translation. The 19th VLDB Conference, Dublin (1993)
52. Batini, C., Cappiello, C., Francalanci, C., Maurino, A., Gianluigi, V.: A capacity and value based model for data architectures adopting integration technologies. AMCIS 2011 Proceedings (2011)
53. Ahituv, N.: A systematic approach towards assessing the value of an information system. MIS Q. **4**, 61–75 (1980)
54. Hanseth, O., Monteiro, E., Hatling, M.: Developing information infrastructure: the tension between standardization and flexibility. Sci. Technol. Hum. Values **21**, 407–426 (1996)
55. Star, S.L., Ruhleder, K.: Steps toward an ecology of infrastructure: design and access for large information spaces. Inf. Syst. Res. **7**, 111–134 (1996)
56. Hanseth, O., Lyytinen, K.: Design theory for dynamic complexity in information infrastructures: the case of building internet. J. Inf. Technol. **25**, 1–19 (2010)
57. Overby, E., Bharadwaj, A., Sambamurthy, V.: Enterprise agility and the enabling role of information technology. Eur. J. Inf. Syst. **15**, 120–131 (2006)
58. Nunamaker, J.J.F., Briggs, R.O.: Toward a broader vision for information systems. ACM Trans. Manage. Inf. Syst. **2**, 20 (2011)
59. Huang, K.T., Lee, Y., Wang, R.Y.: Quality, Information and Knowledge. Prentice-Hall Inc., Upper Saddle River (1999)
60. Batini, C., Cappiello, C., Francalanci, C., Maurino, A.: Methodologies for data quality assessment and improvement. ACM Comput. Surv. **41**, 16 (2009)
61. Sen, A.: Rationality and Freedom. Harvard University, Cambridge (2002)
62. Hanseth, O.: The economics of standards. In: Ciborra, C.U., Braa, K., Cordella, A., Dahlbom, B., Failla, A., Hanseth, O. (eds.) From Control to Drift: The Dynamics of Corporate Information Infrastructures, pp. 56–70. Oxford University Press, Oxford (2000)
63. Webster, J., Watson, R.T.: Analyzing the past to prepare for the future: writing a literature review. MIS Q. **26**, XIII–XXIII (2002)

Key Capabilities of CIOs and IT Managers for Strategic Competitive Advantage: A Qualitative Field Research

Cecilia Rossignoli, Alessandro Zardini and Francesca Ricciardi

Abstract A growing stream of studies is concentrating on *IT management value*, i.e. on how value is created not (only) through IT investment and deployment, but (also, or mainly) through the way IT is idiosyncratically managed by each specific organization. This implies that the capabilities, behaviors and organizational role of CIOs and IT managers could be crucial for the creation of strategic value. Our research question is then the following: in the emerging scenario, shaped by e-business and cloud computing, how can the IT manager's capabilities, behaviors and organizational role influence the generation of competitive advantage? To answer this question, we conducted an explorative study based on interviews to nine managers from as many Italian organizations. The interviews were recorded, transcribed and analyzed through coding. We found that the CIO is perceived as bound to change towards more hybridized roles, whilst the IT department structure is perceived as evolving towards a much deeper cooperation with external partners and with other departments of the organization; this may imply, for example, a matrix organizational re-design. Moreover, our interviews led to the identification of 15 features of the CIO/IT manager, that are perceived as important or crucial for the generation of competitive advantage. Most of these features imply outstanding relational capabilities on the part of the IT managers.

Keywords IT management value · CIO · Capabilities · Qualitative research · Competitive advantage

C. Rossignoli · A. Zardini (✉)
State University of Verona, Verona, Italy
e-mail: alessandro.zardini@univr.it

C. Rossignoli
e-mail: cecilia.rossignoli@univr.it

F. Ricciardi
Catholic University of Milan, Milan, Italy
e-mail: francesca.ricciardi@unicatt.it

L. Caporarello et al. (eds.), *Smart Organizations and Smart Artifacts*,
Lecture Notes in Information Systems and Organisation 7,
DOI: 10.1007/978-3-319-07040-7_10,
© Springer International Publishing Switzerland 2014

1 Introduction

The last decade witnessed a heated academic debate on whether, and how, and under what conditions, ICTs can contribute to firm performances.

Kohli and Grover [1] overviewed literature and concluded: «the "whether" of IT value research now lies in the past. Many recent studies demonstrate that our interlude with the productivity paradox was an artifact of time and measurement (...). We have now accumulated a critical mass of studies that demonstrate a relationship between IT and some aspect of firm value».

But how, and under what conditions, does this relationship between IT and value creation unfold more effectively? A growing agreement has arisen on the idea that «a narrow focus on "IT" is misguided and misleading (...) because technology does not contribute to firm performance in isolation, but instead contributes as part of an activity system that fosters the creation and appropriation of economic value» [2].

But if IT contributes to economic performances as a part of an activity system, then the role of IT management may become pivotal, and potentially more relevant than other variables measuring IT assets *per se*, such as IT investment, infrastructure quality or software innovativeness. Consistently, a growing stream of IT value studies is concentrating on *IT management value*, i.e. on how value is created not (only) through IT deployment, but, more specifically, through IT management [3].

But how does IT management create value? What should IT managers do to allow the best exploitation of IT potentials? What should the organization and the other managers do to allow the CIO and the IT department to get the best out of new technologies? Some traditional answers may be not enough, since the emerging phenomena of globalization, cost pressures, e-business and advanced IT outsourcing are changing the usual landscape of IT managers [4].

Our Research Question is then the following: *in the emerging scenario, how can the IT managers' capabilities, behaviors and organizational role influence the generation of competitive advantage and then the organization's performances?*

2 Literature Review

The role of Information Systems (IS) management within organizations is at the center of many scholarly writings. Literature has been often describing this role in terms of couples of opposing concepts: for example, authors claim that Chief Information Officers (CIOs) should be understood as staff managers [5] or, on the contrary, as line managers [6]; that CIOs should be actively involved in business decisions [7] or, more traditionally, that they should concentrate on ex-post alignment of IT with business strategies decided elsewhere [5]; that they should display relational skills mainly [8] or, on the contrary, technical competences mainly [9].

In other words, the debate has not resulted in a unified view of what a IT manager's desired background should be. «In the world of practice, in fact, different organizations, in different moments of their competitive lives, tend to request different skills and different backgrounds to their CIOs, and this makes the generalization of scholarly surveys quite problematic» [10].

A 2004 survey, involving about 500 CIOs, found that their top priorities were alignment, creating a more adaptable and flexible organization, ensuring security and business continuity and reducing the overall costs of doing business in their organizations [11]. The State of the CIO Report, on the other hand, [12] identified three types of CIO: (i) the Function Head CIO is in charge of managing IT operations and personnel and is expected to face IT problems and crises; (ii) the Transformational Leader CIO is expected to re-design processes, to align IT strategy with business goals, and to lead other change efforts; (iii) the Business Strategist CIO works on developing business strategies, follows market trends, seeks to create competitive differentiation, and develops new sales and distribution channels. These three types of CIO differ as for responsibilities, skills, and compensation levels.

But Moffat Spitze and Lee [13] report that only about 5 % top IS managers seize and achieve opportunities for enduring IT-enabled competitive differentiation, whilst in many firms the IT department is viewed as a necessary, but often annoyingly expensive service. Interestingly, in this writing the growing acceptance of cloud computing as a possible threat to the IT manager's leadership and status.

Another recent paper confirms that this perception is quite wide-spread among IT managers today [10]. This qualitative research, conducted in Italy, revealed that many IT managers «seem to share the idea that a sort of "golden age" is over. In the 1990s, higher budgets corresponded to higher trust in the strategic value of IT on the part of the top management; today, the rationalization of IT spending is a key driver for CIOs' success». Moreover, some IT managers are concerned that the outsourcers' efforts to embed "best practices" into standardized applications result in lower visibility and status of in-house process management, where true competitive advantage can be built, and where the IT management often play a pivotal role.

What are, then, the organizational factors that may allow the rising of a "new CIO", who is not backward-looking and is well adapted to the era of software standardization, cloud computing, e-business and budget constraints?

We selected the following answers from literature:

- Effective management of IT outsourcing contracts/Service Levels Agreements [14, 15].
- Effective strategic cooperation with the Top Management Team (TMT) [16].
- Effective IT strategic alignment /effective co-evolution between IT and business strategies [17, 18].
- Effective operational cooperation between IT and business lines [19, 20].
- Effective management of IT-enabled change and innovation processes [21].
- Effective management of users' IT acceptance and collaboration [22].

- Effective contribution to knowledge sharing and cooperation throughout the organization [2].
- Effective contribution to knowledge sharing and cooperation throughout the value chain [23, 24].

3 Research Method

In order to answer our Research Questions, we decided to conduct a qualitative explorative study by interviewing a number of managers from a sample of firms.

We obtained interviews from nine managers in nine different northern Italy companies. We sought to select the interviewees on the basis of the maximum variety criterion [25], choosing both small and middle/large size enterprises, both businesses and state-owned companies, belonging to five different industrial sectors. The key data on the interviewed managers and their organizations are synthesized in Table 1.

The interviews took place from February to May 2012, and lasted from a minimum of 50 min to a maximum of 2 h. They were all conducted face-to-face by at least two researches, one of which made questions, whilst the other took notes [24]. The conversations were driven by twelve open questions.

The first group of questions was aimed to understand the professional story of the interviewee and his or her relationships with the TMT of the organization. The second group of questions was aimed to enlighten the organization's attitude towards the inter-organizational relationships throughout the value chain, including possible outsourcing agreements. The third group of questions encouraged the interviewee to tell his or her experiences in both successful and unsuccessful cases where competitive advantage had been pursued based on ICT-enabled innovation. The fourth group of questions was aimed to understand the interviewee's opinion about how the role of ICT manager is evolving in the emerging scenario.

Even if our interviews were based on these questions, our information collection process maintained some flexibility, such that unforeseen streams of information could emerge during each interaction with an interviewee.

The interviews were recorded, transcribed, and analyzed with a CAQDAS instrument (Computer Assisted Qualitative Data Analysis Software) that in the specific case was Atlas.ti, through open coding, axial coding [26] and memoing [27].

4 Research Outcomes

We used Atlas.ti coding options to classify the relevant capabilities, behaviors and organizational roles of IT managers according to our interviewees, whilst we used memos to develop reflections about the issue: how is the role of the CIO /IT manager evolving in today's scenario?

Table 1 Data on the nine explorative interviews

Companies	Industrial sector	Company size	Role of the interviewee
Company 1	Utilities	270 employees	CFO
Company 2	ICT	40 employees	CIO
Company 3	ICT	600 employees	CEO
Company 4	Manufacturing	1,000 employees	CIO
Company 5	Manufacturing	1,610 employees	Marketing CIO
Company 6	ICT	510 employees	CIO
Company 7	Health care	4,200 employees	CIO
Company 8	Manufacturing	50 employees	COO
Company 9	Insurance	650 employees	CIO

All the interviewees agreed that the ICT management roles are undergoing important changes, driven by phenomena such as e-business, advanced IT outsourcing and growing cost pressures.

Until recently, ICT just served the organizational structure to make it work... now, it is needed to face the market the interviewee from Company 9 said, highlighting the impact of e-business.

According to the interviewee from Company 6, who discussed thoroughly the impact of advanced outsourcing and cloud computing, these strategic sourcing models *imply new and specific competences within the outsourcee's organization, and then Supplier Management and Project Management skills become most important for the IT managers.* In fact, *even if software development is outsourced in our company, control remains in-house, in terms of quality checking, testing, releasing, training and feedback collection* (Company 7). The IT manager is then *an IT buyer and a manager of human and technical resources... a manager of people mainly. Internal people and external suppliers* (Company 4).

Cost pressures were mentioned as an often harassing concern for CIOs, who complain that *TMT managers tend to allow funding only for specific projects they believe in, but they often don't catch the whole picture and do not understand that IT is not just a sum of projects, it is the nervous system without which nothing could work* (Company 7).

As the use of new technologies becomes more and more widespread, and their strategic role is more and more evident, TMT members tend to take decisions themselves as for IT strategies. CIOs often don't appreciate this, which they perceive as an intrusion: these managers claim that many IT failures *may result from wrong choices by the CEO who often lacks the competences needed to effectively decide between different possible IT investments* (Company 9).

In other words, it seems that we are going towards an hybridization, where both the other CXOs feel capable to contribute to decisions about IT strategies, and CIOs feel capable to contribute to business decisions: *The future CIO should be able to propose the solution, instead of just undergoing it; that's why he/she should thoroughly know his/her company's business and be involved in the Board* (Company 5).

Table 2 Outcomes of the interviews' coding process: main factors enabling the CIO/IT manager to effectively contribute to performances and strategic value generation

No	Identified factor—axial code	Code description: in order to contribute to performances and competitive advantage, *the CIO/IT manager should be...*	Occurrences	Mentioned by (no. of interviewees)
1	Strategic support	Capable to effectively support the organization's competitive strategies	32	7 (77.7 %)
2	Infrastructure reliability	Capable to provide a reliable, secure, standardized and scalable infrastructure (hardware and software)	28	8 (88.8 %)
3	Relationships with the line managers	Capable to build collaborative relationships with line managers and with the other departments of the organization	24	7 (77.7 %)
4	Cost efficiency	Capable to effectively contribute to cost reduction and efficiency	22	5 (55.5 %)
5	Strategic involvement	Actively involved in strategic decisions	21	6 (66.6 %)
6	Innovation promoter	An active promoter of innovation at the organizational level	19	7 (77.7 %)
7	Mgmt of IT providers	Effective in managing contracts and inter-organizational relationships with IT outsourcers and providers	19	8 (88.8 %)
8	Mgmt of IT users	Capable to build collaborative relationships with ICT users and to enhance technology acceptance	18	9 (100 %)
9	Involvement in product innovation	Actively involved in product/service innovation processes	15	6 (66.6 %)
10	Relationships with the value chain	Capable to contribute to good inter-organizational relationship throughout the value chain	12	9 (100 %)
11	Involvement in customer satisfaction	Actively involved in customer satisfaction/customer loyalty initiatives	8	4 (44.4 %)
12	Direct report	A direct report of the CEO or general manager	6	5 (55.5 %)
13	Contribution to reputation	Effective in contributing to the organization's image and reputation	6	4 (44.4 %)
14	SW customization	Effective in managing the customization of the organization's software	6	6 (66.6 %)
15	Professional networking	Actively involved in conferences, workshops and IT professional networks	4	3 (33.3 %)

There is then wide consensus on the fact that the role of IT manager as it was traditionally understood is going to fade, because the "old" competences are being subsumed by IT outsourcers, whilst the "new", emerging competences are more blurred and shared with the other managers.

In certain cases, this trend is perceived as threatening; for example, according to the manager from Company 9, the IT manager is sometimes *in a precarious condition, in which it is impossible for him/her to provide for the future, and even to understand the present.*

In other cases, this trend is more positively seen as an occasion for imminent organizational changes, which are going to involve IT managers in many contexts.

For example, the manager from Company 5 claimed that the IT manager should not be external to business processes, but there should be an IT manager *resident in each specific department (purchase, sales, production, etc.), so that the IT department is not a separated structure any more, but keeps a foot in each core business process. It should physically be inside the processes, and not just behave as a separated entity which sometimes discusses with the users*: in other words, a matrix organizational design is considered a possible solution for the IT management of the emerging era.

The final outcome of the coding process we conducted is synthesized in Table 2. The 15 axial codes, resulting from 21 open codes, highlight the IT manager's capabilities (Codes 1, 2, 3, 4, 7, 8, 10, 13, 14), behaviors/attitudes (Codes 6, 15) and organizational roles (Codes 5, 9, 11, 12) that our interviewees perceive as important for the generation of competitive advantage and for a positive contribution of IT to performances. Our research confirms the importance of the two traditional "pillars" of the CIO performance measures, i.e. the capability to effectively support the organizations' competitive strategies (Code 1) and the capability to provide the organization with a reliable IT infrastructure (Code 2). Beyond these two key factors, it is very interesting to note that the other capabilities and attitudes that are mentioned as important by 77 % interviewees or more, i.e. Codes 3, 6, 7, 8, 10, all imply outstanding relational capabilities on the part of IT managers.

5 Conclusions

Our results confirm many of the IT management success factors already identified as important by literature. On the other side, our outcomes also allow to focus on the fact that the "traditional" technical skills of IT managers are not enough. In fact, according to our interviewees, technology is so strictly linked to business today that unless the CIO is effectively involved in business processes and decisions, the TMT choices are more likely to prove unsuccessful. Moreover, the IT infrastructure's reliability more and more depends on outsourcers. All these emerging phenomena involve paramount relational challenges. In other words, the relational capabilities of the IT managers strongly emerge from our research as the key skills that distinguish successful from unsuccessful IT governance and management.

Our research also indicates that there is a growing feeling among practitioners that the emerging scenario may imply changes in organizational design. In the previous paragraph, we reported the ideas of one of our interviewees about possible matrix solutions for a more effective IT management. There may be, of course, also other solutions, but our interviews are consistent in suggesting that the traditional organizational layout where the IT competences are expected to be concentrated and confined in the classical "IT Department" are more and more perceived as unsatisfactory.

References

1. Kohli, R., Grover, V.: Business value of IT: an essay on expanding research directions to keep up with the times. J. Assoc. Inf. Syst. **9**(1), 23–39 (2008)
2. Piccoli, G., Ives, B.: Review: IT-dependent strategic initiatives and sustained competitive advantage: a review and synthesis of the literature. MIS Q. **29**(4), 747–776 (2005)
3. Melville, N., Kraemer, K., Gurbaxani, V.: Review: information technology and organizational performance: an integrative model of IT business value. MIS Q. **28**(2), 283–322 (2004)
4. Ricciardi, F., Rossignoli C., Zardini, A.: Factors influencing the strategic value of IT: a literature review. In: Proceedings of Singapore ISSGBM Conference 2012. Lecture Notes in Management Science, Social Sciences and Humanities, vol. 7, pp. 86–91. Singapore, 30–31 Dec 2012, ISBN: 978-1-61275-048-4 (2012)
5. Rockart, J.F., Ball, L., Bullen, C.V.: Future role of the information systems executive. MIS Q. (**6:4**), **Dec82**(Special Issue 1982), 1–10 (1982)
6. Gibbons Paul L.: Separate Piece. CIO, section 1, Oct 1998, pp. 50–60 (1998)
7. Earl, M.J.: Are CIOs obsolete? Harv. Bus. Rev. **78**, 2 (2000)
8. Enns, H.G., Huff, S.L., Golden, B.R.: CIO influence behaviors: the impact of technical background. Inf. Manage. (**40:5**), 467 (2003)
9. Brennan, J.: Seeing the whole board: valuable lessons in IT thought leadership—for the CIO and CEO. CIO Mag. September 1 (2002)
10. Ricciardi, F., Rossignoli, C., De Marco, M.: IT commoditization challenging the leadership of information systems managers: an emerging issue for information systems performances. In: Proceedings of the VIII Conference of the Italian Chapter of AIS, Rome, 28–29 Sept 2012
11. CIO Insight: The CIO role. Do you have the right stuff? Ziff Davis Media Inc. http://www.cioinsight.com/article2/0,1397,1551609,00.asp (2004)
12. The State of the CIO 2008. http://www.cio.com (2008)
13. Moffat Spitze, J., Lee, J.J.: The Renaissance CIO project: the invisible factors of extraordinary success. California Manage. Rev. **4**(2), 72–91 (2012)
14. Dos Santos, B.L.: Information technology investments: characteristics, choices, market risk and value. Inf. Syst. Frontiers **5**(3), 289–301 (2012)
15. Han, H.S., Lee, J.N., Seo, Y.W.: Analyzing the impact of a firm's capability on outsourcing success: a process perspective. Inf. Manag. **45**(1), 31–42 (2008)
16. Preston, D.S., Karahanna, E.: Antecedents of IS strategic alignment: a nomological network. Inf. Syst. Res. **20**(2), 159–179 (2009)
17. Benbya, H., McKelvey, B.: Using coevolutionary and complexity theories to improve IS alignment: a multi-level approach. J. Inf. Technol. **21**(4), 284–298 (2006)
18. Chen, Q.D., Mocker, M., Preston, S.P., Teubner, A.: Information systems strategy: reconceptualization, management, and implications. MIS Q. **34**(2), 233–259 (2010)

19. Bharadwaj, S., Bharadwaj, A., Bendoly, E.: The performance effects of complementarities between information systems, marketing, manufacturing, and supply chain processes. Inf. Syst. Res. **18**(4), 437–453 (2007)
20. Liang, T.P., You, J.J., Liu, C.C.: A resource-based perspective on information technology and firm performance: a meta-analysis. Ind. Manage. Data Syst. **110**(8), 1138–1158 (2010)
21. Banker, R.D., Bardhan, I. Asdemir, O.: Understanding the impact of collaboration software on product design and development. Inf. Syst. Res. (**17**: **4**), 352–373 (2006)
22. Ross, J.W., Beath, C.M., Goodhue, D.L.: Develop long-term competitiveness through IT assets. Sloan Manag. Rev. **38**(1), 31–42 (1996)
23. Klein, R., Rai, A.: Interfirm strategic information flows in logistics supply chain relationships. MIS Q. **33**(4), 735–762 (2009)
24. Ray, G., Wu, D., Konana, P.: Competitive environment and the relationship between IT and vertical integration. Inf. Syst. Res. **20**(4), 585–603 (2009)
25. Baskerville R., Spagnoletti P., Kim, J.: Incident-centered information security: Managing a strategic balance between prevention and response. Inf. Manage. (2013)
26. Corbin, J.M., Strauss, A.: Grounded theory research: Procedures, canons, and evaluative criteria. Qual. Soc. **13**(1), 3–21 (1990)
27. Glaser, B.: Theoretical Sensitivity. Sociology Press, London (1978)

The Development of the DDG-Capability in Firms: An Evaluation of Its Impact on Firm Financial Performance

Elisabetta Raguseo and Claudio Vitari

Abstract We examine whether firms that develop the Digital Data Genesis dynamic capability show higher performance. Using detailed survey data on the capabilities developed by companies by the usage of digital data and firm financial performance of 96 firms, we find that the firms that develop the DDG dynamic capability have levels of ROA, ROS and revenue growth higher than others do. Our results provide one of the first empirical evidence on the direct link between DDG dynamic capability and firm financial performance.

Keywords Digital data genesis · Dynamic capabilities · Firm financial performance

1 Introduction

Explaining the variation in the degree of success of business organizations is an evergreen issue in management research, including Information Systems and Strategic Management. Management scholars generally recognize that organizational capabilities can be a major source of firm performance [1], and previous studies have made great strides to extend and refine the conceptualizations and definitions of various types of capabilities (generic, organizational, ordinary,

This research was supported by French Rhône Alpes region (http://www.rhonealpes.fr/).

E. Raguseo (✉)
Politecnico di Torino, Turin, Italy
e-mail: elisabetta.raguseo@polito.it

C. Vitari
Grenoble Ecole de Management, Grenoble, France
e-mail: claudio.vitari@grenoble-em.com

L. Caporarello et al. (eds.), *Smart Organizations and Smart Artifacts*,
Lecture Notes in Information Systems and Organisation 7,
DOI: 10.1007/978-3-319-07040-7_11,
© Springer International Publishing Switzerland 2014

dynamic, heterogeneous, and homogeneous). Specifically, dynamic capabilities have been linked to firm performance in several studies [2], but their contribution is contested, as a firm's ability to deliver superior process performance in a competitive environment does not automatically imply it can achieve sustained competitive advantage, as several variables may intervene to prevent the latter [3, 4]. The concept of dynamic capabilities remains a debated and at times unclear research construct. Therefore, research in this area is clearly important. Hence, in this article, we seek to contribute to the emerging literature on Information Technology (IT) dynamic capabilities and their impact on firm financial performance. In addition, we innovate in the choice of the dynamic capability object of our study: Digital Data Genesis (DDG) [5]. We define DDG as the coming into being of digital data. Specifically, DDG represents the naissance of digital data: it is a phenomenon (an observable fact or event) that involves the direct generation of new data in digital form, and takes place when information representative of a physical action, event or condition is created digitally concurrently with the event taking place. DDG thus enables real time digital representations of objects and events—so that these objects and events can exist as symbolic representations that can interact and be manipulated in the information space. For example, when a waiter takes an order using a palm device, an informational representation of the customer wishes is created in real-time in digital form.

Since dynamic capabilities allow organizations to reconfigure organizational capabilities in response to changes in the business environment, and since data is a precursor to many organizational processes, we decided to study DDG dynamic capability. Indeed, we believe that data can really provide higher financial performance to firms, since nowadays IT solutions are pervasive and ubiquitous and all business or social activities are now generating a corresponding digital data event. Nevertheless, to the best of our knowledge, there is scant evidence in the literature on whether the usage of digital data can provide firms better financial performance. An additional reason to study the emerging DDG dynamic capability. Specifically, we investigate the following research question on a sample of 96 West-European companies: does DDG dynamic capability contribute positively to firm financial performance?

2 Theoretical Background

2.1 DDG as Dynamic Capabilities

Organisations need to constantly match or create market changes and dynamic capabilities are "the firm's processes that use resources—specifically the processes to integrate, reconfigure, gain and release resources—to match and even create market change" [6]. Thus, dynamic capabilities have the potential to create, to evolve and to recombine internal existing resources to allow the firm to adapt continuously to changes [7]. This adaptability has been argued as offering improved customer value [8], and is especially required in fast-paced technological environments [9].

We can define DDG dynamic capability as the three-fold organizational process of: (1) "choosing IT" in order to unobtrusively generate and capture data in digital form; (2) "reconfiguring IT" in the appropriate business processes; (3) "managing digital data" so produced. The technology embedded in a DDG initiative may be emerging IT—a new technology not yet commercially viable (e.g., retinal implants for blind people)—or may be an enabling IT: an established technology used by a firm in an innovative application (e.g., RFID in gaming chips to track table play in a gambling context).

We theorize DDG as a dynamic capability for two complementary reasons. First, it consists of deploying "new configurations of operational competencies relative to the competition" [10]—in other words, a firm with a DDG dynamic capability can identify opportunities for digital data generation and for recombining internal existing resources and data to adapt to changing environmental conditions, through the collection and production of new digital data. Second, the DDG dynamic capability includes the dynamic reconfiguring of the existing combinations of resources for digital data generation [10]. The degree to which an ineffective DDG process can be reconfigured into a more promising one that matches its environment, better, faster, and cheaper than the competition determines the capability's dynamic quality [6]. Therefore, the higher its degree of reconfigurability, the more dynamic the DDG dynamic capability is. Examples of DDG dynamic capabilities exist, such as the Harrah Corporation. For several years now, Harrah has systematically and repeatedly integrated new IT (such as computerized slot machines or RFID chips) to gain—unobtrusively, and always in new ways—valuable digital data on customers' behavior at the Harrah's casinos and exploits these new data to improve its customers' profiles and to better reward customers.

2.2 The Contribution of DDG Dynamic Capability on Firm Financial Performance

Firms use dynamic capabilities to identify and react to opportunities and threats by extending, modifying, changing, and/or creating a firm's ordinary capabilities to accomplish first-order change [11]. This view is also consistent with the study conducted by Eisenhardt and Martin [6, p. 1118] who argued that one could conceptualize dynamic capabilities as tools firms employed to manage and reconfigure existing resource in order to create new resource configurations.

Dynamic capabilities can contribute positively to firm's activities in several ways. First, firms thanks to the dynamic capabilities can improve the speed, effectiveness, and efficiency with which operate and respond to changes that they face in their environment [12]. As a result, this improved response speed,

Fig. 1 Research model

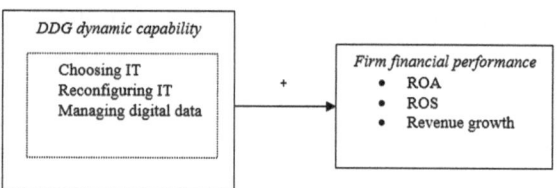

effectiveness, and efficiency with respect to dealing with environmental changes can positively affect firm financial performance by enabling the firm to take advantage of revenue enhancing opportunities and regulate its operations to reduce the incurred costs. Second, dynamic capabilities can positively affect firm financial performance by allowing the firm to recognize and react to opportunities through developing new processes, products, and services [13]. As a result, they have the potential to increase revenue. Third, dynamic capabilities offer new sets of decision options, previously unavailable for the firm, and thus provide the potential for greater firm financial performance contributions [6] such as increased revenues or profits. Therefore, dynamic capabilities can extend existing resource configurations in ways that result in entirely new sets of decision options in order to improve their process and product performance [6].

Based on these arguments, DDG dynamic capability could positively contribute to a firm's financial performance, because the process of choosing IT, managing digital data and reconfiguring digital data, could enable the firm to change its processes, products, and services, using the data in digital form, in order to achieve better financial performance. Therefore, we propose a positive relationship (Fig. 1) between the DDG dynamic capability and the firm financial performance.

3 Methodology

We conducted a questionnaire-based survey in 2012 of firms of any size and that belong to any industries, located in the West Europe, to test the supposed relationship. Given that the best approach to measure dynamic capabilities is at the organizational process level, our key informants were process managers in different companies. In particular, we selected sales managers as the sales department appeared as one of the departments more advanced in using DDG practices to improve customer relation [3]. We adopted the survey method as our main source of empirical data because it enables us to make a quantitative evaluation of the relationships between DDG dynamic capability and firm financial performance.

We operationalized measurement scales that already existed and had been tested for all the model's operationalized all the constructs of the model, with one exception: the 'choosing IT' construct of DDG dynamic capability, which measures the ability to choose IT to collect valuable digital data unobtrusively. We could not find any previously-tested scale for this construct in the literature, so we conducted preliminary testing via a pilot study. This pilot study started from four indicators which were available in the literature [14], but had never been tested empirically. We recruited 35 managers from small, medium and big enterprises in different industries to participate in the test, including the four indicators within a set of 26 other questions to reduce common method bias. Based on the 35 answers, the reliability of the scales satisfied the standard thresholds (Cronbach's Alpha = 0.837) and the scale was then reduced to two items. Specifically, it was operationalized by factoring the two items defined on a Likert scale between 1 and 7. Instead, the existing scales cover the other variables:

(1) Choosing IT: it measures the ability to choose emerging/enabling IT to gain unobtrusively valuable digital data [14];

(2) Reconfiguring IT: it adapts the reconfigurability measurement scale [10] to estimate the potential to reconfigure DDG and it is operationalized by factoring two items defined on a Likert scale between 1 and 7;

(3) Managing digital data: it adapts the information management dimension of the information capability measurement scale [15], to measure the ability to manage digital data and it is operationalized by factoring three items defined on a Likert scale between 1 and 7;

(4) Digital Data Genesis Capability: it is operationalized by computing the mean of the sum of the three variables Choosing IT, Reconfiguring IT and Managing digital data, and finally it was dichotomized on the median value of the variable;

(5) Firm financial performance: we measured profitability using three measures of performance: (1) return on assets (ROA) (2) return on sales (ROS), and (3) sales growth in logarithmic form (SG) [16].

4 Results and Analysis

We collected 96 questionnaires for providing evidence on the relationship between the development of the DDG dynamic capability and the firm financial performance. The respondents were mainly sales department managers (27 %), senior sales managers (15 %), mid-level sales managers (14 %) and business unit managers responsible for sales (10 %). A broad range of industries were represented and the participating companies were of a wide variety of sizes. The descriptive statistics and the correlations between our variables are tabulated in Tables 1 and 2. Specifically, the correlations between the dynamic capability investigated and the ROA, ROS and revenue growth positive and significant if we consider two of the three firm financial performance investigated in this paper: ROA and Sales growth.

Since all the measures that were used for defining the construct related to the DDG dynamic capability were captured on 7-point Likert scales, we conducted confirmatory factor and reliability analysis (Table 3). They were satisfactory for the items that were used for defining each construct on which the DDG dynamic

Table 1 Descriptive statistics

Variable	Minimum	Maximum	Mean	Median	Std. Deviation
ROA	−22.920	40.250	4.456	3.900	7.960
ROS	−28.860	26.070	3.472	3.405	7.391
Sales growth (log)	8.900	37.670	22.019	16.209	9.227
Choosing IT	1.000	7.000	4.992	5.132	1.098
Managing digital data	1.330	7.000	5.036	5.148	1.011
Reconfiguring IT	2.000	7.000	4.585	4.632	1.081
DDG dynamic capability	0.000	1.000	0.260	0.000	0.441

Table 2 Correlations between DDG dynamic capability and firm financial performance

N.	Variable	1	2	3	4	5	6	7
1	ROA	1.000	0.837[a]	0.161	0.104	0.060	0.132	0.178
2	ROS	0.837[a]	1.000	0.187	0.035	0.094	0.057	0.229[b]
3	Sales growth (log)	0.161	0.187	1.000	0.064	0.087	0.109	0.265[b]
4	Choosing IT	0.104	0.035	0.064	1.000	0.618[a]	0.619[a]	0.439[a]
5	Managing digital data	0.060	0.094	0.087	0.618[a]	1.000	0.704[a]	0.600[a]
6	Reconfiguring IT	0.132	0.057	0.109	0.619[a]	0.704[a]	1.000	0.695[a]
7	DDG dynamic capability	0.178	0.229[b]	0.265[b]	0.439[a]	0.600[a]	0.695[a]	1.000

[a] Correlation is significant at the 0.01 level
[b] Correlation is significant at the 0.05 level

Table 3 Factor and reliability analyses

Construct names and construct's items	Factor loading	Cronbach's alpha
Choosing IT		0.779
Our sales personnel have effective methods for the choices of digital data generation	0.914	
The choices of digital data generation make their case for our Sales process	0.910	
Reconfiguring IT		0.871
When our digital data generation must evolve, our sales personnel successfully steer its evolution	0.945	
When our digital data generation must evolve, our sales personnel effectively lead its reorganization	0.950	
Managing digital data		0.879
Our Sales personnel effectively handle the digital data that they obtain	0.937	
Our Sales personnel effectively process the data obtained in digital form	0.917	
Our sales personnel have effective methods for managing the digital data that they obtain	0.900	

Table 4 Mean value of firm financial performance for companies that have developed and not the DDG dynamic capability

	DDG dynamic capability	N	Mean	Std. Deviation	Min	Max	Significance level of the difference
ROA	Low	56	3.362	7.280	−22.920	18.850	5.02 %
	High	22	7.239	9.065	−4.430	40.250	
ROS	Low	56	2.420	6.941	−28.860	18.020	3.70 %
	High	20	6.420	7.983	−5.790	26.070	
Revenue growth (log)	Low	54	20.553	8.880	8.900	37.670	2.90 %
	High	22	25.617	9.268	14.520	37.420	

capability was defined. In terms of collinearity analysis, our tolerance value computations highlighted no risk of multicollinearity, with the correlation coefficients lower than 0.9 and the tolerance values above 0.19.

Our results regarding the level of firm financial performance achieved by companies that have developed the DDG dynamic capability and companies that have not developed such capability are shown in Table 4.

Table 4 shows that companies that have developed the DDG capability (the case where the column "DDG dynamic capability" has the value "High") have achieved higher firm financial performance than the companies that have not developed DDG dynamic capability (column that has the "Low" value). Specifically, companies able to leverage on digital data have achieved higher ROA values (mean value equal to 7.239 regard the 3.362—difference statistically significant at the 5.02 % level), higher ROS values (mean value equal to 6.420 regard the 2.420—difference statistically significant at the level equal to the 3.70 % level), and higher revenue growth (mean value equal to 25.617 regard the 20.553—difference statistically significant at the 2.90 % level).

5 Discussions and Conclusions

The Information Systems and Strategic Management literature suggest a relationship between the dynamic capabilities and the financial performance achieved by firms. However, the literature is scant about empirical evidence on whether the development of DDG capability, leveraging on digital data, determines higher firm financial performance in firms. By analysing a sample of 96 companies, we find that DDG capability is associated with several measures of financial performance, such as the ROA, ROS and the revenue growth. Indeed, our results are consistent with several measures of financial performance.

The results that we found in this research study has important managerial implications. Indeed, managers of firms should become more aware about the potentiality that the usage of digital data can have on the activities that they conduct and should invest more in the capability of use this type of data. Indeed, they can be valuable for firms, as demonstrated in this research study. Future analyses will be based on qualitative studies, in order to understand how the capability emerges, develops and helps companies to gain better performance.

References

1. Peteraf, M.A., Di Stefano, G., Verona, G.: The elephant in the room of dynamic capabilities: bringing two diverging conversations together. Strateg. Manage. J. (2013) (In press)
2. Drnevich, P.L., Kriauciunas, A.P.: Clarifying the conditions and limits of the contributions of ordinary and dynamic capabilities to relative firm performance. Strateg. Manag. J. **32**, 254–279 (2011)
3. Kohli, R., Grover, V.: Business value of IT: an essay on expanding research directions to keep up with the times. J. Assoc. Inf. Syst. **9**, 23–39 (2008)
4. Mithas, S., Ramasubbu, N., Sambamurthy, V.: How information management capability influences firm performance. MIS Q. **35**, 237–256 (2011)
5. Piccoli, G., Watson, R.T.: profit from customer data by identifying strategic opportunities and adopting the born digital approach. MIS Quart. Executive **7**, 113–122 (2008)
6. Eisenhardt, K.M., Martin, J.A.M.: Dynamic capabilities: what are they? Strateg. Manag. J. **21**, 1105–1121 (2000)
7. Teece, D.J., Pisano, G., Shuen, A.: Dynamic capabilities and strategic management. Strateg. Manag. J. **18**, 509–533 (1997).
8. Sambamurthy, V., Bharadwaj, A., Grover, V.: Shaping agility through digital options: reconceptualizing the role of information technology in contemporary firms. MIS Q. **27**, 237–263 (2003)
9. Banker, R.D., Bardhan, I.R., Hsihui, C., Shu, L.: Plant information systems, manufacturing capabilities, and plant performance. MIS Q. **30**, 315–337 (2006)
10. Pavlou, P.A., El Sawy, O.A.: From IT leveraging competence to competitive advantage in turbulent environments: the case of new product development. Inf. Syst. Res. **17**, 198–227 (2006)
11. Dosi, G., Nelson, R., Winter, S.: Introduction: the nature and dynamics of organizational capabilities. In nature and dynamics of organizational capabilities. Oxford University Press, New York (2000)
12. Tallon, P.P.: Inside the adaptive enterprise: an information technology capabilities perspective on business process agility. Inf. Technol. Manage. **9**, 21–36 (2008)
13. Zou, S., Fang, E., Zhao, S.: The effect of export marketing capabilities on export performance: an investigation of Chinese exporters. J. Int. Mark. **11**, 32–55 (2003)
14. Williams, M.L.: Identifying the Organizational Routines in NEBIC Theory's Choosing Capability. HICCS, Hawaii (2003)
15. Marchand, D.A., Kettinger, W.J., Rollins, J.D.: Information Orientation: The Link to Business Performance. Oxford University Press, New York (2002)
16. Qian, G., Li, L.: Profitability of small-and medium-sized enterprises in high-tech industries: the case of the biotechnology industry. Strateg. Manag. J. **24**, 881–887 (2003)

Ideas Sharing Through ICT in Innovation Processes: A Design Theory for Open Innovation Platforms

Barbara Aquilani, Tindara Abbate and Alessio Maria Braccini

Abstract Since Henry Chesbrough's remark on the importance of opening innovation processes to the cooperation of external entities, like partners, competitors or customers, open innovation (OI) gained momentum. Open innovation approach was started and run by different companies around the world. Meanwhile specific platforms were developed to support these processes, either by intermediaries aimed at helping companies to shift to an open innovation approach, or by firms which decided to adopt this approach trough their own created and managed platforms. Through a descriptive design theory perspective the paper analyzes the features (components) that these web-based platforms offer in respect to the requirements they have to fulfill in order to effectively support the open innovation approach.

Keywords Open innovation · Software platforms · Design research · Exploratory design theory

1 Introduction

In the past, firms believed that through investing in their critical R&D activities more strongly than their competitors and protecting their intellectual property, they could innovate more rapidly and radically and, therefore, sustain their competitive

B. Aquilani · A. M. Braccini (✉)
Dipartimento di Economia e Impresa, Università degli Studi della Tuscia, Viterbo, Italy
e-mail: abraccini@unitus.it

B. Aquilani
e-mail: b.aquilani@unitus.it

T. Abbate
Dipartimento di Scienze Economiche, Aziendali, Ambientali e Metodologie Quantitative,
Università degli Studi di Messina, Messina, Italy
e-mail: abbatet@unime.it

L. Caporarello et al. (eds.), *Smart Organizations and Smart Artifacts*,
Lecture Notes in Information Systems and Organisation 7,
DOI: 10.1007/978-3-319-07040-7_12,
© Springer International Publishing Switzerland 2014

advantage in the long run. This model of innovation, later defined closed innovation, was challenged by the reduction of time to market for a larger number of products and services, the mobility of knowledge resources, and the growing availability of private venture capital [1]. In this landscape, a new innovation approach, called open innovation (OI), arose. In OI perspective, firms are increasingly opening up their internal R&D departments and innovation processes to external parties. This innovation approach seems to be an attractive alternative to improve innovativeness and competitiveness [1]. Firms strongly interact and collaborate with external partners, such as suppliers, customers, competitors and research organizations, with the aim of fostering and sustaining innovation processes and, thus, enhancing their performance [1]. To support OI processes and primarily to cooperate with external actors, who are in the position of sharing ideas, organizations make use of software platforms created by innovation intermediaries that help in transferring and sharing ideas among different parties not directly linked and rarely networked [2, 3]. Also, several multinational companies, like P&G, Ducati, Lego, Volvo and Nokia implemented their own software platforms to capture innovative ideas, to build new products/brand, or to improve existing products. Within these platforms the interactions among actors span across one-way exchanges to on-going and continuous dialogue, useful to create and develop innovative solutions to market needs [4].

In this paper we focus on the OI software platforms with a design research perspective. Since OI is frequently adopted as an innovation model [1], and software platforms are commonly used to support the idea sharing [4], there is the need of theories that clarify how to design such platforms. To this regard the paper analyzes both OI processes and OI platforms to propose a first explanatory design theory for OI platforms. We discuss literature on OI and related software platforms to derive requirements and components of the design theory. The paper is structured as follows. After the description of the research design in Sect. 2, both the OI process and the most frequently used software platforms are discussed in Sect. 3. The exploratory design theory is proposed and discussed in Sect. 4. Final thoughts and remarks on future research steps conclude the paper in Sect. 5.

2 Research Design

As described in the introduction, this paper adopts a design research perspective and aims at defining a design theory for OI platforms that states the designing principles for a software platform supporting OI efforts. A design theory is an outcome of a design research effort [5, 6]. According to Walls et al. [5], a design theory is composed by: (a) a design product, and (b) a design process. The design product is in turn composed by: meta-requirements, meta-design, kernel theories, and a set of testable design hypothesis. The design process is instead composed by the design method, the kernel theories, and a set of testable design process hypotheses. A cleaner specification of a design theory is provided by Gregor and

Jones [7] and is based on: kernel theories, meta-requirements, meta-design, design method, and testable design product/process hypotheses. Both frameworks assign to kernel theories the core of a design theory. They are the necessary justificatory knowledge that informs the design process. The kernel theories allow researchers to formulate prescriptions for the other elements of a design theory.

Since in this paper we specifically intend to focus only on the artifact, we find the contribution of Baskerville and Pries-Heje [8] more helpful to this regard. These authors distinguish between practice theory and explanatory design theories. The first are prescriptive theories, which provide prescriptions on how specific artifacts shall be designed. Explanatory design theories explain instead why a generalized set of requirements is satisfied by a generalized set of object components. The essence of an explanatory design theory can be captured by representing general requirements, which can be conditions or capabilities, general components, and relationships between the two [8].

Given the aim of this paper we propose an explanatory design theory that describes the functionalities that shall be found in a software platform to support OI organizational efforts. To this regard the requirements of such a platform are identified with reference to OI literature, which clearly describes the processes that organizations run when they adopt open innovation approach. For the components, the most common platforms for OI are analyzed and discussed in the paper.

3 Open Innovation: Process and Software Platforms

The work of Chesbrough [1] highlights that *open innovation is paradigm that assume that firm can and should use external ideas as well as internal ideas, and internal and external path to market as firm look to advance their technology* (p. vii). The preeminent idea concerns opening up the innovation process outside the traditional boundaries of organizations [1], claiming a higher involvement of external actors in their innovative activities. Organizations cannot merely innovate in their internal R&D functions, but they have to encourage the interaction with their environment and integrate resources and competences derived by external entities to create different opportunities for product development, to exploit new ideas, to meet market demands and, consequently, to stay abreast of competition [1, 9]. External actors can include: customers, suppliers, experts, universities, private/public R&D institutions, partners, competitors, and the general community as a whole.

Consequently, the boundaries of the organizations become porous and permeable, allowing innovative ideas to flow selectively inside and outside [1]. Innovation is getting though more global in nature and is shared among several actors characterized by different expertise and professional experience. The exchange of ideas and the cooperation allow enriching firm's knowledge on a long-term basis and improve its ability to get in touch with other subjects, firms and organizations [10]. Also, such collaboration with different subjects is becoming necessary to increase and to sustain a company's innovativeness [11], to reduce time to market for products/services, and to shrink costs connected to innovation.

Therefore, the OI paradigm challenges the ways to understand innovation. The traditional model is overly linear, sequential and defined by firms that invest in their research labs and in their internal product development processes without any form of interaction with other external forces. The R&D function, traditionally considered critical for innovation, is based on vertical integration logic, through which the firm realizes any aspect of a business. On the contrary, the OI model stresses the concept that innovation process must be more extended, collaborative, and engaged with a wider variety of external participants, combining internal and external ideas into useful contexts, suitable systems, and architectures [12].

3.1 The Open Innovation Process

The opening up of the innovation processes concerned many industries such as pharmaceutical (e.g., Bayer, Pfizer) and biotechnology, software (e.g., Apple, IBM), electronics (e.g., Philips with OI park), high-tech, sports, and food. Both large multinational and small-medium sized firms are engaged in these OI endeavours and in iterative and interactive *probe-and-learn processes* [13].

Literature identifies three important core processes in OI: *outside-in, inside-out and coupled process* [14]. In the outside-in process companies improve their own knowledge through the use of a broad range of external ideas, emphasizing the relevance and the role of dense networks of innovation, the forms of customer integration and the use of third parties that facilitate interactions among different subjects using OI platforms [14].

In the inside-out process companies are oriented to external exploitation of their internal knowledge by carrying out ideas to market, selling intellectual property rights (IPR), licensing mechanisms, and bringing technologies to the outside environment. In other words, this core process aims at allocating and commercializing externally ideas and technological innovation derived by firm's internal R&D activities [14].

In the coupled process the concept of co-creation with complementary partners is relevant, stimulating the definition of forms of cooperation and collaboration with these subjects operating in different sectors of activity and having specific interests [14]. These external and complementary partners can offer *ad hoc* solutions that can improve the company's innovations, or they can exploit solutions developed by the company itself [14]. In addition, these forms of collaboration require strategic decisions, based on the features, the role of involved actors or groups of organizations in the OI networks, and the activities to maintain heterogeneous partners base over time [14].

Many scholars studied OI processes identifying a different number of stages characterized by various activities [15, 16]. These stages demand for both strategic and operational decisions, to define and to manage innovative collaborative projects. Among them, it is possible to include: opportunities seeking to explore internal/external ideas; analysis and evaluation of their market potentiality and inventiveness; evaluation of opportunities linked to the intermediarie's involvement; recruitment of potential developments partners; value capture by commercialization of ideas and technologies brought to the market, and, the innovation proposals extensions to the formal/informal network. However, these activities, in general, and the exchange of ideas and collaboration with different partners (across different contexts and backgrounds), in particular, are not straightforward and characterized by some codifying difficulties. To this regard, Lee et al. [17] suggest the use of the intermediated network model in which the intermediary organizes and manages the network oriented to create both high involvement and trust among different participants.

Defined commonly as organizations that operate as *agent or broker in any aspect of the innovation process between two or more parties* [3], innovation intermediaries can offer different benefits not only to smaller firms, which face many difficulties connected to the opening up of their innovation processes, but also to larger organizations, especially for outbound OI [3, 18–20]. Applied in several ways and across different domain areas, these organizations play a significant role in facilitating the innovation processes, assisting customers to effectively catch the opportunities of customer's business models, connecting innovation requests with potential, globally distributed, innovation providers (e.g., researchers, lead users), creating and maintaining innovation networks and, finally, facilitating outward and inward innovation results commercialization. The main functions, performed by these intermediaries, can be seen as coupled to the diverse phases of the innovation process: (a) the search for innovation stage contains some functions as, for instance, partners identification, suppliers selection, and alternative options evaluation; (b) the innovation transfer step includes other functions, such as: support to deal making, packaging of technology and innovation adaptation to user's needs.

In addition, these intermediaries have been able to change the R&D department and activity configurations for many companies, government agencies, and non-profit actors by using their price-based method to involve innovators from around the world. They enable firms to source (as well as to exploit) innovation globally with limited investments in proprietary structures, reducing the associated transaction costs and information asymmetries through a broad availability of information.

3.2 Open Innovation Software Platforms

Open Innovation Intermediaries (OII) emerged as OI platforms that stimulate, support, and develop innovation communities through interconnected networks of people globally distributed. Some examples of OII are: Ninesigma, Innocentive, IdeaConnection, Big Idea Group, Yet2.com, Mercatodellinnovazione, etc. The OII are able to build and maintain efficient bridges between seekers (companies that seek at and try to solve innovation problems or to take advantages of business opportunities), and solvers (scientists, professionals, post-graduate students, highly qualified individuals around the world), which are potentially able to find innovative solutions [21], or buyers and sellers of intellectual properties. Through the Internet and online web 2.0 tools, these OI platforms promote and facilitate collaborative innovation forms, sustain worldwide R&D projects, and intensify interactions among subjects in a significant and on-going dialogue to explore new solutions. Every day, Internet-based platforms help individuals and organizations across the globe to cross-fertilize their resources and their competences in a wide variety of specialized fields.

Created by both intermediaries of innovation or generated by large multinational companies, the platforms show interesting characteristics [22]: (a) collaboration, facilitating different forms of collaborations between seekers and solvers and stimulating online-communities that involve different subjects as appreciated solvers; (b) interactivity, sharing information between seekers and solvers; (c) networking, in terms of scanning and establishing connections in a network for identifying innovative solutions that meet seeker's requests and other potential needs; (d) articulation, providing different and clear sections that facilitate search of information by users; (e) accessibility, defining search link and screens which facilitate experiences on the web site; (f) multimedia, offering various and efficient web 2.0 tools (e.g., blog, community, forum, etc.) oriented to stimulate suitable relations among participants; (g) groups formation, concerning the creation of a special group of experts for solving problems posted on the platform. With one or more useful characteristics, these Internet-based platforms enable and support open networking of individuals and organizations that move from a closed to an OI approach [22].

4 The Proposal of an Exploratory Design Theory

Following the considerations on the literature on OI and OI platforms, this section proposes an explanatory design theory for OI platforms, which is shown in Fig. 1. Accordingly to Baskerville and Pries-Heje [8], the theory is decomposed into requirements and components.

The literature shows how the OI process presents itself in different flavors according to the decisions of the organization that is opening up its processes for cooperating with external partners. Different stages of the innovation process (i.e., importing innovation from outside, exporting innovation to the external environment, co-innovate with partners) include heterogeneous sets of activities. Since several organizations might choose to perform OI in different ways, we argue that a design theory for OI platforms shall contemplate modularity. We found some difficulties in representing this concept, which is basic in software design and development, into the explanatory design theory blueprint, since it seems not to

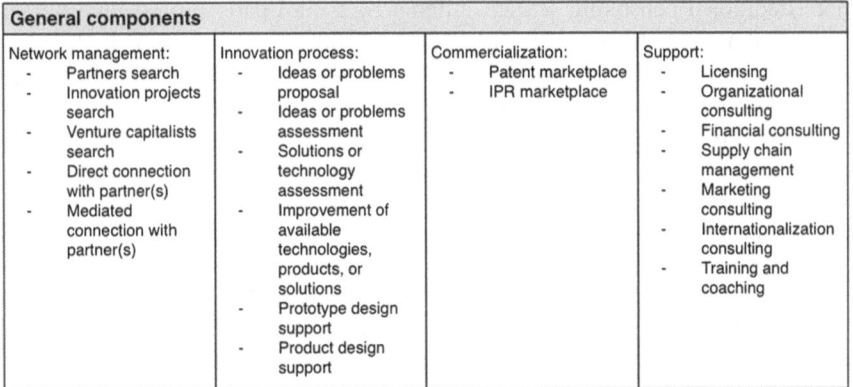

Fig. 1 Explanatory design theory for OI platforms

have been taken into account until now. Therefore, we separated our general requirements and components into groups, each one representing the different ways in which organizations might perform OI (requirements), and the different set of features (components) that a platform to support OI shall integrate to be effective.

On the requirements side, we resorted to Enkel's et al. [14] three different processes: outside-in, inside-out, and coupled. Since each of these processes focus on diverse aspects of OI, requirements are certainly differentiated. In all processes, the ability of the organization to enter in contact with valuable partners is crucial. Network management components in the supporting platforms shall therefore be able to sustain the organization in partners/innovation projects search, in establish and manage the connections, either directly or through intermediaries.

Ideas exchanges are at the core of OI in general, and more specifically are crucial in the outside-in (where ideas are searched externally) and inside-out (where internal ideas are made accessible externally) processes. On the components side the support of the core of OI process requires the platform to be capable of addressing problems/ideas/solutions management (i.e., proposals, discussion, and approval) (i.e., NineSigma, Innocentive, Yet2.com, Mercatodell'innovazione). Product and prototype solutions support are particularly useful in joint efforts (coupled processes) of partners, which aim at co-creating value (i.e., Big Idea Group, Innocentive).

Commercialization happens only when specific IPR elements are sold externally to the market. This happens usually in inside-out processes, when the organization wishes to sell its internal knowledge on the marketplace. On the platform side, at this stage, specific commercialization support components are necessary (i.e., Inpama, Yet2.com, Mercatodell'innovazione).

Finally existing platforms for OI show the presence, in some cases, of supporting/consulting services (i.e., NineSigma, Big Idea Group, Inpama) [22], which are normally accessible to the organization wishing to adopt OI. These services are more traditional consulting services offered by a third party professional organization that might help, in specific aspects, the willing open innovator. In this case, on the components side, the role of the supporting platform is just the provision of information sources necessary to advertise these consulting services (which are most probably human-based). For example, Big Idea Group intermediary proposes several consulting services related to technological-technical aspects, marketing strategies and finance [22]. It also answers to specific needs of the seeker organization, offering useful personalized solutions, through its interface and its specialized personnel. In some cases (depending on the service), the platform shall also be able to let the open innovation company access these services (i.e., NineSigma).

The proposed explanatory design theory is therefore characterized by four different set of requirements (or modules). The core is composed by the set of requirements that support the whole innovation process. The networking requirements are also relevant as they shall support the organization in building the network of relationships with partners. Finally, the commercialization components are expected to be in the platform only in the case of an inside-out-project.

5 Conclusion

This paper aims at proposing an explanatory design theory for OI platforms. Through the discussion of literature on OI, the paper identifies both the general requirements and the general components based on the three specific processes of the OI approach. The main contribution of the paper is the definition of a first canvas to help both OII and firms willing to create their own OI platform, to effectively build and manage this web-based interactive tool. This first insight is still at an exploratory effort and deserves refinements that will be tackled in future research efforts. Besides proposing this explanatory design theory, the paper suggests the need for exploratory design theories to be able to contemplate modularity, which is a basic concept in software development.

Obviously, the selected processes to be run on the OI platform as well as the different weights firms and/or OII assign to processes to be implemented on them, impose also requirements on the necessary resources and on their distribution among the different processes to be realized. The exploratory design theory we propose here is anyhow not focusing on this aspect, which instead results as an implication for its use.

References

1. Chesbrough, H.W.: Open Innovation: The New Imperative for Creating and Profiting from Technology. Harvard Business School Press, Boston (2003)
2. Hargadon, A., Sutton, R.: Technology brokering and innovation in product development firm. Adm. Sci. Q. **42**, 716–749 (1997)
3. Howells, J.: Intermediation and the role of intermediaries in innovation. Res. Policy **35**, 715–728 (2006)
4. Sawhney, M., Verona, G., Prandelli, E.: Collaboration to create: the internet as a platform for customer engagement in product innovation. J. Interact. Mark. **19**, 4–17 (2005)
5. Walls, J.G., Widermeyer, G.R., Sawy, O.A.: El: assessing information system design theory in perspective: how useful was our 1992 initial rendition? J. Inf. Technol. Theory Appl. 6, Article 6 (2004)
6. Braccini, A.M., Federici, T.: New internet-based relationships between citizens and governments in the public space: challenges for and integrated system design. In: Baskerville, R., De Marco, M., Spagnoletti, P. (eds.) Designing Organizational Systems. An Interdisciplinary Discourse. pp. 157–180. Springer, Berlin (2013)
7. Gregor, S., Jones, D.: The anatomy of a design theory. J. Assoc. Inf. Syst. **8**, 312–335 (2007)
8. Baskerville, R., Pries-Heje, J.: Explanatory design theory. Bus. Inf. Syst. Eng. **2**, 271–282 (2010)
9. Laursen, K., Salter, A.: Open for innovation: the role of openness in explaining innovation performance among UK manifacturing firms. Strateg. Manag. J. **27**, 131–150 (2006)
10. Koschatzky, K.: Networks in innovation research and innovation policy—an introduction. In: Koschatzky, K., Kulicke, M., Zenker, A. (eds.) Innovation Networks: Concepts and Challenges in the European Perspective. Physica Verlag, Heidelberg (2001)
11. Diener, K., Piller, F.: The market for open innovation: Increasing the efficiency and effectiveness of the innovation process. The RWTH Open Innovation Accelerator Survey, 1–94 (2009)
12. Chesbrough, H.: Open innovation: where we've been and where we're going. Res. Manag. **55**, 20–27 (2012)
13. Lynn, G.S., Morone, J.G., Paulson, A.S.: Marketing and discontinuous innovations: the probe and learn process. Calif. Manage. Rev. **38**, 8–37 (1996)
14. Enkel, E., Gassmann, O., Chesbrough, H.W.: Open R&D and open innovation: exploiting the phenomenon. R&D Manag. **39**, 311–316 (2009)
15. Fetterhoff, T.J., Volkel, D.: Managing open innovation in biotechnology. Res. Technol. Manag. **49**, 14–18 (2006)
16. Hrastinski, S., M., Edenius, M., Kviselius, N.Z., Ozan, H.: How can software support open innovation? Extending community and marketplace perspective. Int. J. Netw. Virtual Organ. **10**, 1–17 (2012)
17. Lee, S., Park, G., Yoon, B., Park, J.: Open Innovation in SMEs—an intermediated network model. Res. Policy **39**, 290–300 (2010)

18. Abbate, T., R., C.: Knowledge sharing and innovation: the contribution of innovation intermediaries. In: Marco, M. De Te'eni, D., Albano, V., and Za, S. (eds.) Information Systems: Crossroads for Organization, Management, Accounting and Engineering. pp. 251–258. Physica Verlag, Heidelberg (2011)
19. Nambisan, S., Sawhney, M.: A buyer's guide to the innovation bazaar. Harv. Bus. Rev. **85**, 109–118 (2007)
20. Huston, L., Sakkad, N.: Connect and develop inside procter and gamble new model for innovation. Harv. Bus. Rev. **84**, 58–66 (2006)
21. Chesbrough, H.W.: Open Business Models: How to Thrive in the New Innovation Landscape. Harvard Bus. Sch. Press, Boston (2006)
22. Aquilani, B., Abbate, T.: Gli open innovation intermediaries: la prospettiva dei seekers. In: Proceedings XXV Convegno Annualedi Sinergie. Ancona (2013)

Delivering Knowledge to the Mobile Enterprise Implementation Solutions for a Mobile Business Intelligence

Gianmario Motta, Tianyi Ma, Linlin You and Daniele Sacco

Abstract Almost all large companies analyze their performances through KPIs that are processed by Business Intelligence (BI) systems. Specifically, BI is a critical supporting system in service industry where even a little improvement in efficiency allows you to win the competition. It implies a continuous research of excellence in BI, exploiting all technologies supporting the whole information life cycle—collection, processing and distribution. Specifically, within information distribution, mobile devices have increased BI usability, since decision makers can track performance whenever (at any time) and wherever (they do not need to sit at their desk). This paper also illustrates the implementation of a mobile BI system in a customer care company. Our system uses a service-oriented architecture to integrate existing BI systems and our framework allows delivering a cross-platform mobile application to end users. Finally, we summarize the benefits given by a mobile BI solution in small and medium enterprises.

Keywords Mobile business intelligence · Service oriented architecture · Key performance indicators · Dashboard · Analytics · Reporting · Service level

G. Motta (✉) · T. Ma · L. You · D. Sacco
Dipartimento di Ingegneria Industriale e della Informazione,
University of Pavia, Pavia, Italy
e-mail: motta05@unipv.it

T. Ma
e-mail: tianyi.ma01@ateneopv.it

L. You
e-mail: linlin.you01@ateneopv.it

D. Sacco
e-mail: daniele.sacco01@ateneopv.it

L. Caporarello et al. (eds.), *Smart Organizations and Smart Artifacts*,
Lecture Notes in Information Systems and Organisation 7,
DOI: 10.1007/978-3-319-07040-7_13,
© Springer International Publishing Switzerland 2014

1 Introduction

Mobile Business Intelligence (BI) is an asset that enables enterprises to gain business insights through information analysis using applications optimized for mobile devices [1]. BI consists of techniques used to spot, dig out and analyze business data. Even though mobile applications and devices have been around for almost 20 years, only recently mobile BI is becoming a reality [2]. Since smart-phones has led to a new era of mobile computing, mobile BI has shown a momentum of growth. The availability and widespread popularity of easy-to-use touch-based devices like Android devices, iPhones and iPads, along with the reliable availability of wireless bandwidth, has had a strong impact on the potential use cases of BI systems [3]. In order to support an efficient decision making process, companies are undertaking mobile BI systems, because they improve efficiency in business processes, improve productivity of employees and provide better customer service [4].

The purposes of mobile BI solutions can be summarized as follows:

- To integrate existing BI systems and improve their usability.
- To improve business efficiency: decision makers can make decisions anytime, anywhere by using their mobile devices; actually, they do not need to be in their office to monitor business performances.
- To improve information communication timeliness: mobile BI solutions use notification services to message decision makers; therefore they do not need to wait for a result, but they will be alerted when information is ready.

First, we discuss existing solutions for mobile BI. Second, we introduce technologies used to implement mobile BI systems by illustrating three possible solutions, namely native, web, and hybrid applications. Finally, we present a mobile BI solution implemented in a real enterprise and its benefits.

2 Related Work

Since mobile Business Intelligence (BI) is widely spreading across organizations, the benefits of such applications are numerous. Mobile BI benefits can be summarized as increasing enterprise revenue and improving customer satisfaction [5]. Mobile BI enables organizations to track, understand, and manage daily operations anytime and anywhere. As a result, enterprises can enhance efficiency of their processes and create a genuine customer relationship as well as promote new products and services [6]. Mobile BI are an excellent example of aligning IT strategy and enterprise strategy to achieve a competitive advantage among its competitors [7]. Currently, mobile BI mainly provides three functions [8]:

- Exceptions/alerts: some indicators are first defined and tracked. If the performance falls down and is lower than a threshold, the alerts or exceptions report will be sent to users.
- Push reporting: the system generates specific predefined reports, such as key performance indicators (KPIs), are pushed to users (regardless of their location or their device) on a regular schedule.
- Pull reporting: users specify the information they want, using what input method is appropriate for the available device. The user could access almost any type of information available from a centralized server-based system.

Mobile BI systems that are available in the market are mostly proprietary or device specific. Many industry-specific mobile BI systems are also available [9]. The following are the main existing mobile BI systems:

- IBM Cognos Mobile [10]: it extends interactive Cognos Business Intelligence to a broader range of mobile devices, including iPhone and iPad, Android phones, BlackBerry phones, and Playbook. Users can view and fully interact with Cognos reports, dashboards, metrics, analysis and other information by using a thick client. It is a closed-source system.
- Oracle BI Mobile [11]: it allows users to view, analyze and act on Oracle BI content. Oracle BI Mobile provides on-the-go access to the complete range of alerts, ad hoc analyses, dashboards, enterprise reports, geo-spatial visualizations, KPIs/Scorecards, what-if analyses, as well as unified relational OLAP (R-OLAP) and multidimensional OLAP (M-OLAP) content of Oracle Business Intelligence. It supports iOS platform and it is a closed-source system.
- Pentaho Mobile BI (http://www.pentaho.com/mobile-bi/): Pentaho Mobile BI offers a complete business analytics experience, including interactive analysis, rich visualization, dashboards, operational and enterprise reports. It is based on the open source platform but it is not free and only supports iOS devices.
- SAP Business Objects Mobile (http://en.sap.info/an-overview-of-the-new-bi-app/97167): it integrates with SAP Business Objects Explorer. Users have access to information spaces and exploration views to analyze information by filters and search functions. It supports iOS and Android platforms.

3 Implementation Solutions for Mobile Business Intelligence

We have identified three solutions to build a mobile Business Intelligence (BI) system through open source technologies: native apps, web apps and hybrid apps. Native apps are developed by using native APIs on a specific mobile platform; web apps run on web browsers and are developed by web technologies; hybrid apps run as a native app but are developed by web technologies. Each solution has its pros and cons. A detailed description and comparison for each solution is presented, namely native application solutions, web application solutions, and hybrid application solutions.

Native applications are built for a specific platform by using its SDK, tools and languages, typically provided by the platform vendor (e.g. Objective-C/XCode for iOS, Java/Eclipse for Android, C#/Visual Studio for Windows Phone, etc.). They are installed on mobile devices and they can get full access to the hardware of mobile devices by using API calls from mobile device Operating System (OS). Mobile OS directly manages hardware (e.g. camera, GPS, storage, etc.) of mobile devices and returns data to native applications. Native applications can be published on software stores/markets of specific platforms (e.g. Apple store/IOS, Google Play/Android, etc.). Native applications are fast, reliable, and powerful; however they are tied to a specific mobile OS; thus, developers need to duplicate them, when and if they target another platform. This solution is suitable for complex applications, which require high performance, high quality of user experience and full access to hardware.

Mobile web apps are server-side apps, built with server-side technologies (usually HTML5, CSS and JavaScript), so that they can be visualized on a device form factor. Mobile web applications are accessed by browsers on a mobile OS. Here browsers use API calls to access hardware of mobile devices instead of applications themselves. Such applications are easy to develop (single development and deployment) and have a lower cost; however, only few hardware resources can be fully accessed by browsers (e.g. touch screen, keyboard and WIFI); also, they cannot be published to software online stores. So, mobile web apps are not suitable for complex applications.

Hybrid applications are similar to native apps, are installed and run on devices, but they are written with web technologies [12]. Hybrid apps run inside a native container, and leverage the device browser engine (not the browser itself) to render HTML, and process the JavaScript locally. A web-to-native abstraction layer enables access to device capabilities that are not accessible in mobile web applications, such as the accelerometer, camera and local storage. The response speed of hybrid apps is slower than native apps but faster than mobile web apps. In some cases, hybrid apps can also reach native speed, depending on developed functions. Hybrid apps can also be published to software stores of specific platforms.

Hybrid apps are more suitable for mobile BI because mobile BI systems target multiple mobile platforms and require good performance and user experience (Table 1). Also, a mobile BI system needs to access the capabilities of devices that a mobile web app cannot (e.g. mobile web apps do not support notification pushing). Also, hybrid apps cost less than native apps and are almost as reasonable as mobile web apps [13]. Cross-platform capability and performance are the most concerned aspects, so hybrid app solution is chosen to implement a mobile BI system in our case study.

Table 1 Comparison of the different solutions

	Device access	Speed	Development cost	App store	Approval process
Native apps	Full	Very fast	High	Available	Mandatory
Hybrid apps	Full	As much as native apps	Medium	Available	Low overhead
Web apps	Partial	Fast	Low	Not available	None

4 Case Study

Phonetica is a midsize enterprise that operates in Business Process Outsourcing (BPO). Phonetica provides various call center services, such as customer care, back office, remote answering service and reception activities to a wide range of companies. Phonetica also provides marketing services such as market research and opinion surveys, sales support and event organization. Phonetica has a non-integrated information on analyze business performances. In order to get a more comprehensive view, to optimize the workforce, and to improve efficiency, Phonetica commissioned us to build an advanced business intelligence solution. The Phonetica BI suite contains a set of systems based on Pentaho BI platform and includes:

- Dashboard system: it provides dashboards to show Key Performance Indicators (KPIs). The charts contain measures about previous days performances and comparison between last weeks and last months performances. The KPI chart can be displayed according to the service or/and skill set.
- Reporting system: it generates statistical reports automatically and periodically. After generating reports the reporting system sends them to the executives by email. There are three types of different reports: top 10 services reports, exception reports and Interquartile Range (IQR) reports.
- Forecasting system: it forecasts the workload and corresponding workforce for a specific service, skill set or a group of them. The forecasting process is based on the historical data from historical databases in Phonetica.
- Mobile BI system: it integrates the three systems mentioned above through an ad hoc mobile BI server and provides access to users on mobile devices. Provided features are KPI dashboards, statistical reports and forecasting reports.

As shown in Fig. 1, the Phonetica BI suite supports the information cycle transforming from data to knowledge and decision. KPI dashboard system, reporting system and forecasting system use the data stored in the data warehouse by accessing OLAP cubes. These three systems run as web or desktop applications, whereas mobile BI system provides access to the systems on multiple mobile platforms such as Android and IOS. It enables managers to get business insights by mobile devices. Managers can select dashboard or reports using their own mobile

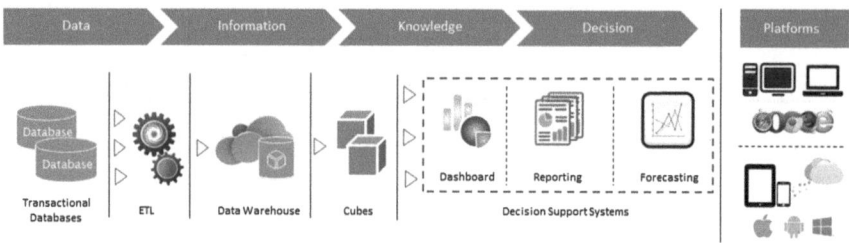

Fig. 1 Information cycle in phonetica BI system

devices also when they are not on site or they are busy in activities not performed on their laptops. In order to provide the same user experience in terms of functions in current Phonetica BI Suite, mobile BI is implemented by two main parts:

- Mobile BI Server which provides an data access layer for mobile devices. Specifically, the mobile BI system server will receive requests from mobile applications, then retrieve data from Phonetica BI Suite in terms of KPIs, reports and forecasting results, finally transfer it into specific format fitting the mobile device.
- Mobile BI Application which presents the results on mobile devices. It can run on different mobile platforms (IOS, Android, Windows Phone, etc.) and different mobile devices (smart phones and tablets).

The Data Access Service provides the orchestration layer for mobile applications by using Pentaho Community Dashboard Access (CDA) to retrieve data defined in the OLAP cubes and stored in the data warehouse. Overall needs of Phonetica for the mobile solution include:

- Dashboard: it enables executives and call center managers to analyze KPIs.
- Reporting: it enables executives to view weekly, monthly and quarterly KPI statistical reports on mobile devices. The reports contain 5/10 top KPI reports, exception reports and Interquartile Range (IQR) reports.
- Forecasting: it enables planners to view forecasting reports and allocate call center workforce based on the resulting workload.
- Push notification: it sends alerts to user's devices when reports are ready.

The mobile application is installed on devices of managers. The mobile application consists of two sub-layers: the first layer is the presentation layer which presents KPI dashboards, forecasting reports and statistical reports; the second layer is business logic layer, this layer contains two parts: (1) data access components to deal with data transmission and processing. (2) UI logic controllers which controls UI rendering and actions of UI components. Functional requirements are identified according to the requirements of Phonetica, as shown in the use case diagram in Fig. 2. It also shows the implementation of the mobile KPI dashboard, organized by service.

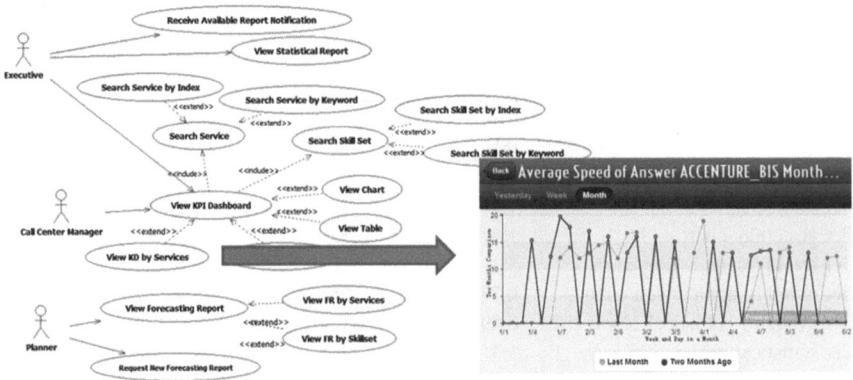

Fig. 2 Use case diagram and screenshot of the Android implementation

Table 2 Comparison of phonegap and appcelerator titanium

	Cross-platform	Native code	Native UI	Performance	Developing tools
PhoneGap	IOS, Android, Windows Phone, BlackBerry, Bada, Symbian	Via native API and plugins	Not native UI (WebView)	Depends on performance of WebView component	Command line and third party developing tools
Titanium	IOS, Android, Windows Phone, BlackBerry	Via JS engine	Truly native UI	Depends on performance of devices	Titanium Studio

The key point of hybrid app solutions is to choose a suitable native app container technology. The most prevalent native container technology products are Adobe PhoneGap and Appcelerator Titanium. All of them support development of native apps by using HTML5, CSS3 and JavaScript. We chose native application container technology according mainly to the following aspects: (a) cross-platform capability and (b) performance; mobile BI application requires running on prevalent mobile platforms with high performance and good user experience.

As shown in Table 2, PhoneGap supports more devices, so cross-platform capability of PhoneGap is better. Both PhoneGap and Titanium use native code, but PhoneGap uses WebView component to build UI which is not truly native. The performance of UI depends on the performance of WebView component. Titanium builds native UI and the performance only depends on the devices. So, on the side of UI performance and experience, Titanium is better than PhoneGap. However, PhoneGap is the better choice for this project because our solution must be available to end user's personal devices, spanning on all possible platforms.

Performance test of our solution has been performed on two Android devices: smartphone (Samsung Galaxy S3 mini) and tablet (Samsung Galaxy Tab 10.1).

Table 3 Performance test of the implemented use cases

Operations	Response time on smart phone			Response time on tablet			Target (s)
	Min (s)	Avg (s)	Max (s)	Min (s)	Avg (s)	Max (s)	
Get KPI list	0.74	1.1	2.3	0.47	0.89	2.15	3
Get service/skill set list	1.3	1.9	2.76	1.1	1.6	2.81	3
Get yesterday chart	1.5	3.88	5.6	1.7	3.2	5.33	10
Get weekly comparison chart	5.4	10.81	20	5.19	9.32	18.5	20
Get monthly comparison chart	6.78	12.6	25	5.19	13.4	25	25
Get available statistical report list	0.89	1.44	1.59	0.71	1.23	1.36	3
Get statistical report	1.3	2.6	4.3	1.4	2.34	4.08	5
Get available forecasting report list	1.2	2.12	3	1.07	1.78	2.7	3
Get forecasting report	1.8	3.73	4.62	1.5	3.56	5	5

The result of performance test against target requirement is shown Table 3 for the implemented use cases. Every operation was recorded 20 times on each device.

The project is currently on-line. Our hybrid solution did not solve only the cross-platform problem, since it supports the most prevalent mobile platforms and devices, but also ensured the performance of the mobile application. However, in the data extraction process, the response time depends on Pentaho CDA components. As Pentaho is an open source system, performance is lower than the mature business intelligence systems, and system response time will be relatively slower.

5 Conclusion

Decision-makers need to monitor performances and make decisions anytime and anywhere. Through a mobile Business Intelligence (BI) they are able to work quickly and effectively. The new BI system can communicate with the existing ones by data access components and these components can be deployed as web services. Mobile apps can access these services to obtain KPI information, reports and forecasting data, as in the system we have developed. Hybrid solutions offer cross-platform capabilities easy to implement.

Our solution provides a reference model for mobile BI based on low cost open source technologies, which fit the needs of small and medium enterprises. Our reference model covers the complete cycle for the control of processes within an enterprise. Planning is supported by the forecasting system, monitoring and control by dashboard and reporting system. Finally, decision-makers can benefit of ubiquitous computing by mobile BI that enhances all the functions offered by our suite of systems.

Next steps include the discussion of Bring Your Own Device (BYOD) policies in enterprises and how they may affect our reference model. On the implementation side we intend to extend our work providing big data analytics, specifically extending the forecasting system implemented, and discussing their visualization on mobile devices.

References

1. Barakat, S.: Business intelligence in the mobile era. Am. Acad. Sch. Res. J.(AASRJ) **5**, 3 (2013)
2. Sutton, N.: Bullish on business intelligence. Comput. Can. Willowdale **30**, 14 (2004)
3. Rud, O.P.: Business Intelligence Success Factors, Tools for Aligning Your Business in the Global Economy, vol. 18. Wiley, New York (2009)
4. Aciar, S., et al.: Adaptive business intelligence for an open negotiation environment. In: 3rd IEEE International Conference on Digital Ecosystems and Technologies (2009)
5. O'Brien, J.A., Marakas, G.M.: Enterprise information systems. McGraw-Hill (2007)
6. O'Donnell, P., Sipsma, S., Watt, C.: The critical issues facing business intelligence practitioners. J. Decis. Syst. **21**(3), 203–216 (2012)
7. Stipic, A., BronzinT.: Mobile BI: the past, the present and the future. In: MIPRO, 2011 Proceedings of the 34th International Convention. IEEE (2011)
8. Airinei, D., Homocianu, D.: The mobile business intelligence challenge. Econ. Inform. **10**(1), 5–12 (2010)
9. Sajjad, B., et al.: An open source service oriented mobile business intelligence tool. In: IEEE International Conference on Information and Communication Technologies (2009)
10. Evelson, B.: Trends 2011 and beyond: business intelligence. Forrester Res. Cambridge MA **31** (2011)
11. Chaudhuri, S., Dayal, U., Narasayya, V.: An overview of business intelligence technology. Commun. ACM **54**(8), 88–98 (2011)
12. Sin, D., et al.: Mobile web apps-the non-programmer's alternative to native applications. IEEE 5th International Conference on Human System Interactions (2012)
13. Charland, A., Leroux, B.: Mobile application development: web versus native. Commun. ACM **54**(5), 49–53 (2011)

Software Agents for Collaborating Smart Solar-Powered Micro-Grids

Alba Amato, Rocco Aversa, Beniamino Di Martino, Marco Scialdone, Salvatore Venticinque, Svein Hallsteinsen and Geir Horn

Abstract Solar electricity is one of the options as innovative approach as primary energy use. It could be deployed decentralised into the urban areas, and could alleviate the carbonised electricity demand drastically. Information and communication technologies (ICT) could be exploited to provide real time information on energy consumption in a home or a building giving the possibility to citizens to take decisions in order to save energy. In this context CoSSMic, an ICT European project, aims at fostering a higher rate of self-consumption of decentralised renewable energy production by innovative autonomic systems for management and control of power micro-grids on users behalf. The paper addresses these challenges and discusses related work dealing with the development of an ICT solution using software agents which collaborate in a neighborhood, and with the central power grid, over a peer-to-peer overlay.

Keywords CoSSMic · Multi-agent systems · Smart grid · Electricity market

A. Amato (✉) · R. Aversa · B. Di Martino · M. Scialdone · S. Venticinque
Second University of Naples, Caserta, Italy
e-mail: alba.amato@unina2.it

B. Di Martino
e-mail: beniamino.dimartino@unina.it

M. Scialdone
e-mail: marco.scialdone@unina2.it

S. Venticinque
e-mail: salvatore.venticinque@unina2.it

S. Hallsteinsen
SINTEF ICT, Oslo, Norway
e-mail: Svein.Hallsteinsen@sintef.no

G. Horn
University of Oslo, Oslo, Norway
e-mail: geir.horn@mn.uio.no

L. Caporarello et al. (eds.), *Smart Organizations and Smart Artifacts*,
Lecture Notes in Information Systems and Organisation 7,
DOI: 10.1007/978-3-319-07040-7_14,
© Springer International Publishing Switzerland 2014

1 Introduction

Cities are increasingly recognised for their ability to play a catalytic role in addressing climate and energy challenges using technologically innovative approaches as energy used in urban areas accounts for about 40 % of total EU energy consumption [5]. A shift to renewable energies is necessary, not only in order to save money, but also for the responsibility that the present population has towards future generations. One of the renewable energy options is solar electricity (photovoltaics or PV for short), which could be deployed decentralised in urban areas, and could alleviate the carbonised electricity demand drastically. In Europe, 21.9 GW of PV-systems were connected to the grid in 2011, compared to 13.4 GW in 2010, which is in line with the average of 40 % increase during the past 15 years. This steady increase has been stimulated tremendously by countries like Germany and Italy, using powerful incentives to install systems both in terms of large power plants and distributed grid-connected roof-top systems for home owners. A combination of IT and telecommunication technologies is necessary to enable the saving of energy and resources: ICT based solutions will allow peer-to-peer sharing of energy produced using renewable schemes allowing households not only to buy but also to sell energy. Furthermore, ICT will provide real time information on energy consumption in a home or a building giving the possibility to citizens to take decisions in order to save energy. Many challenges should be addressed to achieve real benefits. Ideally, we have to let the consumers collaborate in using the local energy production and storage facilities in the neighbourhood to reduce their energy costs by behaving smarter. This objective requires the integration with a variety of appliances and other control systems in the buildings, like solar panels, energy storage units, heating and cooling systems, and various other power consuming devices. Therefore, a technical architecture that enables this connection and control needs to be defined. It requires the integration of information from the many sources mentioned, and in addition from power companies, and weather reporting and forecasting bodies. Moreover, the ICT-solution should encourage the growth of the neighbourhood network and facilitate the interaction with more and other sources of information in the (near) future. It is necessary that the technology is easy to install and to use in order to lower the threshold for households to adopt it and to join a coordinated neighbourhood. The total package of smart grid solutions should be easy to implement, and attractive from a cost perspective. Moreover, the business models used need to be attractive for groups that have shown reluctance to implement sustainable solutions in cases where the benefit was not exactly clear to them. The paper addresses these challenges and discusses related work dealing with the development of an ICT based solution, both for peer-to-peer collaboration between micro-grids in a neighbourhood and for collaboration with the central power grid.

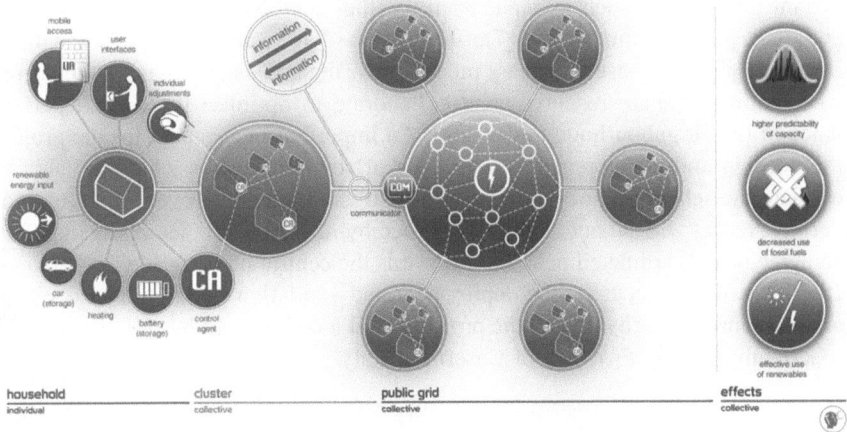

Fig. 1 CoSSMic overview

2 The CoSSMic Project

CoSSMic (Collaborating Smart Solar-powered Micro-grids. FP7-SMARTCITIES, 2013) is an ICT European project that aims at fostering a higher rate for self-consumption ($\succ$ 50 %) of decentralised renewable energy production by innovative autonomic systems for the management and control of power micro-grids on user's behalf. This will allow households and neighbourhoods to optimise consumption and power sales to the network. In addition, a higher degree of predictability of power deliveries will result for the large power companies, and it will satisfy the requirements and achieve the benefits discussed in the introduction. CoSSMic partners are Stiftelsen Sintef, International Solar Energy Research Center Konstanz, Stadt Konstanz, Second University of Naples, Province of Caserta, Norges Teknisk-Naturvitenskapelige Universitet, Sunny Solartechnik, Boukje.com Consulting, University of Oslo. A micro-grid is typically confined to a smart home or an office building, and embeds local generation and storage of solar power, and a number of power consuming devices. In addition, electric vehicles will connect and disconnect dynamically, thus representing a dynamically varying storage capacity or electricity demand. In Fig. 1 an overview of CoSSMic is shown. On the left side, micro-grids, embedded with renewable energy production, storage capacity and consumption, are combined with an intelligent ICT based solution. Such a framework will allow for peer-to-peer collaboration between micro-grids in a neighbourhood forming a cluster. All the cluster members collaborate as one entity with the central power grid that enables the reduction of variation of decentralised renewable energy production to the grid, and a higher rate of self-consumption within the cluster. This system requires sharing of information and the exchange of excess power production and storage capacity in accordance with policies defined by the each cluster member, as well as other relevant information such as input from weather stations, weather forecasts, and habits and plans of inhabitants. The behaviour of the smart micro-grids will be governed by reward based business models ensuring sufficient rewards to the users to be willing to share resources and collaborate to optimise the overall performance of the neighbourhood power grid. An important mechanism for the project is the design and development of a system of software agents which are able to negotiate the scheduling of power sources and energy storage over a peer-to-peer overlay. Agents will act autonomously guided by rules and policies set by the users and agree on a coordinated behaviour towards the central power grid. The research activities will also focus on the deployment and validation of the system over the computational grid provided by the project. Trial locations will be city of Konstanz in Germany and the Province of Caserta in Italy.

3 Related Work

The allocation problem of mapping the consumption demand to the producible or produced energy can be modeled as a negotiation among agents in a marketplace. Negotiation and brokering models have been widely investigated in literature in many field and the complexity of an automated negotiation depends on several factors: the number of negotiated issues, dependencies between these issues, number of agents, representation of the utility, negotiation protocol, constraints, etc. In this section some relevant works within the field of smart grid are presented. [6] proposes a negotiation model to analyze the two-level game strategies for the negotiation process between utilities, Independent Power Producers (IPPs) and customers operating in the partially deregulated environment, in which players intend to maximize their own profits. The derived operation rules based on competition can be viewed as an extension of the conventional equal incremental cost method for the deregulated power system. The method is used for the determination of the electricity transaction volume among market players and the approach is discussed and tested. [8] proposes a Multi-Agent system architecture to simulate and analyse Competitive Electricity Markets combining bilateral trading with power exchange mechanisms. Several heterogeneous and autonomous intelligent agents representing the different independent entities in Electricity Markets are used and a detailed description of a promising algorithm for Decision Support is presented and used to to improve agents bidding process and counterproposals definition. Agents are endowed with historical information about the market including past strategies of other players, and have strategic behaviour to face the market. [9] presents the architecture and negotiation strategy of an agent-based negotiation platform for power generating and power consuming companies in contract electricity market. An intelligent agent implements the negotiation process by selecting a strategy using learning algorithms. Agent uses fuzzy logic modification of basic Genetic Algorithm to accomplish strategy optimization and reinforced learning algorithm to modify the parameter of negotiation tactics and strategy under different situations. [11] presents Open Negotiation Environment (ONE) that provides sophisticated negotiation processes and supports a model of collaboration and trust based on the idea of collaborative multi-agent systems, where agents can work and learn with other trusted agents and develop collaborative learning schemes. ONE allows an organisation to dynamically package and compose complex services by negotiating alliances. Users can define a custom negotiation process taking into account several specification such as negotiation rules, legal rules, pricing policy using a XML based scripting language. The runtime negotiation engine will be in charge of executing the defined process as a facilitator between parties. In [3] and [4] an agent-based approach to manage negotiation among the different parties is presented. The goal is to propose adaptive negotiation strategies for trading energy in a deregulated market. In particular, strategies derived from game theory are used in order to optimize energy production and supply costs by means of negotiation and adaptation. To manage negotiation between agents the El Farol Bar Game is proposed in [13]. Agents act on behalf of end users, thus implying the necessity of being aware of multiple aspects connected to the distribution of electricity. These aspects refer to outside world variables like weather, stock market trends, location of the users etc. Web services are used by agents for retrieving data to be used in adaptive and collaborative aspects. Instead, in [10], a framework (Intelligent Trading Agency) for one-to-many negotiation, by means of concurrent coordinated one-to-one negotiations, is presented. In ITA, a number of agents, all working on behalf of one party, negotiate individually with other parties. ITA uses the multi-attribute utility theory and constraint based reasoning for the evaluation and generation of offers and counteroffers. According to the paradigm presented in this paper there is one single coordinator agent that creates a number of agents, named sub-negotiators, that make many one-to-one negotiations on its behalf. At the end of each negotiation cycle, these agents report the results to the coordinator agent. The latter evaluates all offers, chooses the best and issues instructions accordingly. The advantages of this approach are so many: simplicity and reusability of existent agents that make one-to-one negotiations; the system is customizable since each sub-negotiator can be modified or removed; the system is more robust, in fact, if a sub-negotiator fails, the others continue to work. Besides the development of more advanced environments such as smart grids, has pushed the research about planning and operations of modern Peer to Peer (P2P) infrastructure. In fact agent and P2P concepts are closely related to each other. Agents are able to improve functionality of a P2P system and also P2P architecture can be an environment in which abilities of agents are fully utilized. In [7] it is introduced a P2P architecture consisting of two level where the P2P and the agents paradigms are merged. In particular, the first level regards the functionalities of P2P and the second level autonomous agents. Then, it is created an A2A (Agent to Agent) architecture where every agent acts as a peer to the other agents. The agents can interact e negotiate directly with the other agents using point-to-point communication. The fundamental characteristics of A2A architecture are: virtual P2P platform, agents reside on nodes, P2P community is same as Agent Community, agents have P2P operations and abilities. Authors have previously experiences in building network of agents both in smart cities applications [1] and for negotiation and brokering of computational resources in Cloud markets [2, 12].

4 Beyond the State of Art

CoSSMic is exploiting an agents based marketplace for overcoming the limitations of current solutions by coordinating local energy production and storage resources of neighbourhoods of individual houses, thereby balancing the energy flow and consumption and reducing the fluctuations towards the central power grid, and improving the predictability of consumer behaviour. It relies on a decentralised peer-to-peer approach to the communication and interaction between agents, which represent stakeholders for distributed discovery, negotiation and brokering of those power sources, and storages, to be allocated and scheduled for optimizing the user's and global utility. Autonomy and proactivity of software agents will allow for automating power management task, while still leaving the user in control through the setting of high level policies. In fact acceptability to the consumers will be fostered by a clear interaction model based on constraints and goals which will be full filled by a multi-agent optimisation, where the agents make autonomous decisions on behalf of their users. A distributed P2P overlay will avoid a centralized solution supporting agents to take distributed decisions by advanced learning methods, which will be scalable to larger neighbourhoods. Each peer will behave at the same time as a consumer and a provider. They will handle heterogeneous devices, such as cars that can disconnect from the grid both for a limited period, but at a random or a scheduled time, and solar panel whose efficiency can depend on deterministic parameters and uncertain one. This affects the complexity of agent's task. In fact agents will need to plan their strategy according to the cited issues, taking into account also the consumer flexibility and contingency, and broker the right offers according to the current availability of power and energy in the local pool and the outside conditions. The distributed agents network will also implement a distributed infrastructure for metering and monitoring smart power grids and the related context of relevant information such as the real time whether condition and forecasting, energy cost and market trends.

5 Agent Design and Implementation

The allocation problem of mapping the consumption demand to the producible or produced energy, can be modeled as a negotiation among agents in a local marketplace over a network overlay. Software agents are negotiating using strategies based on short-term micro-economics, increasing their utility and a global one. The emerging capabilities of such a framework will provide users with a

Fig. 2 Agents based
architecture

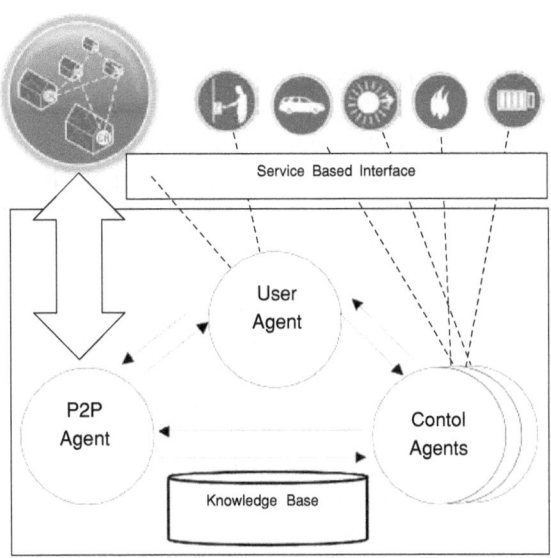

distributed engine with self-capability for decision-making on the effective management of smart power grids, reducing the variation in load towards the grid, hence the need for fossil fuel based backup power. Agents will act autonomously guided by rules and policies set by the users and agree on a coordinated behaviour towards the central power grid. In Fig. 2 the agents based architecture of CoSSMic is shown. The control agent represents a device. It is able to act in real-time mode, controlling the physical equipment, as well as interacting with the other control agents. Note that it is not necessary that the devices are in the household, as for instance an electric car is an example of a mobile device represented by a control agent. The control agents will implement the policies set by the owning user agent for their operation. The policies in the Knowledge Base can be deterministic rules, like telling an electric water heater not to switch on between 8:00 and 10:00 in the morning, or goals, like making a battery last as long as possible. Achieving some of the goals may necessitate peer to peer negotiations with other households and trade offs among several control agents. An example can be that the user would prefer to use first the energy produced by her own solar panels. In other words, there is a finite power budget for all the control agents belonging to the user, and the consumption should be distributed among the control agents such that the utility for the user is maximised. The multi-agent peer-to-peer algorithm will be based on the assumption that the instantaneous amount of energy in the neighbourhood can be modelled as a pool with two main sources: the energy produced by the neighbourhood itself, and the energy the neighbourhood needs to buy from the external grid. Similarly, there are two types of outlet, the energy consumed within the neighbourhood, and the energy they are selling to the outside grid. Ideally, the pool is at the zero level when the energy production within the neighbourhood matches the consumption, and there is no exchange of energy with the outside grid. This energy pool also represents two market places: one for the energy exchange within the neighbourhood and consumed by the neighbourhood, and one for the neighbourhood's exchange with the outside world All members of the neighbourhood will first try to buy or sell energy within their local community, and the role of the external grid is reduced to a buffer that will ensure that local demand will always be met and no energy will ever be lost. The result of this is that there can be only one payoff function for the energy determined by the global energy price. An uniform model of Service Level Agreement (SLA) for the descriptions of offers from providers of power sources and from owner of energy storages. Power market of micro-grid negotiation will be based on publish, discovery and brokering of SLA template over P2P. Learning and self-optimisation technique will be defined for supporting active decisions to be made by the players in neighbourhood energy distribution system, i.e., their strategies or actions. Strategies will be driven by high level policies that need to be easily understood and defined by final users and will use formal SLAs. Examples of goals could be the reduction ore increase of power budget which can result in different actions such as unplugging some appliances from the power network or not consuming energy from the common pool.

6 Conclusion

Comprehensive work has already been conducted on energy strategy plans, research projects and review activities regarding scenario studies for energy system developments to better understand the needs of the energy systems of tomorrow. Here we presented goals and challenges of the CoSSMic project focusing on the optimization of decentralised renewable energy production by a P2P overlay of software agents which implement an innovative autonomic systems for management and control of power micro-grids. We focused on challenges, related work and the expected advance to the state of art we aim at achieving by the application of agents-based techniques and technologies to this application field.

References

1. Amato, A., Di Martino, B., Venticinque, S.: Semantically augmented exploitation of pervasive environments by intelligent agents. In: Proceedings of the 2012 10th IEEE International Symposium on Parallel and Distributed Processing with Applications, ISPA 2012. pp. 807–814 (2012)
2. Amato, A., Liccardo, L., Rak, M., Venticinque, S.: Sla negotiation and broker-ing for sky computing. In: CLOSER 2012—Proceedings of the 2nd International Conference on Cloud Computing and Services Science. pp. 611–620 (2012)
3. Capodieci, N., Alsina, E.F., Cabri, G.: A context-aware agent-based approach for deregulated energy market. In: Reddy, S., Drira, K. (eds.) WETICE. IEEE Computer Society, pp. 16–21 (2012)

4. Capodieci, N., Cabri, G., Pagani, G.A., Aiello, M.: Adaptive game-based agent negotiation in deregulated energy markets. In: Smari, W.W., Fox, G.C. (eds.) CTS. IEEE, pp. 300–307 (2012)
5. Commission, E.: Energy-efficient buildings ppp multi-annual roadmap and longer term strategy. Technical Report (2012)
6. Geerli Yokoyama, R., Chen, L.: Negotiation models for electricity pricing in a partially deregulated electricity market. Power Eng. Soc. Summer Meet. 2000. IEEE. **4,** 2223–2228 (2000)
7. Homayounfar, H., Wang, F., Areibi, S.: Advanced p2p architecture using au-tonomous agents. In: Subramanya, S.R. (ed.) CAINE. ISCA, pp. 115–118 (2002)
8. Isabel P., Carlos R., Z.V., Cordeiro, M.: Intelligent agents for negotiation and game-based decision support in electricity markets. Int. J. Eng. Int. Syst. **13,** 147–154 (2005)
9. Jia-hai, Y., Shun-kun, Y., Zhao-guang, H.: A multi-agent trading platform for electricity contract market. In: Power Engineering Conference, 2005. IPEC 2005. The 7th International, pp. 1024–1029 vol. 2 (2005)
10. Rahwan, I., Kowalczyk, R., Pham, H.H.: Intelligent agents for automated one-to-many e-commerce negotiation. In: Oudshoorn, M.J. (ed.) ACSC. CRPIT, vol. 4, pp. 197–203. Australian Computer Society (2002)
11. Telesca, L., Finnegan, J., Ferronato, P., Malone, P., Ricci, F., Stanoevska-Slabeva, K.: Open negotiation environment: an open source self-learning decentralised negotiation framework for digital ecosystems. In: Proceedings of the the Inaugural IEEE International Conference on Digital Ecosystems and Technologies (2007)
12. Venticinque, S., Tasquier, L., Di Martino, B.: Agents based cloud computing in-terface for resource provisioning and management. In: Proceedings—2012 6th International Conference on Complex, Intelligent, and Software Intensive Systems, CISIS 2012, pp. 249–256 (2012)
13. Whitehead, D.: The el Farol Bar Problem Revisited: Reinforcement Learning in a Potential Game. Ese Discussion Papers, Edinburgh School of Economics, University of Edinburgh (2008) http://EconPapers.repec.org/RePEc:edn:esedps:186

AutoMyDe: A Detector for Pupil Dilation in Cognitive Load Measurement

Davide Maria Calandra and Francesco Cutugno

Abstract Pupil dilation is known to reflect the emotional arousal. Pleasure, effort and fear are examples of stimuli inducing the nervous system to cause dilation *mydriasis*. The work proposes a tool to automatically quantify the mydriasis in order to evaluate mental effort in HCI. The system uses a feature-based approach and monitors the pupil behavior during a given task. As mydriasis is entailed by various reasons, our system distinguishes the cause-effect relationships by synchronizing monitoring and test, dividing the monitoring in fixed intervals and retrieving a survey of the mydriatic events for each determined period of time. We present a case of study analyzing users resolving arithmetical tasks, viewing pictures and using a mobile application. In each scenario, tests intend to impose gradually increasing reactions to the users. The paper will present different techniques for pupil dilation measurements and related results of mental effort evaluation.

Keywords Affective computing · Mental effort · Pupil dilation

1 Introduction

Nowadays, it is widely accepted that the pupillary response represents a reliable information source about human reactions to neuropsychological stimuli [1]. When we want or we need to increase our perception about the external environment, the sympathetic nervous system causes pupils to dilate, allowing more

D. M. Calandra (✉) · F. Cutugno
DIETI, University of Naples, Federico II, Napoli, Italy
e-mail: davidemaria.calandra@unina.it

F. Cutugno
e-mail: cutugno@unina.it

L. Caporarello et al. (eds.), *Smart Organizations and Smart Artifacts*,
Lecture Notes in Information Systems and Organisation 7,
DOI: 10.1007/978-3-319-07040-7_15,
© Springer International Publishing Switzerland 2014

light to reach the *retina*. This is what happens viewing pleasant pictures [2] or when we are stressed by tasks requiring a high cognitive workload [3]. The cognitive theory provides a precious contribute to HCI [4]; it supplies an easy way to evaluate how a typical user can successfully learn to perform a task using a given interface. While the difficulty to learn a specific task is strictly dependent from the material being learned, learning can be improved under conditions that are aligned with human cognitive architecture.

Sweller et al. [5] define as *intrinsic cognitive load* the learning associated with a specific task; as most topics require external knowledge, authors classify the *extraneous cognitive load* as the amount of working memory required by the external activities and highlight the importance of the extraneous cognitive load when intrinsic cognitive load is high, due to the additive property of cognitive load. Unlike the intrinsic, the extraneous cognitive load is influenced by the instructional design, the manner in which information is presented to learners, that is referred by authors as *germane cognitive load*: an efficient instructional design can reduce the amount of resources needed to learn the external knowledge, allowing to allocate the earned working memory capacity for an additional extraneous or germane cognitive load. These definitions allow to formulate the following consideration: if we keep fixed values of intrinsic and extraneous cognitive load, we can measure how much the germane cognitive load influences the total cognitive workload, only by varying the instructional design. It means to audit if the manner to present the information helps learners into the task comprehension, that is, to evaluate if the user interface is well designed.

To suggest the right way to design an user interface is not possible without circumscribing the manner to present the information to specific communities of users: cultural and linguistic backgrounds [6, 7] influence the preferences in interaction as well as different styles to interact are required for old [8] and young [9] users. While special studies should be dedicated to users having disabilities [10, 11], a clear understanding of different personalities and cognitive styles is also helpful in designing interfaces [12, 13] as users recognize slight changes on their displays and begin to issue streams of commands in few milliseconds. These numerous branches of design induce to consider likewise considerations in evaluating the usability degree of the given user interface. Standardized methodologies for the quantitative evaluation of usability often require the use of questionnaires to be given to the test users [14]. While such questionnaires are designed to subjectively evaluate the overall interaction, objective parameters can be extracted from log files that provide information on data such as: number of interactions, duration of the interaction, time for the achievement of a subtask and so on; an example is KLM-GOMS measurement of time performance [15]. Recent studies concentrate on biometric data, as they represent an objective and reliable source of information in the cognitive load theory: Andreassi et al. [16] proved that changes in blood pressure and heart rate were independent from individual personality, thus it could be thought as an objective measurement of the cognitive load, as well as pitches in tonal perception are symptom of high cognitive load [17]. The early mentioned works about the role of mydriasis in the cognitive theory [2, 3] are supported by recent contributes such as [18] in which Sandra Marshall uses pupil dilation as index of the cognitive activity.

In this work, we present AutoMyDe (AUTOmatic MYdriasis DEtector), a multithreading software application which monitors users' pupil and returns a report about its behavior during the entire task duration. Since we synchronize the monitoring with the task execution, it is possible to associate each retrieved value with the corresponding action performed by the user. We present two methods to detect pupil: the first uses a dedicated camera pointed towards user's eye; in the second, we perform detection by means of a hidden camera. To test the system, users have been partitioned in two groups, one for each detection mode. Three experiments have been performed; each group executed all the experiments and the results have been compared. AutoMyDe is thought to support usability evaluation, as we made in [19]: software architectures for evaluating the cognitive workload of a generic application take as input an arbitrary number of input streams containing data reports about the cognitive workload estimated by dedicated modules each concentrating on specific modalities; typically there will be one monitoring module for each available interaction modality. AutoMyDe proposes to be one of these dedicated modules and its output is an input streams for the evaluation architecture.

The paper is organized as follows: Sect. 2 presents the software application, describing the steps needed to detect the pupil and its dilation, and the output structure. In Sect. 3, we expose the cases of study; Sect. 4 concludes the paper discussing the obtained results.

2 AutoMyDe

AutoMyDe is a multithreading software application to detect mydriatic events during a task execution. It is synchronized with the task by means of a dedicated thread querying start and stop time of every connecting process to a remote server; the working thread processes the video stream of the monitored eye, while a reporting thread fills—at regular intervals—a data structure with boolean values representing the mydriatic events. We provide a first version of the software, obtaining the input stream by means of customized glasses, Fig. 1, carrying a 5 MP camera pointed towards user's eye. In the second version, the input source is a 6 MP front camera of a tablet. As AutoMyDe is not presently thought to be run on a tablet, in the second version we just acquire the input from the tablet camera and then we process it offline. The open source OpenCV library (http://opencv.org/) has been used to perform image processing.

Fig. 1 Glasses equipped with a 5 MP camera. The hardware has been initially thought for an eye tracker, thus it was equipped with the leds visible in the figure; leds have not been used in present work

2.1 Pupil and Mydriasis Detection

In order to perform detection, the input image has been firstly grey scaled because colors do not provide contribute to our aim and increase the computational complexity. In the following steps, the image histogram has been equalized to highlight details by increasing the global contrast. A first attempt of detection has been approached applying shape based methods [20]. According to [21], the Hough transform [22] for circles finding has been applied. This attempt returned good results in *iris* detection because the clear contrast between iris and *sclera* permitted an easy detection for both brown colored and bright colored eyes. Some difficulties emerged in pupil detection: the light created some wide white stains which broke pupil circularity preventing Hough transform from a good detection. Thus, this solution has not be applied anymore and a feature based method has been approached. The implemented solution consists of a system of masks created to filter the equalized image by eliminating pixels do not contributing to pupil recognition. The following steps have been performed:

1. the equalized image, Fig. 2a, has been converted into binary format, dropping down to zero (black) all the pixels having cumulative distribution function (CDF) value greater than a certain threshold [23], Fig. 2b;
2. the binary image has been morphologically transformed by a dilation process, Fig. 2c; an elliptical kernel is used to preserve the image natural shape;
3. a binary mask has been created by converting the equalized source through an higher threshold value;
4. the binary mask has been morphologically transformed by an erosion process;
5. the minimum between the equalized image and step 4 has been computed;
6. the minimum between step 5 and step 2 has been computed.

A contours detection function identified the remaining regions: light reflex stains, eyelashes and the pupillary area. As the pupil is the widest area among them, it is selected by a maximum extraction function, Fig. 2d. The residual pixels compose an irregular polygon, thus the minimum ellipse fitting the resulting shape is the best found pupil approximation, Fig. 2e. Once pupil has been identified, Fig. 2f, to

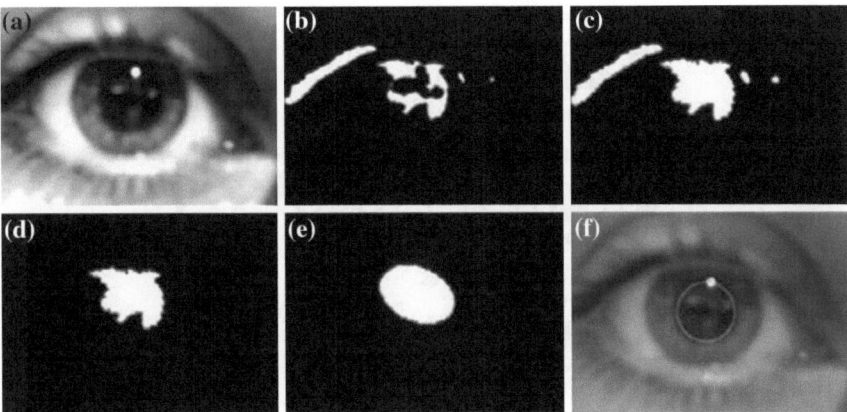

Fig. 2 Pupil detection: main steps

detect mydriasis means to make a comparison between the first stored diameter and those computed during the following iterations: when the comparison exceeds the 40 %, a mydriasis occurs.

2.2 Face and Eye Detection

In the second version, we eliminated the workglasses mounted camera, in favor of the front camera of the tablet where the under test interface is executed. The first step then consisted in locating the face into the image. We used a Haar-based classifier which extends the set of Haar-like features proposed by Viola and Jones [24] with a set of 45″ rotated features, as shown in Fig. 3.

OpenCV provides a simple interface which allows to train the classifiers from a set of samples, but also to load a set of pre-trained detectors arranged in likewise XML documents. To detect the face we used the default pre-trained frontal face detector. The first time, we scanned the entire image; then, the region containing the detected face is used as the center of a dynamically built 3 × 3 kernel. We built the kernel by calculating the previous and the further areas from the center, on both x and y axis. The size of each area is obtained by multiplying the size of the face area for a scale constant δ varying from 0 to 1. If the kernel exceeds the image size, it is cut off to the image size. In general we modeled the region of interest and its size s follows:

$$roi = kernel + offset - \delta * size$$

$$new\_size = 2 * (Kernel + offset - roi) + current\_size$$

The obtained kernel is the base for a face tracking by limiting, at each frame, the search area to it. By reducing the search area, we improve the detection time

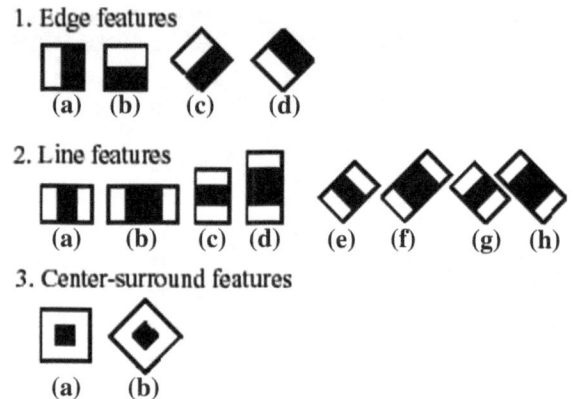

Fig. 3 Viola—Jones Haar-like features

Table 1 Performances of the pre-trained eye detectors provided by OpenCV

Cascade classifier	Reliability (%)	Speed	Eyes found	Glasses
haarcascade_mcs_lefteye.xml	80	18 ms	Open or closed	No
haarcascade_lefteye_2splits.xml	60	7 ms	Open or closed	No
haarcascade_eye.xml	40	5 ms	Open only	No
haarcascade_eye_tree_eyeglasses.xml	15	10 ms	Open only	Yes

and reduce the probability to return false positives. Only when no face is detected, the search area will be set to the entire image. As more than one person could be into the range of the camera, we assume only the nearest face next to the camera—the biggest region containing a face—to be the user. Test proved that limiting the search area to the kernel, the execution time improves of 40 %; if we also look for the biggest face, the execution time improves of 60 %. For images having size of 640 × 480 pixels processed on an Intel Core i7 with 2.2 GHz, we passed from 40 to 16 ms on average. To detect the eyes, we consider that they have a fixed position into the face, thus only the higher half of the face should be investigated. Again, the higher half is divided into two regions each containing one eye. We look for the biggest eye in both regions, by loading the specific pre-trained classifier. OpenCV provides different eye classifiers with different accuracy degrees and different speeds; these are presented in [25] and shown in Table 1.

Test proved that haarcascade_eye.xml is the classifier which returns the highest number of false positives: in particular, when we look for the eyes into the entire face, a semi-opened mouth and the naris are often returned as eyes. By limiting the search area as explained, the same classifier showed an high accuracy. Moreover its low detection time represents an important feature for our aim. Again, only the first time we search eyes into the entire regions; as we did for the face, we dynamically build a 3 × 3 kernel around the first detected eyes. An example is

Fig. 4 3×3 kernel built for each eye

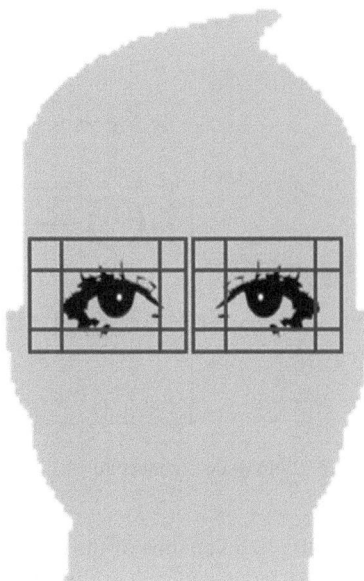

shown in Fig. 4. Once the eyes have been identified, the algorithm exposed in Sect. 2.1 has been applied to detect pupil and mydriasis.

2.3 The Multithreading Architecture

As we want the exact mapping among required actions, current status of the interface in use and how user's pupil reacts, we synchronize the task execution with the monitoring session. We perform the synchronization by modifying the software architecture of the tested interface in a client-server application which logs all the performed events and the timestamps in which they occur. When the tested application starts, it sends a starting signal—composed by the task identifier and the timestamp in which it starts—to a remote server; once the task ends, it sends the stopping signal to the server. When AutoMyDe is launched, the synchronization thread queries the remote server and waits for the task starts. When the starting signal has been received, it runs the working thread and the reporting thread and waits for the stopping signal. During the execution, while the working thread performs the image processing, the reporting thread composes a survey of the pupillary reactions: it stores a boolean value each 200 ms representing the current diameter size (normal or mydriatic) and the timestamp identifying the registration instant. When the stopping signal is received the monitoring ends and an XML document is generated containing the entire report.

AutoMyDe architecture is shown in Fig. 5. In the figure, threads are identified by the T, while the couple (t, w) specifies the workload w measured at the time

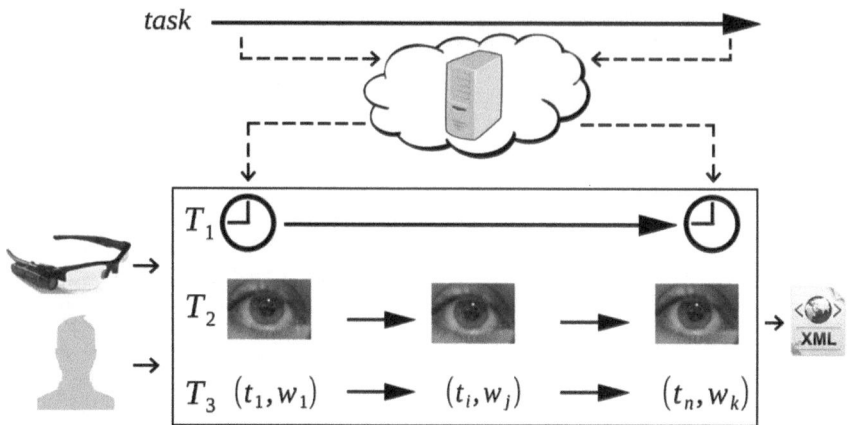

Fig. 5 AutoMyde architecture

t. As the two versions of the software have the same design structure, we reported the two input sources in the same figure; however, we highlight their mutually exclusive usage.

3 Case Studies

To test AutoMyDe, three experiments have been provided. All of them are structured as applications representing the client side of the client-server architecture. The first experiment consists in resolving a sequence of logical-arithmetical tasks: following Kahneman's [3], we propose 10 questions of varying difficulty, intended to impose coherent mydriatic reactions. The second asks users to book a flight by using an accurately modified web interface; the third experiment proposes an interactive session with an Android application.

3.1 First Experiment

The first experiment has been structured as a simple application implementing a sliding presentation. When the application starts, the synchronization signal is sent to the server; then, for each slide, a data structure is updated with the slide identifier and the timestamp in which it has been shown. After that the last task has been accomplished, the stopping signal is sent to the server.

The following tasks have been presented:

1. What is your name?
2. How old are you?
3. 2 * 2;
4. add the last word to the sentence;
5. the bat and the ball problem [3];
6. the Linda's problem [3];
7. 17 * 24 [3];
8. repeat words such as: bread, dog, honorificabilitudinitatibus, floccinaucinihilipilification;
9. words in uppercase and lowercase game [3];
10. words on the left and on the right game [3].

Tasks have been presented one per slide; the interaction time is about 10 min.

3.2 Second Experiment

In the second experiment we ask users to book a flight by using a web interface. We divided the experiment in two tasks and partitioned users in two groups, one for each task. The first task proposes to book the flight by using a well-designed web interface which allows users to choose the departure and arrival airports from an alphabetically sorted list of 15 items; a text box explains users in which format providing the departure and return dates and the error messages identify the field containing the mistakes. The second task proposes to book the flight by using an accurately modified version of the web interface: subjects have to choose departure and arrival airports from a non alphabetically sorted list of about 200 items; moreover, no suggestion is given about the format required for the dates and the alert messages do not specify which fields contain errors. When the web page is opened, the starting signal is sent to the server; the stopping signal is sent when the page is closed. The interaction time is about 5 min.

3.3 Third Experiment

The third experiment proposes an interactive session with an Android application: we realized an application game consisting of a set of geometrical figures with different colors shown on the screen; the user is requested to find and touch an icon showing a specific geometrical shape or one with a specific color within a time limit. The difficulty factor is increased during the interaction by reducing the dimension of the figures on the screen, increasing the number of figures that appear simultaneously and reducing the time limit. The application is provided with an underlying daemon reporting the touch events performed during the execution. Specifically, a parallel thread registered the frequency of touch events occurred

Table 2 First experiment: results

Task	#1	#2	#3	#4	#5	#6	#7	#8	#9	#10
Glasses (%)	60	60	60	60	75	75	80	75	75	75
Hidden camera (%)	10	10	10	10	65	60	70	60	60	50

each 200 ms and the timestamp identifying the registration instant. The events have been interpreted in terms of cognitive workload: the higher is the number of touches, the higher is the cognitive workload. The corresponding values have been then expressed as continuous values normalized between 0 and 1. When the monitoring ends, an XML document is generated containing the entire report.

3.4 Settings

The experiments have been performed indoor and the light conditions are kept under control. Tasks are presented on a tablet to a set of 30 participants who are instructed with the simple rules required by the tasks; they are also explained that it is not they are under examination, but the user interface. The average age was 23 years and all were familiar with the use of smartphones and tablets. Users have been partitioned in two groups, one for each detection mode. Both groups performed the three experiments. When monitoring was made by means of the tablet camera, users did not know to be monitored; they were only asked to concentrate their gaze on the tablet.

3.5 Results

The XML document returned by AutoMyDe represents the cognitive load required to perform the task, using the specific user interface. The following sections provide the obtained results. Each section is associated with an experiment and it presents the related table of the results. Rows represent the experimental setups: workglasses mounted camera and hidden camera, respectively; the columns identify the tasks.

3.5.1 First Experiment

Results shown in Table 2 partially reflect the intrinsic cognitive load associated with the task. Although users were explained that they were not under examination and they would not have been evaluated, Table 2 shows that 60 % of users manifested mydriatic reactions during simple tasks too, in the first setup; this value can be due to focusing the camera on the workglasses as well as it can be

Table 3 Second experiment: results

Task	#1	#2
Glasses (%)	50	60
Hidden camera (%)	10	40

Table 4 Third experiment: results

Bins	#1	#2	#3	#4
Glasses (%)	40	20	60	70
Hidden camera (%)	20	20	50	60

associated to different personalities and emotive reactions. The table even shows how this value is highly reduced to 10 % in the second setup. The task #5 has been particularly interesting: 50 % of users performed the task without initial effort, giving a first fast answer which did not cause mydriatic reactions; only when they were explained that the given answer was wrong, they concentrated on the task, causing their pupils to dilate.

3.5.2 Second Experiment

Table 3 shows how a well-designed user interface can help users in performing a task, while a not usable interface can increase users difficulties. In the specific experiment, 60 % of users in the first setup and 40 % in the second setup had mydriatic reactions while using a not usable user interface; these values decrease when information is presented through a well designed interface.

3.5.3 Third Experiment

To verify that the system detected the increase of the global effort requested to the user, we divided the experiment duration in four bins each representing 25 % of the total interaction time. We considered peaks having a higher value than 0.5 to be representative of high cognitive workload and compute the distribution of these peaks over the considered time bins. Values presented in Table 4 result from the average between the cognitive load associated to pupil dilation and cognitive load computed on touch events. Values show a higher concentration of high effort representatives in the third and fourth time quarter (#3–#4); this matches the increasing of task difficulty. High effort values are also in the first quarter: it is the mydriatic reaction due to focusing the camera on the workglasses or to the cognitive stress of being under examination. It is partially reduced by the low workload values of the touch monitoring. High effort values in the first quarter have been reduced to 20 % in case of users did not know to be monitored, as shows Table 4. We also highlight that the second setup presents a lower general effort level than the first.

Subjects manifested a more natural approach to the second setup; moreover, we asked users to fill an informal questionnaire about their experience: 90 % of participants in first test battery declared to be influenced by the usage of the workglasses and by the awareness to be under examination.

4 Conclusions

We provided a software application which detects mydriatic events during a task execution. We showed that AutoMyDe helps the usability evaluation as the occurred mydriasis can be interpreted in terms of cognitive load values. Results showed that AutoMyDe, with a dedicated head mounted hardware, identified the pupil center and the pupillary radius with an error rate lower than 5 pixels in 85 % of cases, failiuring the detection of black eyed users (No distintcion between iris and pupil was possible). As a head mounted hardware could influence results reliability, with our second solution, we focused on a remote system which detects pupil center and pupillary radius with an error rate lower than 5 pixels in 80 % of cases. A comparison could be made with [23]: algorithm for face detection [24] and CDF value for pupil detection used by authors are the same that we have used in our work; authors detected pupil center with an error rate slightly lower than ours, but they have not identified the pupil boundaries. Future work will consist of an Android based version of AutoMyDe in order to perform the online detection in mobile environment. Moreover, we are going to add remote gaze tracking functionalities to AutoMyDe, in order to know where the user gaze is oriented when her pupils dilate.

Acknowledgments Work supported by the European Community and the Italian Ministry of University and Research and EU under the PON OR.C.HE.S.T.R.A. project.

References

1. Andreassi, J.: Pupillary response and behavior. Psychophysiology: Human Behavior & Physiological Response. 4th ed. pp. 218–233. Lawrence Erlbaum Associates, Publishers (2000)
2. Hess, E.H., Polt, J.M.: Pupil size as related to interest value of visual stimuli. Science 349–350 (1960)
3. Kahneman, D.: Attention and Effort (Experimental Psychology), p. 0130505188. Englewood Cliffs, Prentice-Hall (1973)
4. Polson, P.G., Lewis, C., Rieman, J., Wharton, C.: Cognitive walkthroughs: a method for theory-based evaluation of user interfaces, p. 5. Academic Press Ltd., Int. J. Man-Mach. Stud. **36**, 741–773 (1992)

5. Paas, F., Renkl, A., Sweller, J.: Cognitive load theory and instructional design: recent developments. Educ. Psychol. **38** (1), 1–4
6. Fernandes, T.: Global Interface Design: A Guide to Designing International User Interfaces. Academic Press Professional, Inc., San Diego. 0-12-253790-4 (1995)
7. Marcus, A., Gould, E.: Crosscurrents: cultural dimensions and global web user-interface design. West. pp. 32–46, 1072–5520. ACM interactions, New York (2000)
8. Furlong, M.S., Kearsley, G.: Computers for Kids Over 60. Senior Net, 1993. 9780962670039
9. Druin, A., Inkpen, K.: When Are Personal Technologies for Children? p. 3. Springer, London, Personal Ubiquitous Comput. **5**, 191–194. 1617–4909
10. Edwards, A.D.N.: Extra-ordinary Human-computer Interaction: Interfaces for Users with Disabilities, p. 9780521434133. Cambridge University Press, Cambridge (1995)
11. Paciello, M.G.: Web Accessibility for People with Disabilities, p. 9781929629084. Taylor & Francis, London (2000)
12. Wickens, C.D., Hollands, J.G.: Engineering Psychology and Human Performance, p. 9780321047113. Prentice Hall PTR, Upper Saddle River (2000)
13. Ashcraft, M.H.: Cognition, 3rd edn. Prentice Hall, New York (2002). 9780130307293
14. Kühnel, C., Westermann, T., Weiss, B., Möller, S.: Evaluating Multimodal Systems: A Comparison of Established Questionnaires and Interaction Parameters. Reykjavik, pp. 286–294. ACM, Iceland 2010. 978-1-60558-934-3
15. Bias, R.G., Mayhew, D.J.: Cost-Justifying Usability: An Update for an Internet Age, p. 9780120958115. Morgan Kaufman, San Francisco (2005)
16. Andreassi, J.L., Fichera, L.V.: Cardiovascular reactivity during public speaking as a function of personality variables, p. 3, Int J Psychophysiol, **37**, 267–273. 0167-8760 (2000)
17. Schuller, B., Batliner, A., Steidl, A., Seppi, D.: Recognising realistic emotions and affect in speech: State of art and lessons learnt from the first challenge. Speech Commun. 1062–1087
18. Marshall, S.P.: The Index of Cognitive Activity: Measuring cognitive workload. 2002. In: Proceedings of the 7th IEEE Conference on Human Factors and Power Plants
19. Calandra, D.M., Caso, A., Cutugno, F., Origlia, A., Rossi, S.: CoWME: a general framework to evaluate cognitive workload during multimodal interaction. Proceedings of ICMI (2013)
20. Hansen, D.W., Ji, Q.: In the eye of the beholder: a survey of models for eyes and gaze. **3**, 2010, IEEE Trans. Pattern Anal. Mach. Intell. **32**
21. Aylward, J.J., Erwann, R., Stephen, R.: Automatic quantification of pupil dilation under stress. 2004
22. Duda, R.O., Hart, P.E.: Use of the hough transformation to detect lines and curves in pictures. p. 1, ACM, Commun. ACM, **15**, 11–15 (1972). 0001-0782
23. Shanbezadeh, J., Asadifard, M.,: Automatic adaptive center of pupil detection using face detection and CDF analysis. In: Proceedings of the International MultiConference of Engineers and Computer Scientists, vol. I (2010)
24. Viola, P., Jones, M.: Rapid object detection using a boosted cascade of simple features. Proceedings of the 2001 IEEE Computer Society Conference on Computer Vision and Pattern Recognition. CVPR 2001. vol. 1, pp. 1063–6919 (2001)
25. Baggio, D.L., Emami, S., Escrivá, D.M., Ievgen, K., Mahmood, N., Saragih, J., Shilkrot, S.: Mastering OpenCV with Practical Computer Vision Projects. Packt Publishing, Limited (2012). 9781849517829

Providing a Method for Supporting the Decision Making About a Meaningful XBRL Implementation According to the Specific Situation of an Organization

Claudia Koschtial, Carsten Felden and Bruno Maria Franceschetti

Abstract XBRL is in an increasing number of countries defined as the obligate format for the transmission of financial data to authorities by legal requirements. The legal requirement itself refers solely to the transmission of the information in XBRL format. How a formatting of a company's report becomes realized is not regulated. This decision has to be done by the decision makers of the affected companies. There is no generally recommended realization or global valid implementation process. Each realization (bolt-on, built-in, and embedded) comprises a specific realization effort and offers different potential benefits for the implementing organization. Therefore, it is necessary to decide about the integration depth within an organization. The paper presents a methodology to support the decision process for the adoption of XBRL into the organization. By doing design science research, the constructed artifact enables a structured decision based on facts, individual properties, and needs of the organization.

Keywords XBRL · Information management · Reporting framework

1 Introduction

The US Securities and Exchange Commission (SEC) has required all US-listed companies to provide their financial reports in XBRL since June 2009. Similarly and comparable to other countries (e.g. United Kingdom or South Africa), all

C. Koschtial · C. Felden
Technische Universität Bergakademie, Freiberg, Germany
e-mail: Claudia.Koschtial@bwl.tu-freiberg.de

C. Felden
e-mail: Carsten.Felden@bwl.tu-freiberg.de

B. M. Franceschetti (✉)
University of Macerata, Macerata, Italy
e-mail: bmfranceschetti@unimc.it

L. Caporarello et al. (eds.), *Smart Organizations and Smart Artifacts*,
Lecture Notes in Information Systems and Organisation 7,
DOI: 10.1007/978-3-319-07040-7_16,
© Springer International Publishing Switzerland 2014

German companies have been mandated to use XBRL in the context of reporting to tax authorities from 2011. The rulemaking comes after a development decade of XBRL and after a number of XBRL initiatives around the world (Fig. 1).

XBRL allows, but does not require, a great deal of flexibility in the way that entities report their performance information. Other regulator-driven implementations typically restrict entities to filing only against a standard template of information—enhancing the efficiency of information transfer but arguably reducing the effectiveness. Compared to this, XBRL allows more flexibility of the information inside and outside companies.

The legal requirement itself refers solely to the transmission of the information in XBRL format. How a formatting of a company's report becomes realized is not regulated. This decision has to be done by the decision makers of the affected companies. Sledgianowski [1] have identified three different ways how to realize an XBRL report:

- Tagging financial statements at the end of the reporting process as an extension to the traditional process in order to convert the statements to XBRL format (bolt-on),
- integrating XBRL mapping capability within information systems across the firm's value chain as part of the reporting process (built-in), and
- standardizing the internal reporting process by embedding it in enterprise resource planning (ERP) applications and ledgers (embedded).

There is no generally recommended realization or global valid implementation process. As each realization comprises a specific realization effort and offers different potential benefits for the implementing organization. The deployment of the benefits for an organization depends on its individual situation. Right now, neither there are the properties identified, which need to be regarded for a decision, nor the characteristics of the properties related to a realization type or its potentials.

It is necessary to decide economically sensible about the integration depth within an organization. The paper's contribution is a methodology to support the decision process for the adoption of XBRL into the organization. By doing design science research, the constructed artifact enables a structured decision based on facts, individual properties, and needs of the organization.

The concourse of the paper is as follows: Chap. 2 gives an overview about related work. Chapter 3 describes the research framework. The realization alternatives and their in benefits are explained. XBRL and the reporting process are explained and related in Chap. 4. Herewith the realization or so called implementation approaches are set into relation to the production processes of reports. The evaluation of characteristics of a reporting process and the effect of implementation approaches on them are given in Chap. 5. Chapter 6 gives conclusions and defines further research steps.

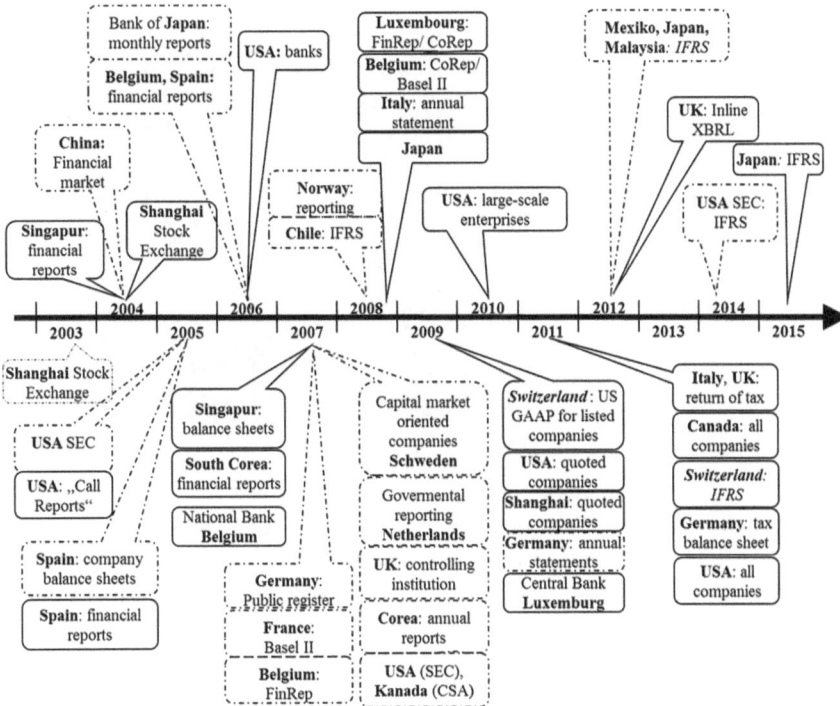

Fig. 1 Time bar of XBRL announcements and projects

2 Related Work

Due to the already globally existing regulator driven XBRL adoptions, we assume that there are appropriate XBRL projects descriptions available. We perform a literature review to gain an understanding about the adoption and implementation of XBRL on a firm level, first. This is done by using Ebsco Host with the search terms (linked with logical and): XBRL adoption, XBRL implementation, XBRL best practice, XBRL lessons learned, XBRL project, and XBRL experience. The discussion is carried out using the parameters shown in Fig. 2.

Why describes the reason for a company's XBRL project. This is relevant to understand the setting up and timeline of a project, and also the effects on organizational and technical entities. *Where* affects processes or spots within processes where XBRL should be implemented. *How* takes a look on the chosen realization and therefore whether it is an internal or external realization or not. *What* concerns the content, which has to be sent by using XBRL. The discussion shows a brief description of category characterizing papers to be able to determine the main content of the defined categories.

Fig. 2 Discussion
parameters

What?   **How?**

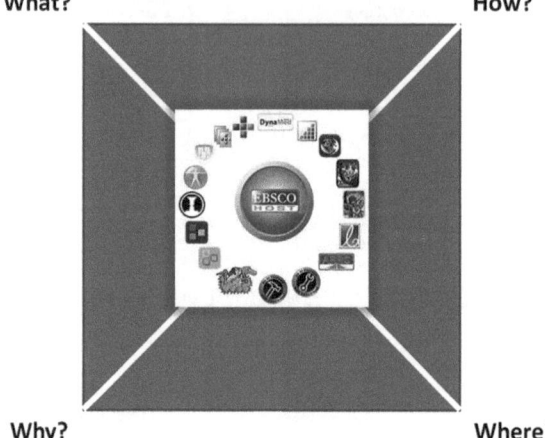

Why?   **Where?**

The database retrieval was done at 05 November 2013 and results in overall 1,164 papers. The differentiation of the identified papers according to the search terms is as shown in Table 1. We ignore practitioner papers on XBRL, because they are mainly coming from software vendors and just describe the vendor's products and XBRL ability within their products.

Having the short time in mind, XBRL is available in the market and adoptions are (usually) mandated by regulators, already a lot of XBRL papers are available (using the term XBRL as search term led to 5,111 results). But, those papers are focusing the general adoption of XBRL and potential benefits of using XBRL and due to this are reflecting behavioral research.

Considering *why* is mainly documented by XBRL adoption papers. Those papers are discussing the introduction of XBRL on a regulator level and therefore, why it is beneficial for a regulator to define XBRL as transmission format in favor of regulatory reporting. One example is [2] "Consequences of XBRL Standardization on Financial Statement Data", which is discussing the effects of using XBRL within financial reporting and due to this the possibility of increased data comparability. This is also discussed in context of auditing to support those activities by standardized reports.

The process orientation, reflected by *where*, is seen in context of implementations. Especially [1, 3–5] discusses implementation strategies and deeply embedded approaches He is one of the authors motivating the usage of XBRL General Ledger (GL) to be able to implement XBRL as deep as possible within a firm's information flow.

How is also discussed by [1, 3–5] looking at the general options of implementing XBRL within companies, but also different authors discuss lessons learned from XBRL projects. Cohen [6] shows integrational efforts of XBRL and Enterprise Resource Planning (ERP) systems to illustrate how an information flow can be supported by XBRL.

Table 1 Ebsco retrieval according to search terms

Search term	Results
XBRL adoption	489
XBRL implementation	299
XBRL best practice	25
XBRL lessons learned	4
XBRL project	254
XBRL experience	93

What is discussed in the area of XBRL projects and implementation studies. Bartley et al. [7] analyzes the usage of defined taxonomy elements of the US SEC reporting. Debreceny et al. [8] take a look on the extensions by analyzing about the need and usefulness of extensions in XBRL filings to the SEC.

Overall, most of the papers discuss the basics of XBRL and its potential benefits. Another part takes a look on different adoption levels and in addition a taxonomy development. Papers reflecting the technical implementation or the implementation depth within companies are not available. Project descriptions, lessons learned papers, or recommendations are not reflecting the decision process about the implementation depth, but they do offer input in such a process. But, due to the reason that companies have to use XBRL as reporting standard, because regulators set the demand, decision makers are requested to decide, how much and how deeply implemented XBRL should be within their enterprise. This shows the existing research gap to model a decision support process about the XBRL implementation depth in companies.

3 Research Framework

The Fig. 3 shows the relation between effort, degree of automation, and implementation type. The first known option is called bolt-on. It refers to the tagging of financial statements at the end of the reporting process. This additional step can be outsourced or handled in-house. Tools supporting this activity are so called mapping tools where each data element becomes assigned to tags. Due to the manual assignment, a tagging of complex structures is not desirable and authors like [1, 3] state that such an implementation does not produce any significant use.

An alternative is the built-in approach. The mapping becomes integrated into the information systems as a part of the reporting process. This option uses the XBRL-GL taxonomy and enables the automatic mapping of reporting information. The data managing systems have to be capable of a mapping to XBRL taxonomies to be able to implement this method. The embedded type relies on a standardization of the internal reporting process by an integration of an XBRL interface with Enterprise Resource Planning (ERP), Accounting, and/or Business Analytics systems [1]. Mertens [9] states that there should be a meaningful automatization as

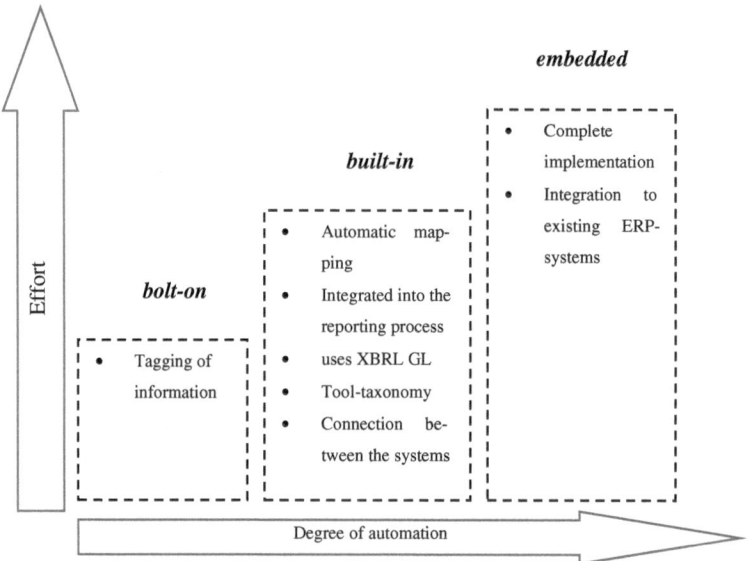

Fig. 3 Implementation types of XBRL

determining parameter of IT implementations in companies. This means that the adoption of IT should be as deep as it makes sense for the supported tasks and can be regarded as theoretical background for the IT related management decision. Depending on the type of implementation the information technology (IT) systems of the organization need to provide the data for an XBRL-tagging or should provide XBRL-tagged-data already.

Therefore task of deciding on an implementation depth of XBRL can be regarded as a management decision among the IT architecture of an organization, which is called enterprise architecture (EA). "The most important characteristic of an enterprise architecture is that it provides a holistic view on the enterprise. ... A well-defined architecture is an important asset in positioning new developments within the context of the existing processes, IT systems, and other assets of an organization, and it helps in identifying necessary changes" [10]. There exist different frameworks, which help to develop and analyze an EA, because they identify all relevant perspectives. The most well-known ones are The Open Group Architecture Framework (TOGAF) or the Zachman Framework [11]. If they are already established among an organization, they will guide the implementation decision for XBRL. Besides, the roll-out of an entire framework on a whole enterprise just in order to decide on an XBRL implementation depth may be not feasible as the underlying complexity of all existing IT solutions are very high and due to this the effort is very high.

As we aim on the discussion of relevant properties of an enterprise we decided to use the perspectives given in a framework and let them guide the identification of the ones which are relevant for the (in the field of enterprise architecture) limited scope of an XBRL realization type. The Zachman framework [11] was chosen because it is layer oriented separation of relevant architecture items starting from the business towards an implementation perspective [11]. Further details on that can be obtained from [11]. Additionally, Zachman's perspectives concurs to some extent with Blohm's reporting framework [12]. Due to this reason, Zachman's framework with the perspectives what (data), how (function), network (where), people (who), time (when), and motivation (why) supports our discussion on the XBRL implementation. Not all items of the entire framework are relevant to guide our discussion, but the used ones make clear where an XBRL implementation affects an enterprise architecture and therefore should be regarded within a management's decision.

The development of the proposed model follows design science guidelines from [13] and [14] on designing and evaluating artifacts (concepts, models, methods, and instances) to solve existing problems.

4 Reporting and XBRL

The identification of basic reporting needs and aspects as evaluation basis is necessary to be able to decide about the implementation depth of an XBRL supported reporting process. Therefore, a discussion about the potentials of XBRL enhances the basis for the decision framework.

4.1 Reporting, Reports and the Reporting Process

Different definitions of the term reporting are reflecting different points of view onto this topic. E.g. [12] defined in 1970 that a report is the exchange of information about facts, events, connections, and processes of the organization and its environment for internal and external recipients. The information itself is supposed to have an economic relevance and is collected under a certain point of view following [15–17] defines such a point of view as an informative purpose referring to a superior goal.

The basic function of reporting, which is derived from the management function, is the transmission of information [18]. Reporting has to support the management within a target oriented planning and control. It is important that a report with a certain purpose contains all relevant information, is clearly arranged and understandable for the recipient. Furthermore, it is essential that the report is available at a particular time, because this influences the effect of the report according to [19]. Due to an increasing amount of information and the dynamic environments, all report types require an increasing IT support. A database access is essential to gain the information faster, more precise, and recipient oriented. It is important to gain a deeper understanding about the report generation in context to the existing properties of a report. The report creation itself, this independent from the reporting style, is usually done by an underlying reporting process. The Fig. 4 visualizes the single steps of a report creation, which are often done simultaneously in practice.

The report becomes defined concerning all properties (information need), which is mentioned in Fig. 2. The second step defines the relevant information sources. This might be enhanced with a data harmonization due to heterogeneous data sources. Harmonization can refer to establishing a common understanding or unifying formats. The different sources can refer to different components of an IT system or structure oriented to different parts of the organizations. Examples are subsidiaries, which have to be consolidated to be able to provide a basis for the data of the parent company. It can be necessary besides the harmonization to connect, update, aggregate, and structure the relevant data [20]. The next step arranges the information in a preferred format to transfer them to recipients for their specific use. The extent to which information becomes reported does not only derive from the influence of different interested parties, but from legal requirements [21]. It is necessary to recognize the accounting discipline as an important aspect of reporting for the analysis of the legal requirements in regard to XBRL. The American Accounting Association (AAA) defines accounting as "... the process of identifying, measuring, and communicating information to permit judgments and decisions by user of the information" [22, 23]. The latter part of the definition constitutes reporting as part of accounting. According to [24], the process of accounting is organized as accounting cycle which "... is defined as a series of activities which begin with a transaction and end with the entries in the general ledger. These processes are repeated during each reporting period" [24]. The financial reports, which base inter alia on the trial balance, have to be prepared at the end of an accounting period. The Fig. 5 shows the reporting process enhanced by the data of the accounting cycle. The shown data flow is between the general process model of reporting and the financial reporting with initiating transaction and entry into a bookkeeping system [8].

The transition of the entries from the general ledger to the trial balance is done by using a chart of accounts [25]. An annual report consists of different parts: the financial statements with explanatory notes and auditors' report and a discussion and analysis of accounts. The scope of financial statements is regulated by accounting standards [24], whereby a variety of different accounting standards exist worldwide. The international accounting standards (IAS) and the "International Financial Reporting Standards (IFRS) are a set of accounting standards which are developed by the International Accounting Standards Board (IASB). It is becoming the global standard for the preparation of public company financial statements" [26]. The IAS/IFRS are therefore detached from national regulations and are invented to enable a comparison on an international level. A complete set of financial statements in harmony with IAS/IFRS should include a statement of financial position (balance sheet) at the end of the period; a statement of profit and loss and other comprehensive income for the period, a statement of changes in equity for the period, a statement of cash flows for the period, notes, comprising a summary of accounting policies and other explanatory information and a statement

Fig. 4 General reporting process

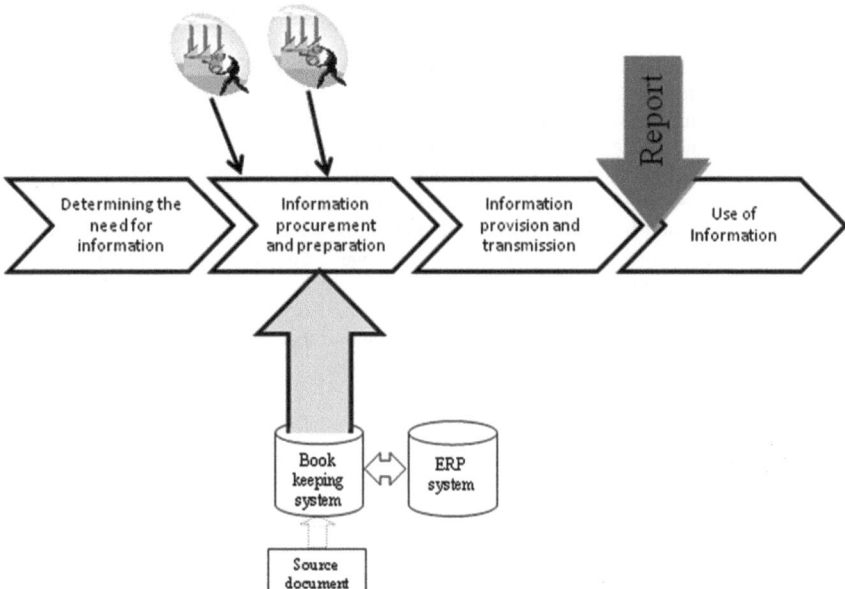

Fig. 5 Reporting process connected with the financial reporting process

of financial position as at the beginning of the earliest comparative period when an entity applies an accounting policy retrospectively or makes a retrospective restatement of items in its financial statements, or when it reclassifies items in its financial statements [27]. Therefore, the IAS/IFRS are one example of legal requirements concerning the possible content of reports. Piechocki [24] defines seven different reporting scenarios for financial reporting, which are given in Table 2.

Whereas principles like IFRS deal especially with the reporting content, other regulations affect the formatting of the report as well. One example is the German tax bureaucracy reduction act [28], which reregulates the transmission of the data in § 5 of the German income tax act. The exact realization of the transmission—the formatting of the electronic data—is regulated by the tax administration. XBRL is explicitly announced as the official format (letter of the Federal Office of Treasury, 19th January 2010). The SEC enabled a voluntary filing in XBRL in 2005, which became mandatory in 2009. XBRL is considered in these projects,

Table 2 Financial reporting scenarios with potential clientele

Reporting scenario	Description	Potential receivers
Auditor reporting	Conveying of the financial reports to the auditor for the needs of audit procedures	The big four auditors: Deloitte Touche Tohmatsu, Ernst & Young, KPMG, PricewaterhouseCoopers
Group reporting	Reporting of a subsidiary to its parent entity	Parent entities
Capital markets reporting	Reporting of public companies regulated by stock exchange regulations to the investors, analyst and stock exchange but not related to supervisory reporting	Stock Exchanges like SEC
Statutory reporting	Reporting regulated by local GAAPs and related to the publication of financial report in generally accessible media	German Business Register
Supervisory reporting	Reporting regulated by the stock exchange supervision of the publicly traded companies	Federal Financial Supervisory Authority
Tax reporting	Reporting related to the submission of the financial reports to the tax offices for the purpose of calculating tax values	Local tax offices
Credit risk reporting	Reporting to the credit risk management divisions of commercial banks for the needs of credit risk assessment and ratings	Deutsche Bank, Deutsche Bundesbank, Federal Reserve System

because it is discussed with several advantages, which are relevant for improvements in the supervising or regulation process.

4.2 Potential Benefits of the eXtensible Business Reporting Language

XBRL is a derivate of the eXtensible Markup Language (XML). Its principle is the so called tagging of information. Each single data becomes attached with an identifying tag. A tag is a set of metadata enhancing the number with semantic information [29]. A set of tags forms a taxonomy. A taxonomy is a defined, classified, and comprised description of elements in a coherent structure [30]. Taxonomies do not define an accounting standard [31]. They map existing standards like IFRS in an appropriate way for processing. Three different kinds of XBRL technologies are established according to the semantic complexity:

- XBRL General/Global Ledger (GL),
- XBRL Financial Reporting (FR), and
- XBRL Dimensions.

XBRL GL is data oriented and focuses on an internal reporting and the origin of data from business processes. In contrast, XBRL FR is semantically more sophisticated, document oriented and is developed for external reporting. The hinges semantic complexity can be seen in XBRL Dimensions, which becomes used for the transmission of multidimensional data. Hoffman and Strand [32] states that "XBRL can be viewed as a framework of controlled flexibility." The Fig. 6 presents the different XBRL technologies, their embedding into different processes and different interest groups.

XBRL is a set of concepts to reflect the heterogeneous needs of different processes and therefore the different participants of the respective process.

In context to reporting, "XBRL is a language for the electronic communication of business and financial data which is revolutionizing business reporting around the world. It provides major benefits in the preparation, analysis and communication of business information. It offers cost savings, greater efficiency, and improved accuracy and reliability to all those involved in supplying or using financial data. ... It is one of a family of "XML" languages which is becoming a standard means of communicating information between businesses and on the internet. XBRL is being developed by an international non-profit consortium of approximately 600 major companies, organizations and government agencies. It is an open standard, free of license fees" [33]. This statement contains a list of discussed benefits of XBRL. The Fig. 7 shows abstract benefits of XBRL.

Dynamic market developments are forcing supervisors to provide international platforms for controlling activities. Supervisory reporting in this area requires a precise, efficient and up-to-date flow of information. The use of international standards allows national regulators to introduce high-quality control processes while ensuring compatibility with global markets. This is supported by XBRL due to the development of international taxonomies based on the respective reporting standards. Adoption of the above standard taxonomies allows organizations to:

- limit the risk of development of new standards;
- increase market transparency;
- rely on internationally developed, implemented and maintained solutions; and to
- limit resistance of organizations and software vendors for implementation of new standards.

Especially public organizations are often criticized for the introduction of custom and proprietary reporting solutions. Consequently, transparency of reporting procedures together with intelligible reporting systems becomes a key requirement for national supervisors and regulators. International XBRL taxonomies developed by independent authorities and utilizing an open standard, provide a foundation for transparent and efficient reporting systems. Analysis and verification of submitted supervisory data presents a challenge in rapidly developing markets. Analysts and statisticians are often faced with requirements to manually input data into validation systems, which increases both time and cost of data examination. The use of international XBRL taxonomies in automatic data processing systems allows the supervisory institutions to increase performance while

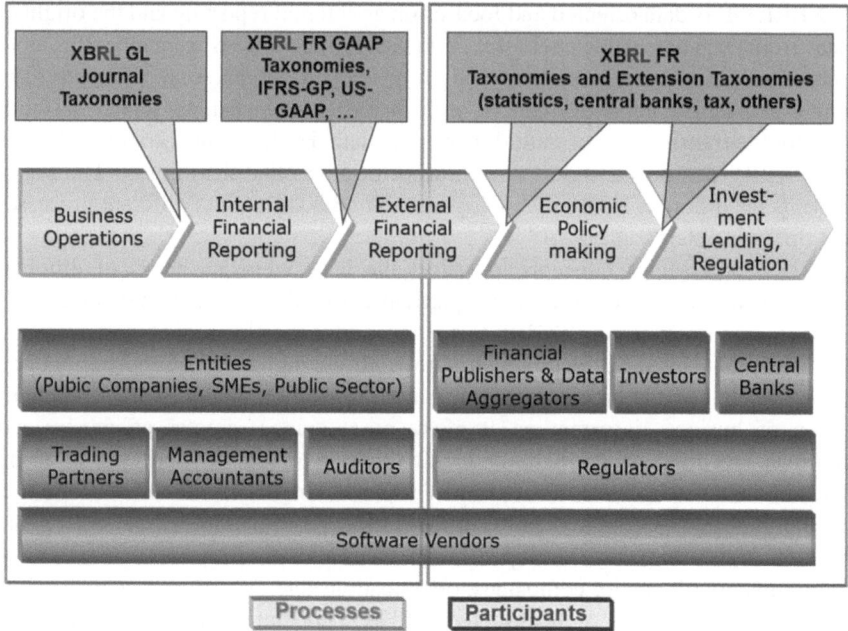

Fig. 6 XBRL technologies in relation to processes and participants

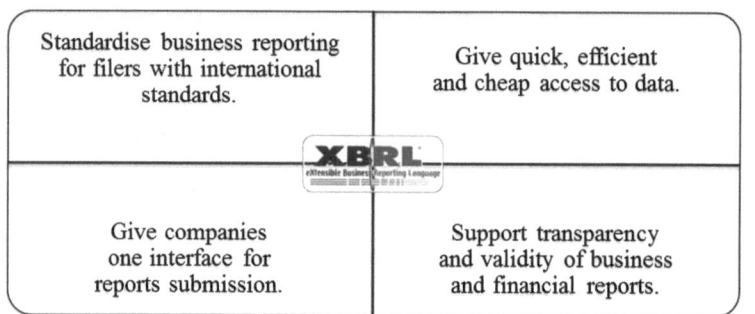

Fig. 7 Discussed XBRL benefits

reducing the cost of data collection and validation. The XBRL standard allows the enhancement and optimization of the internal data processing flow, which results in an efficient data management and improved supervision. Reports submitted by supervised entities may be structured in precise groups of data and reflected in XBRL taxonomies. This feature allows preparing consistent and standardized data points enhanced by references to underlying legal documentation and enriched by multilingual labels and filling guidance information. Data reported using XBRL taxonomies can be automatically validated on several levels: technical (validity of information against data types and reporting attributes) domain (validity against a structured XBRL taxonomy) and custom (business rules or statistical verification). Strong validation capabilities may be combined with automated reporting platform responsible for collection, validation, and processing of submitted data. Business activities of organizations often concern multiple markets. Fulfilling various supervisory reporting obligations present a significant burden, which combined with importance of the data submitted may impact the domestic and global market. One of the challenges of companies is to establish a single platform, which enables the companies to satisfy majority of reporting obligations. XBRL taxonomies allow the development of one-interface solutions to reduce reporting burdens. Supervised entities are able to select appropriate reporting schemes and pre-validate their submissions. Reporting companies may be required to submit various reports regularly or instantly after evoking event occurrence. Revisions and corrections of reports submitted create a significant flow of information, which requires an appropriate management in the companies. The proposed benefits motivated national supervisors or regulators to introduce XBRL into their reporting process. Such regulatory driven adoption of XBRL forces companies, to make decisions about the XBRL implementation in their company to fulfill the official demand in context of an external reporting. The XBRL standard allows the development of easy-to-use solutions like predefined and pre-mapped templates for the creation of reports. This offers the opportunity for transparent and efficient reporting environments, where participants are not only obliged to fulfill, but also support e.g. the supervisory processes. But additionally, the discussed benefits will also lead to questions for the companies itself, if a broader XBRL adoption can gain benefits within the own reporting processes.

4.3 The Reporting Process and the Different Implementation Stages

The reporting process is enhanced by parts of the financial reporting. This leads to the next step to project the defined stages of XBRL implementation to the appropriate phases. It is not important for the transmission and dissemination of the reports how XBRL tags are added. Therefore and concerning the use of the information, the depth of such a tagging is not relevant. The Fig. 8 shows the covering of the different stages on the reporting process.

The bolt-on approach, which refers to a simple tagging or the information, affects the final reporting process step. Therefore the effects on the reporting process and the identified properties for an evaluation itself are reduced. The duration time of the process does not change. Additionally, the number of media discontinuities is not reduced (on the producer side), Furthermore, parties concerned within an organization are not better connected, which means that the more often reports have to be tagged the higher the effort is (complex tagging is connected to a high effort, amount of errors and combined formats is not reduced, the harmonization of metadata is not affected). But further data processing and analysis from reports is enabled and regulations concerning the formatting by consumers can be kept. The built-in approach covers two steps of the reporting process. Within the provided support the duration time of the reporting process can be reduced for example by the time needed for a manual tagging. The number of media discontinuities can be reduced, concerned parties intra or extra organizational can be connected in a better way by a common standard, the number of errors for example due to less manual work is reduced, the manual effort can be reduced and metadata is provided via XBRL. The embedded approach has the greatest impact on the reporting chain. All positive effects of the built-in approach are realized or intensified. An additional advantage is the general metadata harmonization, which can be realized by connecting heterogeneous systems. The Table 3 gives a structured overview of the mentioned benefits related to the stages.

In order to evaluate the necessity for the realization of the potential benefits they will be considered for the analysis of an implementation as well.

5 Decision Support for XBRL Implementation's Depth

As explained, the decision on a realization type of XBRL has to regard the specific situation in an enterprise. This leads to a need to identify the characteristics of the reporting processes being carried out by the company.

A methodical approach is provided to support the identification of relevant process and organizational characteristics to be able to choose an XBRL implementation level. The phases of the approach are explained. Using elements of Zachman's framework, the process oriented parameters are evaluated. Therefore, the implementation depth becomes linked to the process model. Later on, the report oriented part is evaluated as well.

5.1 Relevant Reporting Attributes

Here, we discuss the relevant characteristics for the decision on an XBRL implementation and hereby for the implementation scheme. As stated earlier, each report is generated among a reporting process. In correspondence to each process assessment, the instances of the process of reporting, which is instantiated with every report, can be characterized by quantitative and qualitative aspects [34]. The performance of a process becomes measured in a quantitative assessment. A qualitative assessment unveils whether the process shows special characteristics or not. The qualitative attributes being used are partly a conglomerate of given ones in literature of [12, 17–19, 35], and [36]. They are enhanced by attributes derived from the potential benefits XBRL explained in Chap. 4. A quantitative assessment of a reporting process identifies by the parameters duration time or number of

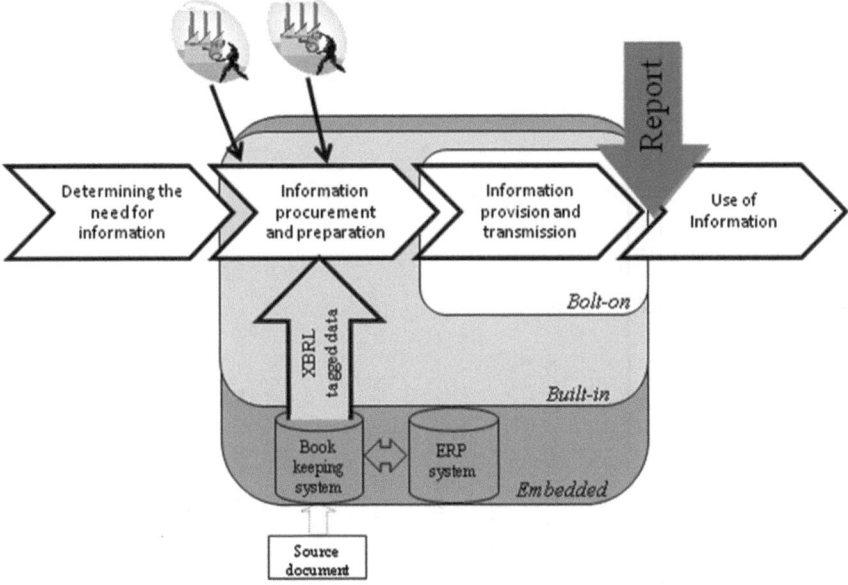

Fig. 8 Reporting process and its coverage by XBRL implementation stages

errors. The potential effects of an XBRL support have to be determined for further investigations. All kind of attributes are structured according to the perspectives of Zachman's framework (Table 4).

5.2 Evaluation of the Reporting Attributes Concerning Relevance for the Implementation Decision

Table 5 gives the results of the analysis of different report properties and possible surplus values coming from the different stages of an XBRL implementation.

Three basic types of reports can be distilled among the varied property combinations. The initiating event of a report is used to distinguish the implementation types.

The standard report is characterized by [19] as a regular creation, a predefined content, and its uniformity. The content is defined once and usually stable in time according to [17]. It is not adjusted to specific information needs. So, it is the additional task of the recipient to take the relevant information out of the report for analytical tasks [35]. For a standard report with a standardized information subject, the type of creation should be an automated and regular (electronic) transmission to different internal and external recipients. It is important to organize the creation of the report as effective as possible. Hereby, the support of this report type is the better the deeper the integration of XBRL is.

Table 3 XBRL Implementation Style Benefits derived from literature

	Bolt-on	Built-in	Embedded
Use of information			
Providing the data in recipient oriented way	X	X	X
Enabling an easier data distribution	X	X	X
Supporting further analysis and processing and automated integration (for receiver)	X	X	X
Tagging			
Prevention of a time consuming manual data tagging		X	X
Automated loading of a standard taxonomy (e.g. IFRS) → Standard reports		X	X
Reducing errors by decreasing media discontinuities within the report generation		X	X
Information procurement			
Harmonization of different formats of data sources → data in an unified format			X
Support of data consolidation			X
Internal reporting enhancement (thereby Business Analytics) → exception reports and reports on demand			X
Integration support of different departments into the generation process			X
Automated reports			X
Linking of heterogeneous data sources/systems via a unified interface			X
Enabling a common understanding by providing metadata (search cost reduction)			X
Reduced generation time for all kind of reports			X

Table 4 Zachman's perspectives applied to reporting properties

Zachman's perspective	Reporting process's attributes
What (data or reporting content)	Information subject: standardized, not standardized
	Type of message: facts, explanatory, normative, prognostic preciseness
	Degree of consolidation
	Homogeneity of data
How (function or reporting process)	Type of creation: manual, automated → information procurement, preparation, provision and transmission
	Visual formatting: verbal, graphical, table based
	Media discontinuities
	Heterogenity of data formats
	Errors
Network (where or reporting logistics)	Type of transmission: oral, in written form, electronic (different formats)
People (who)	Reporting author: single person, department, group
	Reporting recipient: internal, external
Time (when or reporting date)	Reporting cycle: regularly; unregularly
Motivation (why or reporting purpose)	Reporting purpose: management, control, plan, documentation, decision support, information

An exception report will be initiated, if a defined threshold is exceeded. It contains information on the deviation and does not have any regularity. The main task is to adjust a useful threshold, which is initiating the report. For an exception report, the effort for the creation is higher, because it is more individual and the relevant information have to be determined in advance whereby the identification and usage of metadata can play an important role. The effectiveness of its creation is less important compared to the speed. The speed can be increased by the reduction of manual work. But in comparison to standard reporting, the number of properties, which are affected positively by XBRL, is reduced. Therefore, it is supported less compared to standard reporting.

A report on demand is initiated by an individual request and is motivated by the special needs of the recipient. Often this type of report means a higher effort, because the collection of the information is more expensive (transaction cost) and the utilization of the provided information is limited. The report on demand is equal concerning the need for speed to an exception report. Therefore, it is supported by XBRL. There is nevertheless a huge effort concerning the generation of the report in most cases. Therefore, the support by XBRL is the lowest one in comparison to the other two types.

5.3 Implementation Scheme

The extracted and assessed reporting attributes set the basis for an evaluation among an enterprise. Among a second step, the relevant properties have been converted into a set of statements. Each statement specifies an argument for a

Table 5 Effects of Report Properties to the XBRL Implementation

Attribute	Characteristics	Bolt-on	Built-in	Embedded
Information subject	Standardized	No effect	Production costs for XBRL reports can be reduced as the manual tagging is omitted	Especially the repetitive character of standard reports enhances the potential savings which can derive from a production costs reduction
	Not standardized	No effect	Production costs for XBRL reports can be reduced as the manual tagging is omitted	Relevant information may be found much easier, because metadata is provided
Type of message	Facts/explanatory/ normative/ prognostic	No effect		
Precise-ness		No effect		
Degree of consoli-dation		No effect		
Homogenity of data		No effect	No effect	The embedded approach results in homogeneous data. Homogenization of data may cause errors
Type of creation	Automated	No effect		
	Manual	No effect	Manual effort especially in tagging data is reduced	Manual effort especially in the tasks information procurement, preparation (consolidation, harmonization) and XBRL-tagging of data is reduced
Visual formatting	V., gr., table based	No effect		
Media discontinuities		No effect	No media discontinuities for the XBRL production	As all data will be available electronically from the same system and herewith media discontinuities will not appear
Heterogeneity of data formats		No effect	No effect	As all data is harmonized as it is available from an integration layer
Errors		No effect	Errors resulting from manual tagging can be reduced	Errors appearing all along the reporting process due to heterogeneity or manual task can be reduced

(continued)

Table 5 (continued)

Attribute	Characteristics	Bolt-on	Built-in	Embedded
Type of transmission	Oral/written	No effect	No effect	No effect
	Electronic	No effect	No effect	No effect
Reporting author	Single	No effect	No effect	No different understanding or formatting of the data between different departments
	Group	No effect	No different understanding or formatting of the data between different departments	If all members of a group share data within XBRL the effort for consolidation is reduced very much
	Department	No effect		
Reporting recipient	External/Internal		The transmission of meta-data connected to data reduces the effort to explain the data	
Reporting cycle	Regular	No effect	Especially within regular reports it is necessary to think about reducing the production cost like tagging, transformation, manual activities and time. The more often and the more reports the higher is the cost reduction	Most positive effect, because within the stringent use of taxonomies most steps can be automated and very low manual activity → highest cost reduction and faster
	Non-regular	No effect	No effect	Non-regular reports like exception reports and reports on demand often have a time critical effect → metadata enriched data reduces effort of searching a specific information → positive effect
Reporting purpose	Management, control, plan, documentation, decision support, information	No effect		

Table 6 Set of statements

Zachman's perspective	statement	Bolt-on	Built-in	Embedded
What	There is no a need for a harmonization of data among the process	X		
	There is a need for a harmonization of data among the process			X
How	The report creation is already automated to a high degree	X		
	The report creation happens manually concerning the information procurement			X
	The report creation happens manually concerning the preparation of data			X
	The report creation happens solely manually concerning the XBRL-tagging of the data		X	
	The report creation happens manually concerning the XBRL-tagging of the data			X
	There are media discontinuities among the process of report creation		X	
	There exist heterogeneous data formats which need to get integrated			X
	There are no errors appearing—neither among the report creation nor within the tagging of the data	X		
	Some errors occur among the process of manual tagging. There are no errors among the process of report creation		X	
	Some errors occur among the process of the report creation. Additionally but not necessarily errors occur among the manual tagging			X
Who	The report is solely produced by one person which has all information needed. There is no need to establish a common understanding	X		
	There is a group of people concerned with the report development which therefore needs a common understanding about the data			X
	There are different departments concerned with the report development which therefore need a common understanding about the data			X
When	The report is a regularly provided report with no need for the reduction of production costs or is a non-regular report which needs no time saving	X		
	The report is provided on a regular basis and there is a need for a reduction of the production costs			X
	The report is a non-regular report and therefore time critical. There is a need to provide the information faster			X
Amount		5	3	10

realization type. If there is an agreement on that statement the marked approach will be supposed to help with the specified issue. Each statement leads to exactly one realization type. The list of statements has to be applied for each reporting process.

The result of the assessment of all reporting processes is the amount of crosses for each category. Ideally, the result for each reporting process is homogenous. If there are crosses for more than one category the deepest implementation approach marked will be the result, because the strongest demand sets the rule for the remaining ones. The Table 6 replies to the question What specifics of a reporting process may lead to a realization of benefits of a XBRL realization type? It asks for the implementation in correspondence to existing need for improvement. According to each implementation depth, the effects on the reporting process or the different kinds of reports can be seen. Therefore, depending on the necessary support, the implementation depth can be identified by tagging to the different attributes.

Once the set of statements has been checked for all reporting processes, there will be a realization recommendation for each reporting process. In order to generate an overall realization decision, the deepest indicated realization decision is the relevant one.

6 Conclusions

It is the paper's goal to provide a support for the decision about the implementation depth of XBRL into any organization by doing design science research. Relevant aspects for the evaluation of a reasonable depth become identified and a method is designed. Therefore, the reporting process and reports are analyzed and the process of reporting and the potential support by an XBRL implementation is integrated.

Regarding the statement set there is right now an identification of the needs of the regarded organization and a connection to the potential benefits. From a practitioner's point of view it remains critical that the cost perspective is not regarded, yet. But they are highly enterprise individual as they depend on the existing IT landscape, the qualification of the staff and of course from the price of an eventually needed consulting service.

Furthermore, it can be argued that with the current approach the deeper realization methods have a higher weight, because already one cross for the deeper implementation leads to its choice. In order to understand how much an implementation type would fit for the specific reporting process, the percentage to all crosses among that category may be calculated. But the percentages of the implementation types may not be compared, as the total of crosses for each type is different. Therefore the direct comparison is not helpful.

The defined method and the implementation scheme have been applied in a couple of case studies. Therefore the applicability of the approach has been proven. Of course, this is no generalized contribution, yet, but it has shown in a very first step that the method supports the decision making in context of XBRL in a way, to make relevant parameters more obvious. Usually, decision makers in companies just have little knowledge about the XBRL characteristics and due to this reason a meaningful decision about an XBRL implementation. The proposed implementation scheme offers a helping hand to support the project definition in a company according to their specific needs. Further research is necessary to analyze XBRL projects to gain more information about different approaches in practice and their related project efforts like cost or time.

Next research steps contain a more advanced implementation and the assessment of project experiences, which can be gained only during the implementation. The mandatory filing of the German tax balance sheet starting from 2011 offers the opportunity to analyze decision making and projects in practice. This enables us, starting with the proposed model, to improve the model with arising aspects or characteristics.

References

1. Sledgianowski, D., Fonfeder, R., Slavin, N.S.: Implementing XBRL reporting. CPA J. **80**(8), 68–72 (2010)
2. Vasarhelyi, M.A., Chan, D.Y., Krahel, J.P.: Consequences of XBRL standardization on financial statement data. J. Inf. Syst. **26**(1), 155–167 (2012)
3. Garbellotto, G.: XBRL implementation strategies: the bolt-on approach. Strateg. Finance **92**, 56–58 (2009a)
4. Garbellotto, G.: XBRL implementation strategies: the built-in approach. Strateg. Finance **92**, 56–57 (2009b)
5. Garbellotto, G.: XBRL Implementation Strategies: The Deeply-Embedded Approach, Strategic Finance, **92**, 56–58 (2009c)
6. Cohen, E.E.: XBRL's global ledger framework: exploring the standardised missing link to ERP integration. Int. J. Discl. Gov. **6**(3), 188–206 (2009)
7. Bartley, J., Chen, A.Y.S., Taylor, E.Z.: A comparison of XBRL filings to corporate 10-ks-evidence from the voluntary filing program. Acc. Horiz. **25**(2), 227–245 (2011)
8. Debreceny, R.S., Farewell, S.M., Piechocki, M., Felden, C., Gräning, A., d'Eri, A.: Flex or Break? Extensions in XBRL disclosures to the SEC. Acc. Horiz. **25**(4), 631–657 (2011)
9. Mertens, P.: Wirtschaftsinformatik: von den Moden zum Trends. In: König, W. (ed.) Wirtschaftsinformatik '95: Wettbewerbsfähigkeit, Innovation, Wirtschaftlichkeit, pp. 25–64. Physica, Heidelberg (1995)
10. Jonkers, H., Lankhorst, M.M., ter Doest, H.W., Arbab, F., Bosma, H., Wieringa, R.J.: Enterprise architecture: management tool and blueprint for the organisation. Inf. Syst. Frontiers **8**(2), 63–66 (2006)
11. The Zachman Framework (2013). http://www.zachman.com/about-the-zachman-framework
12. Blohm, H.: Die Gestaltung des betrieblichen Berichtswesens als Problem der Leitungsorganisation. Herne/Berlin, NWB (1970)
13. Hevner, A.R., March, S.T., Park, J., Ram, S.: Design science in information systems research. MIS Q. **28**(1), 75–105 (2004)
14. March, S.T., Smith, G.F.: Design and natural science research on information technology. Decis. Support Syst. **15**(4), 251–266 (1995)
15. Bramsemann, R.: Handbuch Controlling, 3rd edn. München, Wien (1993)

16. Blohm, H.: Berichtssysteme. In: Grochla, E. (ed.) Handwörterbuch der Organisation, 2nd edn, pp. 315–320. Poeschel, Stuttgart (1980)
17. Horváth, P.: Controlling, 11th edn. München, Vahlen (2011)
18. Koch, R.: Betriebliches Berichtswesen als Informations- und Steuerungsinstrument. Peter Lang, Frankfurt am Main (1994)
19. Weber, J., Schäffer, U.: Einführung in das Controlling, 11th edn. Schäffer-Poeschel, Stuttgart (2006)
20. T-Rex-Terminosaurus Rex - Die Informationswissenschaft in Begriffen: Information-saufbereitung (information work), http://server02.is.uni-sb.de/trex/index.php?id=1.3.1.4. &suche=N
21. Bieg, H.: Buchführung, 2nd edn. NWB, Herne/Berlin (2004)
22. American Accounting Association: A Statement of Basic Accounting Theory. American Accounting Association, Sarasota (1966)
23. American Accounting Association: A Statement of Basic Accounting Theory. American Accounting Association, Sarasota (1966)
24. Piechocki, M.: XBRL financial reporting chain architecture (2007)
25. Eisele, W.: Technik des betrieblichen Rechnungswesens – Buchführung und Bilanzierung, Kosten und Leistungsrechnung, Sonderbilanzen, Verlag Franz Vahlen, München (2002)
26. Internet Source: IFRS. http://www.ifrs.com/ifrs_faqs.html#q1 (2010)
27. International Accounting Standards n. 1 as issued at 1 January 2013
28. Steuerbürokratieabbaugesetz, http://www.authentidate.de/fileadmin/pdf/Grundlagen/GER_08_Steuerbuerokratieabbaugesetz_Jan2009.pdf (2008)
29. Leibfried, P.: Finanzberichterstattung mittels XBRL - Mögliche Erleichterungen durch die Vermeidung von Datenbrüchen, in: Audit Committee News, no. 29, 10–13. http://www.alexandria.unisg.ch/Publikationen/61865 (2010)
30. XBRL Deutschland: Glossar, http://www.xbrl.de/index.php?option=com_content&view=article&id=79&Itemid=71 (2010)
31. XBRL Deutschland: Einführung in XBRL, http://www.xbrl.de/index.php?option=com_content&view=article&id=80&Itemid=77
32. Hoffman, C., Strand, C.: XBRL Essentials. American Institute of Certified Public Accountants, New York (2001)
33. Internet Source: XBRL International (2013). www.XBRL.org. Last call 10/31/2013
34. Beckert, T.: Prozesse in Produktion und Supply Chain optimieren. Springer Verlag, Wiesbaden (2005)
35. Küpper, H.-U.: Controlling, 2nd edn. Schäffer-Poeschel, Stuttgart (2008)
36. Weber, J., Bramsemann, U., Heineke, C., Hirsch, B.: Wertorientierte Unternehmenssteuerung: Konzepte – Implementierung - Praxisstatements, 1. Auflage, Wiesbaden, Gabler (1997)

A Knowledge Management Strategy to Identify an Expert in Enterprise

Matteo Gaeta, Rossella Piscopo, Luigi Rarità, Luigi Trevisant and Daniele Novi

Abstract The aim of this paper is to define a strategy to identify, manage and take advantage of competences in the enterprise via figures of opportune experts, with consequent advantages for workers and users in terms of problem solving. In such a context, industrial aspects, such as resources localization, research time and accessibility to the organizational hierarchy and the work load, are also considered. This allows to distinguish three different phases in finding the experts: Initialization, in which a score is assigned to workers on the base of competence levels; Propagation, where the search accuracy is improved using trust and closeness measures; Localization, where updates of scores are made in terms of social and geographical positions of users/enterprises and experts. The three phases allows to identify inside an enterprise the expert, who has the best competence and is close to the resource, that is in the shortest delay possible.

Keywords Social network analysis · Enterprise 2.0 · Trust · Candidate experts

M. Gaeta (✉) · R. Piscopo · L. Rarità
Dipartimento di Ingegneria dell'Informazione, Ingegneria Elettrica e Matematica Applicata, University of Salerno, Via Giovanni Paolo II, 84084 Fisciano, SA, Italy
e-mail: mgaeta@unisa.it

R. Piscopo
e-mail: rpiscopo@unisa.it

L. Rarità
e-mail: lrarita@unisa.it

L. Trevisant
Dipartimento di Ingegneria dell'Informazione, Ingegneria Elettrica e Matematica Applicata, Centro di Eccellenza su Metodi e Sistemi per Aziende Competitive, University of Salerno, Via Giovanni Paolo II, 84084 Fisciano, SA, Italy
e-mail: trevisant@cemsac.it

D. Novi
Dipartimento di Informatica, University of Salerno, Via Giovanni Paolo II, 84084 Fisciano, SA, Italy
e-mail: daniele.novi@dia.unisa.it

L. Caporarello et al. (eds.), *Smart Organizations and Smart Artifacts*, Lecture Notes in Information Systems and Organisation 7, DOI: 10.1007/978-3-319-07040-7_17,
© Springer International Publishing Switzerland 2014

1 Introduction

Expert finding procedures are useful to identify appropriate persons with particular skills and knowledge within a reference domain [1]. This contingent necessity is highly crucial, as it concerns general industrial frameworks, especially for private and public enterprises, with the aim of minimizing the time to market, seen as the development time for new marketing strategies and/or products. Moreover, the increasing number of processes makes the expert finding a necessary effort for avoiding some typical phenomena, such as bottlenecks, dead times, and optimizing the operations along supply processes. In such a context, the expert, who has to be found, is a person that gives opinions and solves problems, due to his/her personal knowledge and experience. Methodologies for expert finding are mainly of content-based type, namely candidate experts are searched via their personal data, such as local information and documents. From one side, such approaches have been very effective as for the identification of the most knowledgeable people on a given topic; but, on the other hand, they are quite far from the usual operations of search. This is a common situation within the Information Retrieval [2–5], and some aspects of experts selection are also ignored, such as the time needed to contact a person within the organizational hierarchy and workload [6, 7]. This task is highly non trivial, because the optimization of Knowledge Management procedures implies that candidate experts have to be chosen either in terms of knowledge and skills, or considering physical distances and contact times with other users/enterprises.

In this paper, the aim is the definition of a strategy to identify, manage and take advantage of competence in the enterprise [8], considering skills and knowledge of users, their geographical position and the time to contact them. The approach foresees that, for a given topic, there must be a classification of resources [9] and candidate experts through some opportune scores. Such experts are the nodes of an abstract reference Social Networks and their expertise values, namely their scores, are then updated [10] using an iterative procedure, based on the propagation theory [11], that also considers trust [12] and closeness centrality [13]. Finally, further approximations of the expertise are made considering the distance and the contact time [14] between users/experts in a Social Network. Hence, we distinguish three different phase for an expert finding methodology: Initialization, for which a vector space model [15, 16] is used to compute scores for resources and candidate experts; Propagation, in which expertise values are updated; Localization, in which the expertise of each expert is corrected via geographical, distance and time information.

In the future, the just described strategy will be analyzed on a real enterprise network through some experimentation activities. In particular:

1. connections of a typical social network, determined by interactions, such as replying to a post, following an author/post, liking an author/post, will be considered;
2. the social network dataset, consisting of user profiles and the above mentioned connections, will be partitioned to obtain a subset on a particular topic t;

3. a subgraph of interactions about t will be constructed. In this way, all people involved in the subgraph will be considered potential experts about t;
4. the proposed procedure for expert finding will be applied to just obtained subgraph.

The paper is organized as follows. Section 2 shows the basic ideas for a possible methodology of expert finding, while Sect. 3 concerns all possible steps (Initialization, Propagation, and Localization) useful for the identification of opportune experts on given reference topics. Conclusions and future perspectives are reported in Sect. 4.

2 Identification of an Expert

In considering some types of problems, especially for the enterprises, suitable persons are required. This is a hard task in general, as profiles and competence have to be accurately studied. In general, for such an analysis, we give the following definitions.

Definition (*Expertise need*) An expertise need is an information set, that concerns specific skills and/or knowledge.

Definition (*Expert*) The expert is a person with high skills degree and/or knowledge on a given topic, gained over the years, as a result of his/her experience and/or training. He/she will be able to give advice or recommendations for the verification of matters/facts/topics for problem solving or for the right comprehension of situations.

Notice that an expertise need refers to at least one domain of interest and can be of various types: from a natural language question to a more structured information, such as documents and papers. Moreover, candidate experts are a subset of workers of enterprises, or external persons who, in some way, have work relationships with the enterprises themselves. Hence, candidate experts refer to a part of users within a reference Social Network, mainly of enterprise type.

A correct methodology for the Knowledge Management foresees that experts of some fields of interest allow to answer the following questions: *focusing on a reference enterprise Social Network, which is the most suitable subset of such a network in order to achieve the aims of an assigned expertise need? And which is the best way to contact the experts?*

A possible strategy is represented in Fig. 1: an enterprise formulates an expertise need, whose characteristics are mapped with the users resources of a reference Social Network. A score is associated to each resource and this computation is useful for the formulation of the expertise values of candidate experts, namely the scores for each member of an abstract Social Network, whose nodes are the most suitable users who can address the assigned expertise need. The computation of scores for resources and then for candidate experts defines the

Initialization phase, the first step of an expert finding procedure. Then, using the propagation theory [12], expertise values are updated (second step, Propagation) for each node of the abstract Social Network. Finally, the third phase, Localization, allows a further update of the expertise values, according to: the geographical position between the experts and other experts/enterprises; the contact time [14] between experts and enterprises, measured via the "social distance", namely the shortest path in terms of faster connections.

In order to improve the estimations for the various scores, an accurate resource analysis must be made. Indeed, resources are composed by text, often including URLs to external Web pages. Hence, different resources must be first extracted (*Extraction* phase), then foreign languages must be identified (*Language identification* phase), and finally, we have the *Text Processing* and *Entity Recognition and Disambiguation* steps. *Text Processing* deals with standard Information Retrieval phases, such as tokenization, stop word removal and stemming. *Entity Recognition and Disambiguation*, instead, aims at the identification of named entities (people, enterprises, places, and so on) from texts, and then at the enriching of the found terms via some semantic annotations. Details are found in [9]. It is quite obvious that resources processing, although it is not the fundamental step for an expert finding strategy, plays an important role for the accuracy of scores computations.

3 Methodological Steps

We describe now the methodological steps for an expert finding strategy, with the aim of a more opportune management of skills and knowledge procedures. In particular, a mathematical description of the just described three phases, Initialization, Propagation and Localization, is made.

3.1 Initialization

The steps for the Initialization phase are the computation of:

1. the score for a generic resource with respect to an assigned expertise need;
2. the expertise, namely a further score, for the considered candidate experts.

Such two steps are not independent, as considered in what follows.

3.2 Score for Resources

Consider the necessity of computing the score for a given resource, once an expertise need is assigned. In this case, it is suitable to refer to a vector space model [15, 16], that allows a uniform formulation for all entities involved in the problem. For this, assume that:

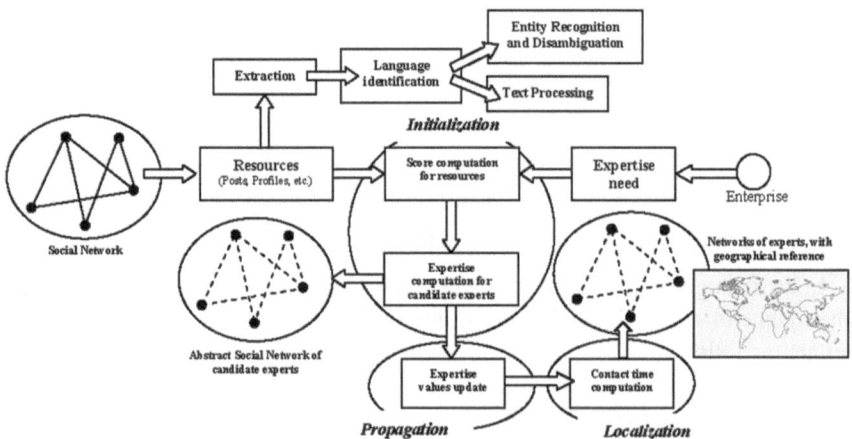

Fig. 1 Scheme of a knowledge strategy for the identification of experts

1. $Q = \{q_1, q_2, \ldots, q_N\}$ is the expertise need, whose i-th term is represented by q_i, $i = 1, \ldots, N$;
2. $R = \{r_1, r_2, \ldots, r_M\}$ is the set of resources. Each resource r_j, $j = 1, \ldots, M$, has cardinality $|r_j|$;
3. $U = \{u_1, u_2, \ldots, u_P\}$ is the set of the expertise need suitable users, found by the procedure of *Entity Recognition and Disambiguation*;
4. $R_{r_j, q_i} = \{r_j \in R : q_i \in r_j\} = \{\bar{r}_1, \bar{r}_2, \ldots, \bar{r}_{M_{i,j}}\}$ is the subset of R that keeps all resources $\bar{r}_l$, $l = 1, \ldots, M_{i,j}$, that contain the term q_i, $i = 1, \ldots, N$;
5. $U_{r_j, u_k} = \{u_k \in U : u_k \rightarrow r_j\} = \{\bar{u}_1, \bar{u}_2, \ldots, \bar{u}_{P_{kj}}\}$ is the subset of U, where the term $\bar{u}_m$, $m = 1, \ldots, P_{kj}$, is the user who is in relation with the resource r_j, namely $u_k \rightarrow r_j$, $j = 1, \ldots, M$;
6. $A = \{\varphi_{i,j}(q_i, r_j), i = 1, \ldots, N, j = 1, \ldots, M\}$ is the set of the generic functions $\varphi_{i,j}(q_i, r_j)$ that represent, for fixed i and j, the occurrences of q_i in r_j;
7. $B = \{\psi_{k,j}(u_k, r_j), k = 1, \ldots, P, j = 1, \ldots, M\}$ is the set of the generic functions $\psi_{k,j}(u_k, r_j)$ that indicate, for fixed k and j, the number of suitable users involved in the resource r_j.

The importance of r_j, $j = 1, \ldots, M$, for Q, due to the generic term q_i that appears in r_j, is given by the Keyword Matching Function (KMF), defined as:

$$KMF(r_j, Q) := \sum_{i=1}^{N} \alpha_{i,j} \varphi_{i,j}(q_i, r_j), \quad j = 1, \ldots, M, \tag{1}$$

where:

$$\alpha_{i,j} := \frac{1}{|r_j|} \log \frac{M}{M_{i,j}}, \quad i = 1,\ldots,N, \, j = 1,\ldots,M. \tag{2}$$

We observe that (1) is a linear combination of elements of A via the coefficients (2), and it is built considering, $\forall i = 1,\ldots,N$, $j = 1,\ldots,M$, the *term frequency* $\frac{\varphi_{i,j}(q_i,r_j)}{|r_j|}$ and the *inverse term frequency* $\log \frac{M}{M_{i,j}}$.

In an analogous way, the Entity Matching Function (EMF), that measures the importance of r_j, $j = 1,\ldots,M$, for Q, due to the generic user u_k, $k = 1,\ldots,P$, is defined as follows:

$$EMF(r_j, Q) := \sum_{k=1}^{P} \beta_{k,j} \psi_{k,j}(u_k, r_j), \quad j = 1,\ldots,M, \tag{3}$$

where:

$$\beta_{k,j} := \frac{1}{|r_j|} \log \frac{P}{P_{k,j}} w_u(u_k, r_j), \, j = 1,\ldots,M, \, k = 1,\ldots,P. \tag{4}$$

Notice that (3) is a linear combination of elements of B through the scalars (4), $\frac{\psi(u_k,r_j)}{|r_j|}$ and $\log \frac{P}{P_{k,j}}$ are interpreted, respectively, as the *user frequency* and the *inverse user frequency*, while $0 \leq w_u(u_k, r_j) \leq 1$ is a value, that measures the disambiguation confidence of u_k for r_j, computed during the *Entity Recognition and Disambiguation* step.

Finally, the score $S_{r_j}(Q)$ of a resource r_j, $j = 1,\ldots,M$, due to the expertise need Q, is constructed as:

$$S_{r_j}(Q) := \lambda KMF(r_j, Q) + (1 - \lambda)EMF(r_j, Q), \tag{5}$$

where $0 \leq \lambda \leq 1$ is a weight, that indicates the importance of the contribution of KMF and EMF.

Notice that function (5) defines a possible criterion for the importance of all resources with respect to the expertise need.

3.3 Expertise

Assume that a reference Social Network is described by the graph $G' = G'(V', E')$, where V' is the set of nodes, that represent the users, while E' is the set of relations of type ζ (coauthor or college, for example) between two different users.

Given the expertise need Q, we construct a sub-graph $G = G(V, E)$ of G' for which: $V' \supseteq V = \{v_1, v_2, \ldots, v_n\}$ is the set of the candidate experts; $E' \supseteq E =$

$\left\{ e_{ij}^{\zeta} \right\}$, $i = 1, \ldots, n$, $j = 1, \ldots, n$, $i \neq j$, is the set of relations of type ζ between v_i and v_j. Notice that G is an abstract Social Network of candidate experts, seen as a part of a reference network, that can describe, in general, relations among users of an enterprise.

Consider the set:

$$\tilde{R} = \left\{ r_j \in R : S_{r_j}(Q) \geq \rho_{r_j} \right\} = \{ \tilde{r}_1, \tilde{r}_2, \ldots, \tilde{r}_T \},$$

that contains all resources r_j, $j = 1, \ldots, M$, whose score $S_{r_j}(Q)$ is greater than an assigned threshold value ρ_{r_j}.

The preliminary expertise $\tilde{E}^{(0)}$ of a candidate expert v_i, $i = 1, \ldots, n$, for the expertise need Q is:

$$\tilde{E}_{v_i}^{(0)}(Q) = \sum_{t=1}^{T} S_{\tilde{r}_t}(Q) w_r(v_i, \tilde{r}_t), \quad i = 1, \ldots, n, \tag{6}$$

where $0 \leq w_r(v_i, \tilde{r}_t) \leq 1$ is a weight, that quantifies how the expertise inferred from the resource $\tilde{r}_t$ can be associated to the expert v_i.

3.4 Propagation

Notice that formula (6) represents only the initial value of expertise for each candidate expert. It is possible to define an iterative procedure to update the expertise values $\forall v_i$, $i = 1, \ldots, n$, with respect to the whole Social Network. The basic idea [10] is that a given user is seen as an expert if he/she knows other experts and/or collaborates with them. Such an approach is based on the propagation theory [11]. We have that $\tilde{E}_{v_i}^{(\eta+1)}(Q)$ is computed by $\tilde{E}_{v_i}^{(\eta)}(Q)$ as follows:

$$\tilde{E}_{v_i}^{(\eta+1)}(Q) = \tilde{E}_{v_i}^{(\eta)}(Q) + \sum_{v_j \in \Omega} \sum_{e \in X_{ji}} s\big((v_j, v_i), e\big) \tilde{E}_{v_i}^{(\eta)}(Q), \quad i = 1, \ldots, n, \tag{7}$$

where Ω is the set of all neighbouring nodes to v_i in the graph, X_{ji} indicates all relationships from v_j to v_i, $e \in X_{ji}$ is one kind of relation from v_j to v_i, while $s\big((v_j, v_i), e\big) \geq 0$ represents the propagation coefficient, computed considering, for v_i, the trust parameter [12], the closeness centrality [13] and the communication entities. For a given $\varepsilon > 0$, after K iterations the propagation process stops if $\left| \tilde{E}_{v_i}^{(K)}(Q) - \tilde{E}_{v_i}^{(K-1)}(Q) \right| < \varepsilon$ $\forall$ $i = 1, \ldots, n$, and the obtained expertise values $\tilde{E}_{v_i}^{(K)}(Q)$, $i = 1, \ldots, n$, are normalized, i.e. dividing by $\max \left\{ \tilde{E}_{v_i}^{(K)}(Q) \right\}_{i=1,\ldots,n}$.

Formula (7) allows to obtain better expertise values, also considering all types of relations between experts on the considered Social Network.

3.5 Localization

The last step of an expert finding strategy foresees an update of the expertise values considering the position of the experts. Notice that the contact time between a generic user and an expert can be estimated via their "social distance", namely the shortest path is considered either as the faster or the most efficient connection between the nodes of a Social Network. Hence, greater is the number of nodes between the user and the expert, higher is the time required to have real contacts.

Starting from the graph G, we define a new graph $\tilde{G} = \tilde{G}(V, U, \Gamma, L)$ where: nodes U represent the geographical units (users and/or enterprises in the industrial context); $\Gamma = \{V \times U\}$ is the set of relations that indicate that a given user belongs, from a geographical point of view, to a precise enterprise; $L = \{U \times U\}$ represents the geographical distance among the various enterprises.

Define the set $Z = V \cup U = \{z_1, z_2 \ldots, z_R\}$ and let $\tilde{w}(z_j, z_i)$ be the weight (of value 1) of the arc, that connects nodes z_j and z_i, $j \neq i$. Then, the weight $W(p(z_1, \ldots, z_k))$ of a path $p(z_1, \ldots, z_k)$ that connects, in the order, nodes $z_1, z_2, \ldots, z_k$, is:

$$W(p(z_1, \ldots, z_k)) = \sum_{i=1}^{k-1} \tilde{w}(z_i, z_{i+1}).$$

The contact time $T(z_j, z_i)$ between two different nodes z_j and z_i, $j \neq i$, that can represent users, experts or enterprises, is computed as the length of the minimal path between z_j and z_i, normalized by the diameter of the network [14]. Hence,

$$T(z_j, z_i) = \frac{\min_{\substack{p \\ z_j \to z_i}} W(p)}{\max_{z_j, z_i} \left(\min_{\substack{p \\ z_j \to z_i}} W(p) \right)}. \tag{8}$$

Formula (8) allows to discriminate among all the suitable experts, searching for the "nearest" candidate to the enterprise/user, that requires him.

4 Conclusions

We have considered an approach to describe the possibility of identifying expert users in opportune industrial contexts.

The original problem has been decomposed into three different steps: Initialization, Propagation, and Localization.

The first phase has been useful to compute the expertise values for workers. The second one has allowed to refine the found expertise through an iterative procedure involving an abstract Social Network of possible candidate experts. Finally, in the third step an update of experts has been made in terms of their social/geographical positions and contact time.

From a numerical point of view, further research should be developed. Some preliminary simulations, extended to some industrial Social Networks, are nowadays giving meaningful results for the correctness of the proposed approach w. r. t. already different ones. Indeed, the identified approach seems to give positive answers to practical difficulties within the Enterprise 2.0, with consequent resolution of industrial problems.

References

1. Balog, K., Azzopardi, L., de Rijke, M.: Formal models for expert finding in enterprise corpora. In: Proceedings of ACM SIGIR, pp. 43–50 (2006)
2. Bailey, P., Craswell, N., de Vries, A.P., Soboroff, I.: Overview of the TREC 2007 enterprise track. In: The Sixteenth Text REtrieval Conference Proceeding (2008)
3. Craswell, N., de Vries, A.P., Soboroff, I.: Overview of the TREC-2005 enterprise track. In: The Fourteenth Text Retrieval Conference Proceedings (2006)
4. Foggia, P., Percannella, G., Vento, M.: Graph matching and learning in pattern recognition in the last ten years. Int. J. Pattern Recognit. Artif. Intell. (In Press) (2013). doi: 10.1142/S0218001414500013
5. Soboroff, I., de Vries, A., Crawell, N.: Overview of the TREC 2006 enterprise track. In: The Fifteenth Text REtrieval Conference Proceedings (2007)
6. Ackerman, M., Wulf, V., Pipek, V.: Sharing Expertise: Beyond Knowledge Management. MIT Press, Cambridge (2002)
7. McDonald, D.D., Ackerman,M.: Just talk to me: a field study of expertise location. In: CSCW 1998, pp. 315–324 (1998)
8. Loia, V., De Maio, C., Fenza, G., Orciuoli, F., Senatore, S.: An enhanced approach to improve enterprise competency management, In: 2010 IEEE World Congress on Computational Intelligence, WCCI (2010)
9. Finkel, J.R., Grenager, T., Manning, C.: Incorporating non-local information into information extraction systems by gibbs sampling. In: Proceedings of ACL 2005, pp. 363–370 (2005)
10. Zhang, J., Tang, J., Li, J.: Expert finding in a social network. In: Kotagiri R., et al. (eds.) DASFAA 2007. Lecture Notes in Computer Science vol. 4443, pp. 1066–1069. Springer, Heidelberg (2007)
11. Felzenszwalb, P.F., Huttenlocher, D.P.: Efficient belief propagation for early vision. Int. J. Comput. Vision. 70(1), 41–54 (2006)
12. Golbeck, J.: Combining Provenance with trust in social networks for semantic web content filtering. In: Moreau L. et al (eds.) IPAW 2006. Lecture Notes in Computer Science, vol. 4145, pp. 101–108. Springer (2006)
13. Okamoto, K., Chen, W., Li, X.Y.: Ranking of closeness centrality for large-scale social networks. In: Preparata F.P. et al. (eds.) FAW 2008. Lecture Notes in Computer Science, vol. 5059, pp. 186–195. Springer, Heidelberg (2008)
14. Smirnova, E., Balog, K.: A User-oriented model for expert finding. In: Clough P. et al. (eds.) ECIR 2011. Lecture Notes in Computer Science, vol. 6611, pp. 580–592. Springer, Heidelberg (2011)

15. Bozzon, A., Brambilla, M., Ceri, S., Silvestri, M., Vesci, G.: Choosing the right crowd: expert finding in social networks. In: EDBT '13 Proceedings of the 16th International Conference on Extending Database Technology, pp. 637–648. ACM, New York (2013)
16. Demartini, G., Gaugaz, J., Nejdl, W.: A vector space model for ranking entities and its application to expert search. In: Boughanem M. et al. (eds.) ECIR 2009. Lecture Notes in Computer Science, vol. 5478, pp. 189–201. Springer, Heidelberg (2009)

User Evaluation Support Through Development Environment for Agile Software Teams

Shah Rukh Humayoun, Yael Dubinsky and Tiziana Catarci

Abstract User evaluation is generally performed early in the development process to reveal usability problems, design flaws, and errors and correct them before deploying. Due to the short iterations of agile development, implementing user evaluation as part of the development process is a challenge that is often neglected. In a previous work, we proposed an approach that would enable the integration of user evaluation throughout the development process, by managing and automating user evaluation activities from with the integrated development environment (IDE). In this work, we focus on a case study in which small-sized agile software teams, made up of students in an annual software engineering project course, applied our integrated user evaluation approach for developing their software projects. The feedbacks from these agile teams show the intuitiveness and effectiveness of our integration approach.

Keywords User evaluation · Automated evaluation · Integrated development environment (IDE) · Software development · Agile development

S. R. Humayoun (✉)
Computer Graphics and HCI Group, University of Kaiserslautern, Gottlieb-Daimler-Str., 67663 Kaiserslautern, Germany
e-mail: humayoun@cs.uni-kl.de

Y. Dubinsky
IBM Research—Haifa, Mount Carmel, 31905 Haifa, Israel
e-mail: dubinsky@il.ibm.com

T. Catarci
Dipartimento di Ingegneria Informatica, Automatica e Gestionale "A. Rubert", SAPIENZA Università di Roma, Via Arisoto 25, 00185 Rome, Italy
e-mail: catarci@diag.uniroma1.it

L. Caporarello et al. (eds.), *Smart Organizations and Smart Artifacts*,
Lecture Notes in Information Systems and Organisation 7,
DOI: 10.1007/978-3-319-07040-7_18,
© Springer International Publishing Switzerland 2014

1 Introduction

Poor usability and inefficient end-product design are common causes [3, 19] of failed software products. These causes can be avoided by involving end users in design, development, and evaluation activities. The current state of the art includes many approaches and techniques for involving end users throughout the software lifecycle for different purposes [7, 22]. The *user-based evaluation*, or *user evaluation* approach, deals with methods that involve real end users in the evaluation process for judging the design and the usability level of the product [7, 22]. A big challenge with this approach is collecting the end users' feedback and then analyzing their behavior in an effective and efficient manner, so as to draw useful conclusions. Moreover, these conclusions must be applied accordingly to the ensuing development process to improve user experience in the final product.

The agile approach [1, 2, 23] is a software development approach that has emerged over the last decade. It is used for constructing software products in an iterative and incremental manner, in which each iteration produces working artifacts that are valuable to the customers and to the project. Since most of the user evaluation activities are performed manually [17], they are time-consuming and effort-intense. Examining projects in which the agile development approach is implemented, we found that due to budget and schedule concerns, software teams typically hesitate to perform user evaluation activities. Neglecting them totally or partially applying only near the end of the process increases the risk of software failure. Automating user evaluation encourages the agile software teams to engage in these activities throughout the software lifecycle. Moreover, the automation provides several benefits, including reduced time and costs, improved error tracing, better feedback, and increased coverage of evaluated features [17].

We previously proposed a way to manage and automate the user evaluation activities from within the integrated development environment [9, 10, 14–16]. The motivation behind this IDE-level user evaluation integration is clear. The method equips development teams with a mechanism to monitor and control a continuous user evaluation process tightly coupled with the development process. This keeps the time and resource constraints of short-term development iterations, especially the agile iterations, well in control. Providing support for user-centric design and evaluation in software development is not a new idea. Many studies have been done in this regard. Examples of studies in which user-centric design, development, and evaluation was applied or integrated into software development, specifically into agile development, can be found in [5, 6, 11, 12, 20, 21, 23]. The main difference between our approach and these is that ours tightly integrates user-centric design, development, and evaluation with the software development environment. The management, automation, and traceability at the IDE level bridges the gap between the user evaluation and the software teams and fuses the user experience with the development process, thus achieving a high level of usability and an efficient design in the resulting product.

In this paper, we focus on a case study in which we worked with agile software teams in academia who applied our integrated user-evaluation approach during development of their software projects. These agile development teams were made up of fourth-year computer science majors taking the Annual Project in Software Engineering course. These agile software teams used our developed evaluation tool, called UEMan [10, 14], for automating and managing the process of user evaluation at the development environment level. In this work, we focus on the development methodology used while working with these teams and the evaluation strategy applied for performing the user evaluations. Moreover, we highlight the teams' feedback to show the effect of our integrated approach on these teams during the development. The feedback shows that the team members were engaged in performing user evaluation on an iteration basis in a natural and intuitive manner.

The remainder of this paper is structured as follows: Sect. 2 gives an overview of the integrated approach and Sect. 3 describes the given project, the development approach, the evaluation strategy, and the teams' feedback in the case study. Finally, we conclude in Sect. 4.

2 Background: The Integration Approach

We emphasize the management and automation of user evaluation activities to be done at the development-environment level, as it helps to overcome the challenges of short-time development iterations. This IDE-level integration makes the agile development teams to feel the user evaluation as an integral part of the development process. Therefore, they feel more comfortable with applying the evaluation activities alongside the development activities. Our integration approach means performing the following activities, from the agile software teams' perspectives, alongside the regular development activities from within the development environment:

- **Experiment Entity**: Our approach toward integrating user-evaluation automation at the IDE level means that we can add a new kind of an object in the development area of a software project. These objects, which we refer to as *experiments* because of the controlled environment in which they are performed, can be created and executed to provide evaluation data. Furthermore, an experiment's results can be associated with future development tasks as they emerge. We categorized these experiments into two categories: *user-based* experiments (e.g., question-asking protocol), in which the evaluating users perform different tasks on the target system or evaluate the system based on any given criteria, and *system-based* experiments (e.g., log file or task-environment analysis), in which the automated tools are used to record users' and system behavior while end users work on the system.

- **Derived Development Tasks**: Each kind of evaluation experiment has its own criteria for judging the product. Support for the analysis of the experiments' results enables the comparison of these results against the targeted criteria (e.g., usability criteria or some design standard). If the results show a failure to achieve the target level, then new development tasks can be defined accordingly. Each development task is associated with the relevant data, thus providing its rationale.
- **Code Traceability**: Automating the process of backward and forward traceability among different evolving parts, at the development-environment level, provides a better traceability of the refinement carried out in the design to improve the product. Such parts could include code parts, experiments, and derived development tasks. One of the benefits of this mechanism is that it helps to reveal the impact of the evaluations.
- **Developing Evaluation Aspects**: Automating user-evaluation activities in the development environment can enable developers to add automatic evaluation hooks to the software under development. For example, an aspect could be created to control the use of a specific button or key that is part of the developing software. System-based methods that include such measures provide insights about the users' behavior. A practical example of this is the use of Aspect-Oriented Programming (AOP) [18] to facilitate such automatic evaluation.

Figure 1 shows the relationships between the above-described activities. Adding automatic evaluation hooks provides the desired user behavioral data (e.g., a specific key stroke at a particular phase of task) either to other evaluation experiments or directly for the analysis. The evaluation entities also provide users' evaluation data and their feedback. The software team analyzes the users' data, received from the evaluation entities and the automatic evaluation hooks, to determine new development tasks if the results were not satisfied. Throughout this process, the code is associated to these evaluation activities (shown in the figure by the dashed-lines) for keeping the backward and forward traceability among different evaluation activities and software parts. This helps the software team in understanding how the software evolves given the effects of performing different evaluation activities.

3 The Case Study

In this section, we describe the case study in which agile software teams, made up of students, used our integrated user-evaluation approach for automating and managing the user evaluation from the development environment, alongside performing the development activities.

The agile teams were made up of 4th year computer science majors participating in the Annual Project in Software Engineering course of the Computer Science Department at the Technion—Israel Institute of Technology. Thirty-seven

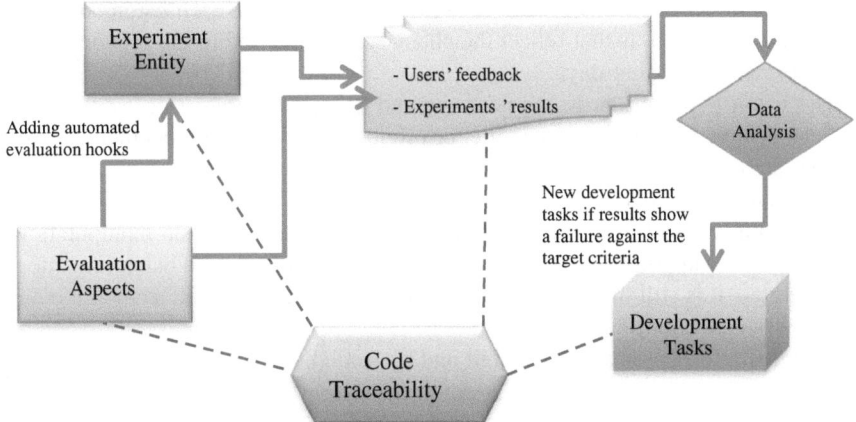

Fig. 1 The relationship among different evaluation activities. The *arrows* show the data flow, while the *dashed lines* show the connectivity among the different activities and the related code parts for keeping the backward and forward traceability

students were divided into six agile teams, with each team consisting of six or seven students. Specification for a project called *FTSp (Follow the Sun Plug-in)* [4] was given to all teams, and our previously-developed tool, UEMan [10, 14], was presented for performing the evaluation experiments at the IDE level. UEMan is an Eclipse[1] plug-in that supports the automation and management of different user and usability evaluation activities as part of the Eclipse IDE. Furthermore, it provides a library to enable development of Java aspects for the creation of automatic measures to increase the breadth of the evaluation data.

In the next sections, we briefly introduce the FTS project and then we describe the development methodology we used while working with the agile teams. We then explain our evaluation strategy, and finally, we summarize the integrated user evaluation effects on development and give the teams' feedback. We do not describe the conducted experiments' details and results, as our focus in this paper is on highlighting how these teams worked with the integrated approach.

4 The FTS Project

The Follow the Sun project (FTS) aims at supporting the synchronization among distributed teams that have no synchronous communication due to time zone difference. The FTS project consists of the following features:

---

[1] http://www.eclipse.org/

- A Java project can contain a set of objects named *batons*; each baton contains a set of change objects that reflect the changes that occurred in the product during the previous working day.
- The baton is passed on to the next site and accepted there.
- Each change in source file, test file, or product design can be documented using text, audio, or video.
- The plug-in supports a time view of the different sites, calendar features (including support for different calendars and clocks), and event manipulations.
- The plug-in supports alerts for generating or not generating the baton (e.g., don't generate—it is still in "our" site; generate—the vacation of the team at the next site was cancelled).
- Automatic measures are calculated and presented.

4.1 The Development Methodology

In this section, we describe the development methodology we used while working with these software development teams. Our approach is based on agile development [2] and is presented using three main perspectives: human/social (H), organizational (O), and technical (T). More information about the HOT framework that provides case analysis using these three perspectives can be found in [13].

As part of the human/social perspective, the main ideas we foster are teamwork, collaboration, and reflection. Teams meet every week for a four-hour compulsory meeting in which they communicate regarding the product development and the process management. Periodically, team members reflect on their activities. From an organizational perspective, this project was defined by two releases. Each was composed of two iterations of three weeks, i.e., four development iterations. Roles were ascribed to each of the team members as part of the team management; e.g., in charge of unit testing, tracking, or designing (see more details regarding the role scheme at [8]). Each of the role holders presented measure(s) for the relevant responsibilities.

From a technical perspective, the following practices were used: automated testing, continuous integration, and refactoring to ensure simple design. The role scheme supported these practices by emphasizing the appropriate practices for specific iterations and changing the role scheme accordingly in other iterations. For instance, the person in charge of continuous integration worked mainly at the first iteration to provide the infrastructure and work procedure, refactoring activities were the responsibility of the designer at the third iteration, and so on.

The user evaluation of the product being developed is yet another practice that was implemented as part of this project. Based on our experience with guiding the implementation of the agile approach [8, 13, 24], and the integration of user and usability evaluation in the last few years in agile projects in the industry and academia [9, 10, 13, 15], the main practices we used are as follows:

- Iterative design activities that included cycles of development containing development tasks that were derived from user and usability evaluation.
- Role holders in the subject of user and usability evaluation and using UEMan.
- Measurements taken by the role holders as part of fulfilling their responsibilities.

4.2 The Evaluation Strategy

User evaluation was done as a team exercise. The six FTS development teams, each consisting of six or seven members, used UEMan to evaluate FTS version 1.0, and accordingly derived development tasks to implement as part of FTS version 1.1. The teams were asked to define and execute two kinds of evaluation experiments. The members of each *team i*, in addition to running their evaluation exercises, served as inspectors for *team i-1* in the first type of experiment and as users for *team i-2* in the second type of experiment. This way, each team worked with 12 participants, 6 for each experiment.

Teams were asked to summarize the results including their own evaluation and severity rankings, group brainstorms, and final results. Based on the final results, teams were asked to suggest three specific development tasks for subsequent iterations.

4.3 Effects on Development and Teams' Feedback

Teams summarized their results, including the observers' notes, the complete data gathered, and the results' analysis. Based on these results, several development tasks were defined, which were then implemented in the next iterations. For example, one significant suggestion was to make the content of the baton more accessible. It was also suggested to introduce more direct means for viewing the code changes. Indeed, reviewing a particular code change directly from within a dedicated view became possible in the next development iteration.

The different teams provided feedback on the contribution of our integrated user-evaluation approach. Among other comments, teams mentioned the good collaboration between the team and the participants, the benefit of recognizing new issues, and the ability of UEMan to automate the results summary, enabling them to identify significant problems and define development tasks accordingly.

As part of the evaluation study, we found that the software teams' members engaged in user evaluation activities in a natural and intuitive manner. They were able to analyze experiments' results for their project and they successfully derived significant development tasks accordingly.

Note that although we focused on studying the contribution of UEMan to the evaluation of FTS, we found a high severity problem in UEMan related to the Expert Evaluation Form (see [14] for the detail of the Evaluation Form). The information that the participants fill in using this form is lost once the unification is done. This problem, along with other issues, was solved in a subsequent version of UEMan.

5 Concluding Remarks

In this paper, we focused on a case study in which small-size agile teams from the academia adopted our integrated approach for the evaluation of their software project. They used the UEMan tool for managing and automating the process of user evaluation from within their development environment. We believe that implementing user evaluation into the development tooling, such as in the case of UEMan, ensures an explicit process that is documented and realized by the entire development team. This was shown in the feedback provided by these teams, in which they cited a higher identification of significant problems found through working this approach. Moreover, we highlighted the development methodology we used while working with these agile teams. In this development methodology, we also incorporated our integrated user-evaluation approach. The teams recognized an improvement in team members' collaboration while working with this development methodology and were able to recognize issues that they had not before seen. Overall, the feedback shows that an IDE-level integration approach encourages the agile software teams in engaging in evaluation activities. In the future, we intend to apply our approach to medium-to large-scale software projects to properly check its feasibility and effectiveness.

References

1. Abrahamsson, P., Salo, O., Ronkainen, J., Warsta, J.: Agile software development methods—review and analysis. Technical Report 478, VTT Publications (2002)
2. Agile-Alliance.: Manifesto for agile software development. Technical re-port. http://www.agilealliance.org (2001)
3. Anderson, J., Fleek, F., Garrity, K., Drake, F.: Integrating usability techniques into software development. IEEE Softw. **18**(1), 46–53 (2001)
4. Carmel, E., Espinosa, J.A., Dubinsky, Y.: "Follow the sun" workflow in global software development. J. Manag. Inf. Syst. **27**(1), 17–38 (2010)
5. Chamberlain, S., Sharp, H., Maiden, N.A.M.: Towards a framework for integrating agile development and user-centred design. In: Abrahamsson, P., Marchesi, M., Succi, G. (eds.) XP 2006. LNCS, vol. 4044, pp. 143–153. Springer, Heidelberg (2006)

6. Constantine, L.L., Lockwood, L.A.D.: Usage-centered software engineering: an agile approach to integrating users, user interfaces, and usability into software engineering practice. In: ICSE '03, IEEE Computer Society, Washington, DC, USA, pp. 746–747 (2003)

7. Dix, A., Finlay, J.E., Abowd, G.D., Beale, R.: Human-Computer Interaction, 3rd edn. Prentice-Hall Inc, Upper Saddle River (2003)

8. Dubinsky, Y., Hazzan, O.: The construction process of a framework for teaching software development methods. Comput. Sci. Educ. **15**(4), 275–296 (2005)

9. Dubinsky, Y., Catarci, T., Humayoun, S.R., Kimani, S.: Integrating user evaluation into software development environments. In: 2nd DELOS Conference on Digital Libraries, Pisa, Italy (December 5–7, 2007)

10. Dubinsky, Y., Humayoun, S.R., Catarci, T.: Eclipse plug-into manage user centered design. In: Workshop on the Interplay between Usability Evaluation and Software Development (I-USED), Pisa, Italy (2008)

11. Göransson, B., Gulliksen, J., Boivie, I.: The usability design process—integrating user-centered systems design in the software development process. Softw. Process Improv. Pract. **8**, 111–131 (2003)

12. Gulliksen, J., Goransson, B., Boivie, I., Blomkvist, S., Persson, J., Cajander, A.: Key principles for user-centered systems design. Behav. Inf. Technol. **22**(6), 397–409 (2003)

13. Hazzan, O., Dubinsky, Y.: Agile software engineering. In: Undergraduate Topics in Computer Science Series. Springer, London (2008)

14. Humayoun, S.R., Dubinsky, Y., Catarci, T.: UEMan: a tool to manage user evaluation in development environments. In: ICSE, pp. 551–554. IEEE press, Vancouver (2009)

15. Humayoun, S.R., Dubinsky, Y., Catarci, T.: A three-fold integration framework to incorporate user-centered design into agile software development. In: Kurosu, M. (ed.) HCD'11, pp. 55–64. Springer, Berlin (2011)

16. Humayoun, S.R.: Incorporating usability evaluation in software development environments. Künstliche Intelligenz **26**(2), 197–200 (2012)

17. Ivory, M.Y., Hearst, M.A.: The state of the art in automating usability evaluation of user interfaces. ACM Comput. Surv. **33**, 470–516 (2001)

18. Kiczales, G., Mezini, M.: Aspect-oriented programming and modular reasoning. In: ICSE '05. ACM, New York, NY, USA, pp. 49–58 (2005)

19. Landauer, T.K.: The Trouble with Computers: Usefulness, Usability, and Productivity. The MIT Press, Cambridge (1996)

20. Lohmann, S., Rashid, A.: Fostering remote user participation and integration of user feedback into software development. In: I-USED (2008)

21. Patton, J.: Hitting the target: adding interaction design to agile software development. In: OOPSLA 2002. ACM, New York (2002)

22. Rogers, Y., Sharp, H., Preece, J.: Interaction Design—Beyond Human-Computer Interaction, 3rd edn. Wiley, Chichester (2012)

23. Sy, D.: Adapting usability investigations for agile user-centered design. J. Usability Stud. **2**(3), 112–130 (2000)

24. Talby, D., Hazzan, O., Dubinsky, Y., Keren, A.: Agile software testing in a large-scale project. IEEE Softw. (Special Issue on Software Testing) **23**(4), 30–37 (2006)

"Each to His Own": Distinguishing Activities, Roles and Artifacts in EUD Practices

Federico Cabitza, Daniela Fogli and Antonio Piccinno

Abstract End-User Development (EUD) studies how to empower end users (among which, e.g., professionals and organizational workers) to modify, adapt and extend the software systems they daily use, thus coping with the evolving needs of their work organizations and the shop-floor environment. This research area is becoming increasingly important also for the cross fertilization of ideas and approaches that come from the fields of Information Systems and Human-Computer Interaction. However, if one considers the variety of research proposals stemming from this common ground, there is the risk of losing denotational precision of the key terms adopted in the common vocabulary of EUD. To counteract this natural semantic drift, the objective of this paper is to distinguish within three EUD complementary important notions, namely activities, roles, and artifacts, in order to help researchers deepen important phenomena regarding the "meta-design" of systems built to support EUD practices.

Keywords End-user development · User task · Meta-design · Intermediary object · Knowledge artifact

F. Cabitza
Università degli Studi di Milano-Bicocca, Milan, Italy
e-mail: cabitza@disco.unimib.it

D. Fogli
Università degli Studi di Brescia, Brescia, Italy
e-mail: fogli@ing.unibs.it

A. Piccinno (✉)
Università degli Studi di Bari, Bari, Italy
e-mail: antonio.piccinno@uniba.it

L. Caporarello et al. (eds.), *Smart Organizations and Smart Artifacts*, 193
Lecture Notes in Information Systems and Organisation 7,
DOI: 10.1007/978-3-319-07040-7_19,
© Springer International Publishing Switzerland 2014

1 Introduction

Humanist studies and disciplines have often provided Information Systems (IS) and Human-Computer Interaction (HCI) researchers with sets of so-called "sensitizing" concepts, that is terms and expressions that "help analysts unpack the social organization of cooperative activities" [1]. However, a natural semantic drift usually occurs when such sensitizing concepts are borrowed by scholars of different disciplines. This has occurred, especially in the HCI field, with regard to the concepts of boundary object [2], community of practice [3], and appropriation [4], as well as to the recent concept of meta-design [5]. In this drift, as also argued in [6], subtle but yet important nuances of the original concepts are either completely lost or get blurred in the description and analysis of social settings; in this way, they fail to inform requirement elicitation and Information Technology (IT) design to their full potential.

The objective of this paper is to shed light on three necessary notions, which could help researchers better analyze subtle but yet important phenomena for a more successful meta-design in End-User Development (EUD) initiatives [7, 8]. Indeed, in 2003, EUD has been defined as "the set of methods, techniques, and tools that allow users of software systems, who are acting as non-professional software developers, at some point to create, modify, or extend a software artifact" [9]. However, if one analyses the variety of proposals in the EUD field, like those included, for example, in the book on EUD [9] or in the proceedings of the so far four editions of the International Symposium on EUD, it is possible to observe that, over the years, such a definition became blurred and too general, due to the possibilities provided by technology today (e.g., the advent of the Web 2.0 and 3.0) that ten years ago people could not anticipate. Indeed, the objective of this paper is to propose a clear distinction in the EUD discourse between complementary articulations around three perspectives: namely, the perspectives of *activities*, *roles* and *artifacts*, according, respectively, to the aim and scope of the EUD practice, to whom is to take advantage of the product of such a practice, and lastly to the role of mediation played by IT artifacts in EUD scenarios. This threefold articulation is based on a series of field studies that the authors have performed in the last years in heterogeneous and unrelated EUD projects, whose main element in common has been the endeavor of adapting the meta-design framework to real communities of practice and practitioners.

The paper is organized as follows. Section 2 presents a classification of EUD activities. In Sect. 3 the roles in EUD practices are discussed, while in Sect. 4 a classification of the artifacts as a result of the different EUD activities is presented. Finally, in Sect. 5 the implications that the three articulations may have on meta-design activities and on the role of meta-designers are discussed.

2 Activities

To disentangle EUD articulations, we propose at first to classify EUD into *individual EUD* and *public EUD* (see Fig. 1). Individual EUD encompasses all those activities that lead to the creation, modification or extension of a software artifact for personal use only. Typical examples of individual EUD regard spreadsheet programming [10], where end users create or modify formulas and macros for their own purposes, or scripting environments for statistical computing and graphics, like R and MatLab, by which experts in scientific domains (biology, statistics, geology, etc.) write usually short bunches of software code to analyze and display their data autonomously [11]. Individual EUD is the main research subject of End-User Software Engineering (EUSE) [12], which proposes a variety of methods for requirement analysis and specification, system design and reuse, verification and testing, code debugging, specifically devoted to non-professional software developers.

However, in many situations, single end users either program or configure software artifacts that are used by (or also by) *other* people, as in the case of multi-tiered proxy design problems [13, 14]. Usually these people are colleagues and co-workers (as in the case of the Electronic Patient Record in [15]), but also people working in other departments, contexts, and communities (as in the case of e-government in [16]): In this case, we speak of public EUD, since the outcome of the EUD activity is aimed at being shared and publicly available to others than the end user involved in the programming activity. The main difference between public and individual EUD is then the explicit intention behind the programming effort: either making something intended to be shared or not, respectively.

Public EUD can be further specialized into *inward EUD* and *outward EUD*. In the former case, the people carrying out any EUD activity work for a community they also belong to, with or without the intention to build an artifact that could be adopted also in other, possibly different, settings. Although this cannot be a priori excluded, EUD activities are intended to support members of small teams and groups of people sharing sets of conventions, assumptions and practices, i.e., in many cases what are called "communities of practice" [17]. In these settings many things can be given for granted and computational support is intentionally adjusted in a "quick and dirty" fashion to achieve effectiveness and flexibility, rather than maintainability and transferability. An example is a "pipe" in Yahoo!Pipes: this is usually developed for personal use, but it can also (either intentionally or unintentionally) be shared among the Yahoo!Pipes community. In the outward EUD case, conversely, the quality of the software artifacts is more likely to be purposely pursued, as the EUD activity is intentionally aimed at building and improving tools that are to be used across different communities or, even, in other communities.

In the case of inward EUD, who undertakes EUD tasks is usually denoted with a number of different names, like "power user", "gardener" or "local developer" [18]; these terms are usually used to indicate someone who, belonging to a given community, works for the proficiency of the community itself, in virtue of a deep

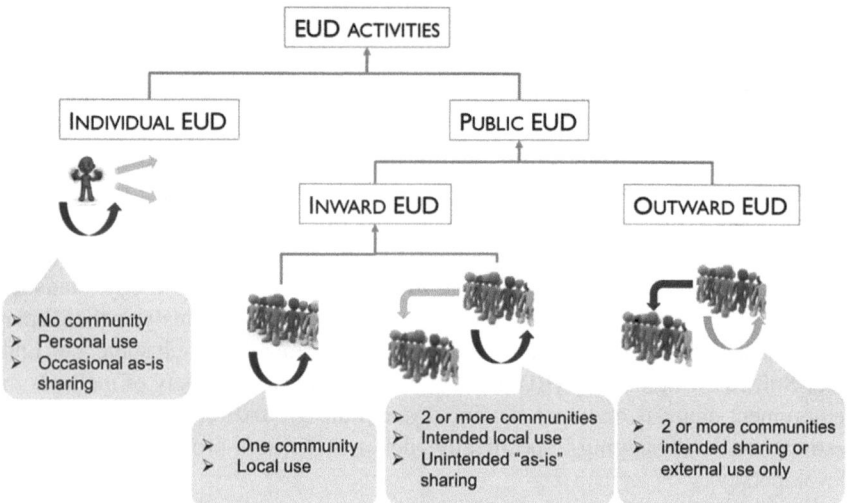

Fig. 1 EUD activities articulation

and often tacit knowledge of the characteristics and skills of its members. For example, in the case of the Electronic Patient Record discussed in [15], the head physician is called to visually compose the software environment, i.e., the electronic patient record that will be used in her/his ward by her/his colleagues and co-workers. In [19], the authors report of a system in which doctors could create simple rules so that relevant information displayed in their medical records could be highlighted according to the context. Another example is in the archaeological context: in [20], it is described how professional guides use different software solutions that allow them to create personal information spaces, which could be shared with other colleagues through annotation mechanisms.

Conversely, in outward EUD, at least two communities are involved and there is no guarantee that those who carry out EUD activities will also take advantage of the product of these activities; this case has been investigated to a lesser extent by the EUD community, but, nevertheless, can occur in complex and important domains. For instance, in [21] the authors report how civil servants, acting as non-professional software developers, are called to create e-government services for citizens; in [13] it is described how, in a similar way, mobile user interfaces for disabled patients can be easily developed by caregivers (parents or assistants) by means of a script-based system; in [22], it is reported and discussed how editorial staff members of a Web shop portal may be asked to personalize systems for shop owners, and, finally, in the archaeological context mentioned above [20, 23], each guide can retrieve and compose, via a desktop application, the material for his/her personal information space to be shown to a group of visitors during a visit of an archaeological park.

This classification, far from being a rigid taxonomy of EUD practices, hints rather at a spectrum of possible uses (see Fig. 1) and is provided for its role in pointing to specific design implications that will be discussed in Sect. 5.

3 Roles

Distinguishing between kinds of activities allows also to consider more precisely scopes and roles involved in those activities. In particular, in addition to the oft-cited roles of the *end user* and *meta-designer,* we propose to consider also the roles of *domain developer* and *maieuta-designer*, according to the task these people are supposed to undertake in an EUD process of IT artifact construction.

As widely known, the end user is a passive user of the IT artifact and consumer of its products and services.

We propose the term "domain developer" to subsume all those roles that are in charge of carrying out EUD activities, like the above mentioned "power user", "local developer", "gardener", "end-user developer" [14], "bricolant bricoleur" [24]. Therefore, a domain developer is a domain expert actively involved in the so-called *meta-task* of improving the system used in the domain-specific task: such a task is "meta" in that it is aimed at creating better artifacts for the main tasks in the work domain at hand.

Likewise, the meta-designer is someone involved in the design of the EUD environment and tools by which domain developers can build their own artifacts. Therefore, s/he is usually a professional software developer in charge of creating the *technical* conditions for EUD practice, according to a vision of meta-design as a two-phase process [7, 25]: The former consisting of designing the design environment, the latter consisting of designing the artifacts for end users using the design environment.

On the other hand, the maieuta-designer specializes some of the activities that previous literature contributions assigned to the meta-designer and which are more concerned with the establishment and conservation of the most favorable social conditions for empowering and motivating users in shaping their tools at use time [5, 8]. This role actually encompasses and subsumes those that are involved in the task of supporting the meta-task of the domain developers, that is of having the domain experts (playing the role of domain developers) internalize the design culture and the technical notions necessary for the meta-task of artifact development. The maieuta-designer is therefore supposed to facilitate the evolution of single users from being passive end users of their tools to become domain developers, that is domain experts capable to develop their own tools and make them more fit to their settings, or at least to empower and help end users appropriate their IT artifacts more actively and consciously, so that they can commit themselves in improving the artifact e.g., by simply reporting shortcomings and system faults, and expressing due modifications and appreciated improvements to whom it concerns or is able to intervene (i.e., the domain developers or the IT professionals, if available). For this reason we call such a designer a maieuta-designer, partly in analogy with the Socratic method of getting people acquire notions, motivations and self-confidence to undertake challenging tasks by themselves, and partly in clear assonance with the term meta-designer, of which it is a specialization more oriented to work practice and EUD activities than to IT design and development [24]. The maieuta-designer role is also in line with a new and more recent vision of EUD that considers it (and meta-design) as one of the foundations of the cultures of participation rather than a mere technical instrument [8].

Domain developer and maieuta-designer are just new roles that we have introduced to specify the activities of the end user and meta-designer in EUD practice (see Fig. 2). However, nothing prevents that the same person plays different roles at different degrees: for example, especially in individual EUD, the end user actually becomes, at some time, a domain developer. Similarly, the roles of meta-designer and maieuta-designer could be played by a software engineer and by a HCI expert respectively, as in the case described in [26], or both roles may be played by a professional software developer as in [13]. In the same vein, the maieuta-designer could be occasionally just the most passionate one of the practitioners involved in an EUD initiative, who tries to convince his/her colleagues to join the initiative as well and have an active stake in the continuous improvement of the IT artifacts that are in their partial or total control.

Indeed, as Fig. 2 shows, these four roles are also aimed at representing a sort of continuum in the attitude towards the IT artifact, from the less active one, i.e., the end user that just uses the IT artifact and occasionally gives feedback to the person who is officially accountable for its quality, often on a professional basis (i.e., the meta-designer). Compliant with the EUD tenets, our categorization does not force domain analysis to fit actors into narrow boxes that do not reflect the complexity of real work settings; quite the opposite we recognize such a complexity considering that no wall should be established between roles, and that responsibilities, although clear at any given time, can change as the project unfolds over time and contributions are given on a voluntary basis irrespective of the intended planning. The unpredictability and necessary openness of EUD projects is what makes them substantially different from traditional software engineering projects and urges for role and activity models that could cope with situated processes of IT appropriation and collaborative development of the technology in a community context.

4 Artifacts

The classification proposed above, which distinguishes between individual EUD and public EUD, as well as between inward and outward EUD, allows also to distinguish in a finer-grained manner the IT artifacts used by the roles involved in those activities.

In particular, it is useful to distinguish between: *personal artifacts*, which are used by single users that employ the EUD environment for their own purposes, as

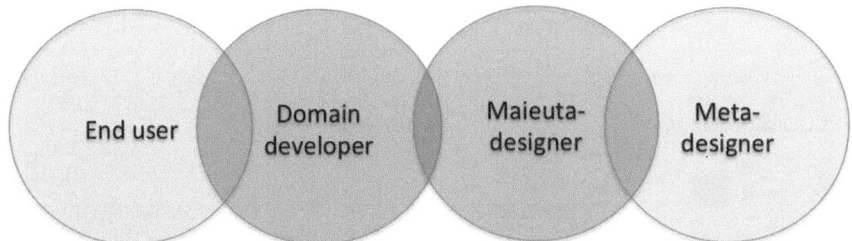

Fig. 2 Roles in EUD practices

in the case of spreadsheet programming; and *intermediary objects*. These are objects that are shared, exchanged and circulated among members of networks and communities to mediate their interactions [27]; in so doing, they represent the intermediate steps of any design or meta-design task [28], i.e., "the traces as well as the outputs of a collaborative transformational process" [29] and thus support the continuous process by which they and other objects evolve over time. Personal artifacts and intermediary objects mirror the EUD activities that they support: individual and public EUD, respectively. Intermediary objects can be further distinguished in *knowledge artifacts* and *boundary objects*, as extremes of a continuous range that do not only cross boundaries but also contribute in shaping them [29, 30]. Boundary objects is the notion introduced by Bowker and Star in [31] to account for those artifacts that enable a sort of standardized and effectively simplified communication and coordination between members of different communities of practice; knowledge artifacts, on the other hand, are artifacts that enable and support learning and innovation within a specific community of practice, that is processes of knowledge acquisition, circulation and creation among its members [32]. This spectrum of EUD artifacts is illustrated in Fig. 3.

In the EUD literature, boundary objects are often recognized between the community of end users and the community of the IT professionals (i.e., meta- and maieuta-designers) involved in the digitization process (e.g. [33]). Although this can be perfectly the case, we should always remember that, in a real EUD scenario, IT professionals should be present only at the inception of a digitization project, as EUD is ultimately aimed at making end users autonomous in the long run. For this reason, in standard use, speaking of EUD software artifacts as intermediary objects seems more appropriate. That notwithstanding, either boundary objects or knowledge artifacts, as particular instances of intermediary objects, cannot be rigidly associated with either Inward or Outward EUD activities: it is a matter of analysis to understand what roles an IT artifact is playing in an organizational domain and understand how to support it computationally. Indeed, on one hand, inward EUD addresses IT artifacts that often play the role of knowledge artifact; moreover, hosting or being the objective of inward EUD activities make those IT artifacts become also knowledge artifacts in the process itself of development, as these latter end up by "mirroring and reflecting" how the community (or its

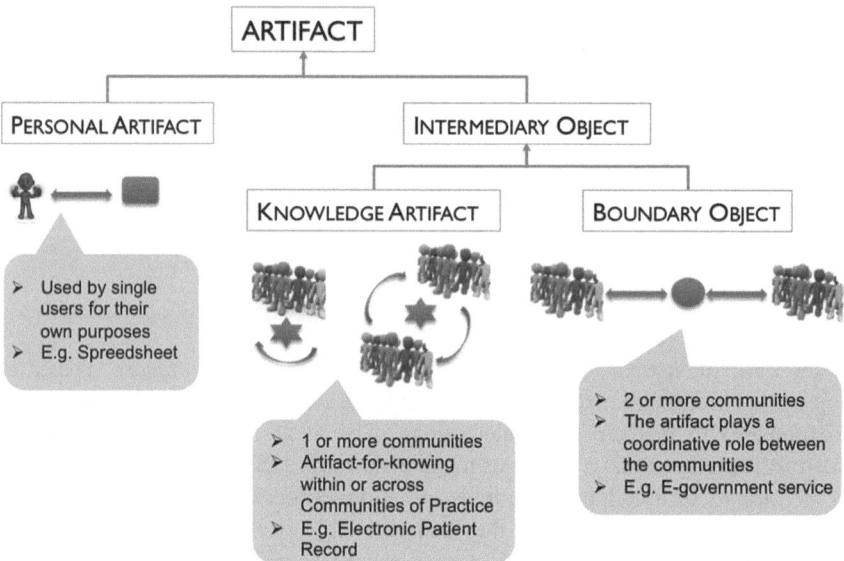

Fig. 3 EUD artifacts articulation

domain developers) has improved both the work tasks and the meta-tasks that characterize the community itself. This is for example the case of the Electronic Patient Record in the medical domain [15, 19, 23], which represents a shared artifact within a hospital ward and among different wards, useful for accumulating and sharing knowledge about each patient. In outward activities IT artifacts can "fertilize" different communities, by enabling activities that require some learning by the members of the "receiving" community: therefore also in this case it is possible to speak of knowledge artifacts "across communities of practice" [32]. On the other hand, outward EUD always encompasses the transfer of more or less full-fledged IT artifacts from one community to another, but this does not necessarily imply that these latter will play any coordinative role between these two communities, thus being boundary objects as Bowker and Star defined them originally [31]. However, one of the main reasons why a community could want to develop tools to be given to other communities is to achieve a better communication and alignment of meanings, purposes and activities, so as to make those tools effective boundary objects: for instance, an administrative office could provide a commercial office with a partially precompiled spreadsheet to have commercial agents fill in expense accounts more accurately and completely, as reported in [34]. Another example is in the e-government domain, where a civil servant may create the description of an e-government service, which gives rise to the automatic generation of both the web pages to be used by citizens to apply for the service, and of the web pages to be used by administrative employees to manage citizens' requests [16].

Once again, our point is that distinguishing between different activities, roles and artifacts is not a nominalist effort, but rather an analytic stance that allows for detecting nuances that could call for different design approaches, quality requirements and EUD solutions.

5 Discussion and Conclusion

In this paper we proposed a threefold "activity, role and artifact" perspective in EUD, in order to address complementary and mutually affecting components of an EUD project. As said above, our effort is not merely taxonomic, but rather oriented to the situated practices of requirement analysis and design. Indeed, a fine-grained articulation of roles can help in understanding how to deploy efficient training programs and apply effective rewarding mechanisms; for instance, distinguishing between end-user, domain developer, and meta- and maieuta-designer, according to the level of involvement in the process of artifact production, can help in detecting different tasks to be supported in different ways and hence in shedding light on specific meta-design principles. On the other hand, distinguishing what kind of preexisting artifact has to be digitized in an organizational domain, that is focusing on what main role a traditional artifact is playing, which has to be substituted by a software application or IT artifact, would help designers invest on more critical functionalities that are typically necessary in one case, but redundant if not detrimental in the other one, or in detecting a palette of reusable off-the-shelf EUD components to offer to domain developers. In the same light, the analysis we outlined above on the distinction between individual and public EUD suggests to reconsider meta-design priorities and the meta-designer's role.

To this aim, we find it interesting to recall the seminal work of Grudin [35], who discusses the different emphasis put on utility and usability of software systems in different development contexts: whilst in in-house and internal system development emphasis is rightly put more on utility since IT artifacts are built around their intended functionalities, in commercial projects it is conversely usability the most important characteristic, as one of the priorities is to facilitate system acceptance by users and therefore increase the likelihood of success of the digitization process. This tension between utility and usability has also influenced different approaches to IT artifact development that have been pursued in the IS and HCI communities over the years respectively. Nowadays, the cross-fertilization of these two research fields can provide insights for dealing with this controversial relation between usability and utility that in the EUD discourse revives as a primary concern and can find, hopefully, an effective solution.

On the one hand, if one considers individual EUD and public/inward EUD, emphasis should be mainly put on utility: indeed, EUD activities encompass system adaptation and extension to increase effectiveness of the individual user and/or of the whole community. Usually this is achieved through development techniques that are very close to traditional programming languages, such as macro or script development, component-based development and programming by examples. This requires that domain experts are trained (or even self-trained) in programming methods and languages, so as to become what we have therefore called "domain developers", that is domain experts that develop IT artifacts for their own domain or setting. More specifically, in individual EUD, end users and domain developers coincide as people who are in control of modifying the IT artifact for their own purpose.

Conversely, in public/outward EUD, domain developers modify the IT artifact by constantly taking into account the requests of other end users, for the sake of the whole community's advantage, a community they often do not belong to.

As a consequence, to support the meta-task of domain developers in individual EUD and public/inward EUD, meta-designers must focus on the design of EUD tools and infrastructures for communication within the community, whilst the maieuta-designer must focus on the proper training of the domain developers, and on managing the risk and the impact that the system under evolution may have on the organization and its work practices.

On the other hand, in public/outward EUD, artifacts must be designed more carefully for at least two reasons: first, because these artifacts will be used by people that did not participate in the development process and could find contacting the developers very hard, if not impossible at all. In fact, an EUD artifact is not guaranteed by any commercial company, nor a help desk exists to troubleshoot its problems or provide guidance about its proper use. Secondly, it is possible that other non-professional software developers will have to adjust the artifacts to make them more suitable and fit to the community of end users where these are eventually adopted. This means that public/outward EUD requires a greater emphasis on usability: not only tools supporting domain developers must fit their characteristics, skills and background, but also the artifacts created for end users by the domain developers must be usable as well. Thus, in this case, EUD techniques must be both informed by domain-specific concepts and oriented toward the support of daily work practices: for instance, EUD environments in e-government [21] and medical projects [36] adopt the metaphors of the form-based interaction and of the active document because these recalls the usual ways work is accomplished in those domains. Furthermore, the activity of domain developers consists of creating software artifacts for people that belong to a different community; thus, proper mechanisms for making artifact creation easier and code generation transparent, that is free of unnecessary implementation details or language-specific technicalities, must be defined, along with procedures that guarantee the creation of usable artifacts [37]. Both aspects still regard the meta-task of domain developers, which should be supported no more with training in programming, but rather with user-friendly and visually engaging EUD systems [38], along with proper incentive and rewarding mechanisms. Therefore, in public/outward EUD, the meta-designer must pay more attention on easy-to-use EUD techniques and automatic code generation mechanisms (for example through meta-modeling [39]), whilst the maieuta-designer must focus on motivation strategies.

In light of the considerations mentioned above, novel meta-design guidelines emerge and should be refined and put to the "test of life". Therefore, our future work will be aimed at extending the current proposals on meta-design and making them more concretely applicable in the challenging context of the communities of practice for the creation of supportive EUD tools and infrastructures that can evolve more easily along with the needs and objectives of the members of those communities.

References

1. Hughes, J.A., Randall, D., Shapiro, D.: Faltering from ethnography to design. In: ACM Conference on Computer-Supported Cooperative Work, pp. 115–122. ACM Press, New York (1992)
2. Star, S.L.: This is not a boundary object: reflections on the origin of a concept. Sci. Technol. Human Values **35**(5), 601–617 (2010)
3. Duguid, P.: Prologue: community of practice then and now. In: Amin, A., Roberts, J. (eds.) Community, Economic Creativity, and Organization, pp. 1–10. Oxford University Press, Oxford (2008)
4. Dix, A.: Designing for appropriation. In: 21st British HCI Group Annual Conference on People and Computers: HCI...but not as we know it, vol. 2, pp. 27–30. British Computer Society, Swinton (2007)
5. Fischer, G., Giaccardi, E.: Meta-design: a framework for the future of end user development. In: Lieberman, H., Paternò, F., Wulf, V. (eds.) End User Development, vol. 9, pp. 427–457. Springer, Dordrecht (2006)
6. Alter, S.: Work systems and IT artifacts—does the definition matter? Commun. Assoc. Inf. Syst. **17**, 299–313 (2006)
7. Costabile, M.F., Fogli, D., Mussio, P., Piccinno, A.: A meta-design approach to End-User Development. In: IEEE Symposium on Visual Languages and Human-Centric Computing (VL/HCC), pp. 308–310. IEEE Computer Society (2005)
8. Fischer, G.: End user development and meta-design: foundations for cultures of participation. J Organ. End User Comput. **22**(1), 52–82 (2010)
9. Lieberman, H., Paternò, F., Wulf, V. (eds.): End User Development. Springer, Dordrecht (2006)
10. Burnett, M., Rothermel, G., Cook, C.: An integrated software engineering approach for end-user programmers. In: Lieberman, H., Paternò, F., Wulf, V. (eds.) End User Development, vol. 9, pp. 87–113. Springer, Netherlands (2006)
11. Letondal, C.: Participatory programming: developing programmable bioinformatics tools for end-users. In: Lieberman, H., Paternò, F., Wulf, V. (eds.) End User Development, pp. 207–242. Springer, Dordrecht (2006)
12. Ko, A.J., Abraham, R., Beckwith, L., Blackwell, A., Burnett, M., Erwig, M., Scaffidi, C., Lawrance, J., Lieberman, H., Myers, B., Rosson, M.B., Rothermel, G., Shaw, M., Wiedenbeck, S.: The state of the art in end-user software engineering. ACM Comput. Surv. **43**(3), 1–44 (2011)
13. Carmien, S., Dawe, M., Fischer, G., Gorman, A., Kintsch, A., Sullivan Jr, J.F.: Socio-technical environments supporting people with cognitive disabilities using public transportation. ACM Trans. Comput. Hum. Inter. **12**(2), 233–262 (2005)
14. Fogli, D., Piccinno, A.: Co-evolution of end-user developers and systems in multi-tiered proxy design problems. In: Dittrich, Y., Burnett, M., Mørch, A., Redmiles, D. (eds.) End-User Development. LNCS, vol. 7897, pp. 153–168. Springer, Berlin (2013)

15. Ardito, C., Buono, P., Costabile, M.F., Lanzilotti, R., Piccinno, A.: End users as co-designers of their own tools and products. J. Vis. Lang. Comput. **23**(2), 78–90 (2012)
16. Fogli, D.: Towards a new work practice in the development of e–government applications. Electron. Gov. Inter. J. **10**(3), 238–258 (2013)
17. Wenger, E., McDermott, R.A., Snyder, W.: Cultivating Communities of Practice: A Guide to Managing Knowledge. Harvard Business Press, Boston (2002)
18. Gantt, M., Nardi, B.A.: Gardeners and gurus: patterns of cooperation among CAD users. In: ACM Conference on Human Factors in Computing Systems (CHI), pp. 107–117. ACM, New York, NY, USA (1992)
19. Cabitza, F., Simone, C.: Affording mechanisms: an integrated view of coordination and knowledge management. Comput. Support. Coop. Work (CSCW) **21**(2–3), 227–260 (2012)
20. Ardito, C., Bottoni, P., Costabile, M.F., Desolda, G., Matera, M., Piccinno, A., Picozzi, M.: Enabling end users to create, annotate and share personal information spaces. In: Dittrich, Y., Burnett, M., Mørch, A., Redmiles, D. (eds.) End-User Development. LNCS, vol. 7897, pp. 40–55. Springer, Berlin (2013)
21. Fogli, D., Provenza, L.P.: A meta-design approach to the development of e-government services. J. Vis. Lang. Comput. **23**(2), 47–62 (2012)
22. Ardito, C., Barricelli, B.R., Buono, P., Costabile, M.F., Piccinno, A., Valtolina, S., Zhu, L.: Visual mediation mechanisms for collaborative design and development. In: Stephanidis, C. (ed.) Universal Access in Human-Computer Interaction. Design for All and eInclusion. LNCS, vol. 6765, pp. 3–11. Springer, Berlin (2011)
23. Ardito, C., Buono, P., Costabile, M.F., Lanzilotti, R., Piccinno, A., Zhu, L.: On the transferability of a meta-design model supporting End-User Development. Univ. Access Inf. Soc. J. (UAIS) (in print)
24. Cabitza, F., Simone, C.: Building socially embedded technologies: implications on design. In: Randall, D., Schmidt, K., Wulf, V. (eds.) Designing Socially Embedded Technologies: A European Challenge. Springer, Berlin (in print)
25. Sutcliffe, A., Mehandjiev, N.: End-user development (Introduction to Special Issue). Commun. ACM **47**(9), 31–32 (2004)
26. Costabile, M.F., Fogli, D., Marcante, A., Mussio, P., Provenza, L.P., Piccinno, A.: Designing customized and tailorable visual interactive systems. Inter. J. Softw. Eng. Knowl. Eng. **18**(3), 305–325 (2008)
27. Vinck, D., Blanco, E.: Everyday Engineering: an Ethnography of Design And Innovation. MIT Press, Cambridge (2003)
28. Boujut, J.-F., Blanco, E.: Intermediary objects as a means to foster co-operation in engineering design. Comput. Support. Coop. Work (CSCW) **12**(2), 205–219 (2003)
29. Lee, C.P.: Boundary negotiating artifacts: unbinding the routine of boundary objects and embracing chaos in collaborative work. Comput. Support. Coop. Work (CSCW) **16**(3), 307–339 (2007)
30. Cabitza, F.: At the boundary of communities and roles: boundary objects and knowledge artifacts as complementary resources for the design of information systems. In: Mola, L., Pennarola, F., Za, S. (eds.) From Information to Smart Society: Environment, Politics and Economics. LNISO. Springer, Berlin (in print)
31. Bowker, G.C., Star, S.L.: Sorting Things Out: Classification and Its Consequences. MIT Press, London (1999)
32. Cabitza, F., Colombo, G., Simone, C.: Leveraging underspecification in knowledge artifacts to foster collaborative activities in professional communities. Int. J. Hum. Comput. Stud. **71**(1), 24–45 (2013)
33. Hess, J., Reuter, C., Pipek, V., Wulf, V.: Supporting end-user articulations in evolving business processes: a case study to explore intuitive notations and interaction designs. Inter. J. Coop. Inf. Syst. **21**(4), 263–296 (2012)
34. Batini, C., Barone, D., Cabitza, F., Grega, S.: A data quality methodology for heterogeneous data. Inter. J. Database Manag. Syst. (IJDMS) **3**(1), 60–79 (2011)

35. Grudin, J.: Utility and usability: research issues and development contexts. Interact. Comput. **4**(2), 209–217 (1992)
36. Cabitza, F., Simone, C.: WOAD: a framework to enable the end-user development of coordination-oriented functionalities. J. Organ. End User Comput. **22**(2), 1–20 (2010)
37. Fogli, D., Piccinno, A.: Enabling domain experts to develop usable software artifacts. In: Spagnoletti, P. (ed.) Organizational Change and Information Systems. LNISO, vol. 2, pp. 419–428. Springer, Berlin (2013)
38. Cabitza, F., Gesso, I., Simone, C.: Providing end-users with a visual editor to make their electronic documents active. In: IEEE Symposium on Visual Languages and Human-Centric Computing (VL/HCC), pp. 171–174. IEEE Computer Society (2012)
39. Fogli, D., Provenza, L.P.: End-user development of e-government services through meta-modeling. In: Costabile, M.F., Dittrich, Y., Fischer, G., Piccinno, A. (eds.) End-User Development. LNCS, vol. 6654, pp. 107–122. Springer, Berlin, (2011)

Understanding User Visiting Behavior and Web Design: Applying Simultaneous Choice Model to Content Arrangement

Lianlian Song, Geoffrey Tso, Zhiyong Liu and Qian Chen

Abstract A common problem encountered in web design is how to arrange content on the homepage of a website. This paper uses a random-utility theory in studying visitors' choice behaviors to optimize web design. Classical discrete choice models are not suitable. A total of six multiple-choice demand models are proposed in this paper. These models are applied to web log file data collected from an educational institute over a seven and a half month period, and the parameters are estimated consistently across all models. The best model based on the forecasting accuracy rate is selected as the tool for resolving the problem of web design. Two metrics, utility loss and compensating time, are constructed using the selected utility model to facilitate web design. Empirical results show that the proposed metrics are highly efficient to develop web design to resolve the problem of how to allocate the information resources of a website, and the algorithms can also be utilized to assist the study of the feasibility of introducing a new function in a website.

Keywords Web design · Random utility theory · Web log file · Utility loss

L. Song (✉) · Z. Liu · Q. Chen
USTC-CityU Joint Advanced Research Center, Suzhou, China
e-mail: songll@mail.ustc.edu.cn

Z. Liu
e-mail: liuzy@mail.ustc.edu.cn

Q. Chen
e-mail: qianch@mail.ustc.edu.cn

G. Tso
City University of Hong Kong, Hong Kong, China
e-mail: msgtso@cityu.edu.hk

L. Caporarello et al. (eds.), *Smart Organizations and Smart Artifacts*,
Lecture Notes in Information Systems and Organisation 7,
DOI: 10.1007/978-3-319-07040-7_20,
© Springer International Publishing Switzerland 2014

1 Introduction and Literature Review

The fast development of web technologies has revolutionized the living patterns of our lives. The Web provides a direct communication medium between users and the outside world. The website has become an indispensable unit for any organization to stay connected with the outside world. The question now faced by a company is not whether, but rather how to build effective websites that can attract and retain internet visitors [1].

Studies that investigate web design are emerging rapidly [2–5]. However, many of these studies lack solid empirical support, and some are simply derived from existing print-design guidelines. They do not approach the web design problem from the perspective of visitors' preferences. Many works using web log files present us with simple and basic aggregated statistics such as influential factors, frequency and time of visit, or navigation patterns and users' future movements. However, it is difficult to generalize these results to develop website design guidelines without the use of statistical models to measure the competing and satiation effects of web pages. This paper presents a first attempt to transform information contained in a web log file into useful statistical models to help to produce an instrument of web design guidelines. In this paper, we illustrate how to use the 'click' behavior of visitors of a website of an educational institute to develop models that measure the utilities gained by visitors when viewing certain web pages, and then construct metrics to facilitate optimal web design.

In order to study the tine that a viewer allocates to visiting a variety of pages, we could use the concept of "utility" in economics to measure the reward of viewing a particular page. The utility that we defined here is the utility of information. The more time a visitor spends reading a particular page, the more information he or she would obtain, the more utility he or she would get; however, this occurs at a decreasing rate due to satiation. The concept of utility has a wide application in many areas, including product purchase [6], brand choice [7], activity-travel choice [8], etc. The most popular choice model using utility is the multinomial logit model, which deals with situations in which only one alternative is chosen from a set of mutually exclusive alternatives [9]. However, the issue that consumer demands are characterized by the choice of multiple alternatives simultaneously in many real situations was not studied until [10], who proposed a utility-based demand model, called the Kim et al.'s model, using a translated, nonlinear but additive structure, with multivariate normal error terms. It is noted that the Kim et al.'s model is a special choice model which goes beyond the restricted meaning of "choice" in DCM (discrete choice model), where one can only choose a single alternative, and the alternatives are substitutable.

We illustrate the use of the developed models by answering questions related to website design, such as "Which items should be presented in the homepage of a website and how should useful information be arranged?" Given the limited space of webpages, key descriptions of only a subset of a website's pages can be displayed on the homepage, which saves visitors' searching time. Consequently, understanding visitors' preferences of choosing web pages can help web design by identifying what information should be shown on webpages. By using our developed models, we are able to create one metric, *utility loss*, to measure the relative importance or attractiveness of categories of web pages.

2 Modeling Methods in Time Analysis

We define the total reading time (TRT) as the sum of the time that a visitor spends in reading the information on all of the pages that he or she chooses, excluding search time. Under the assumption that the TRT is limited and based on the random-utility framework principle, a website visitor would allocate his or her time efficiently to maximize the utility gained. Based on the model of Kim et al. [10], three versions of utility models are proposed here. In order to choose the best model to improve website design, we consider both the multivariate normal distribution and extreme value distribution [11] for the error term of each model. Thus, we have six different new models. There are three important parameters in our models. The first is the baseline utility parameter, denoted as ψ; the more popular a variety, the bigger the value of ψ. The second is the satiation parameter, denoted as α, which influences the rate of diminishing marginal returns. The third is the translation parameter, which is set to be 1 without a loss of generalization.

We use the following structure model to describe the development process of our model (Fig. 1):

The first set of models (model 1 and model 2), with utility function $U(t) = \sum_{i=1}^{5} \psi_1 \ln(t_i + 1)$, is the simplest one, containing only one baseline utility parameter for each category. However, it still possesses the features of additive, nonlinear and translation with a diminishing marginal utility function. It serves as a baseline model for comparison with other models.

The second set (model 3 and model 4), with utility function $U(t) = \sum_{i=1}^{5} \psi_i (t_i + 1)^{\alpha}$, is similar to the one used in the Kim et al.'s model, but all α_i's are assumed to be equal across varieties. This form is considered as the simplest version of the utility function that uses a satiation index. It can be utilized as a baseline model to supply initial values of parameters and for comparisons with other more complicated models.

The third set (model 5 and model 6), with utility function $U(t) = \sum_{i=1}^{5} \psi_i (t_i + 1)^{\alpha_i}$, relaxes the assumption of equal satiation index. Different categories can have different rates of diminishing marginal utility, which can supply us with more information about the heterogeneity of the diminishing effect. Since there could be a confounding effect between α and ψ, we assume some alternatives of a similar nature to have the same satiation parameter α.

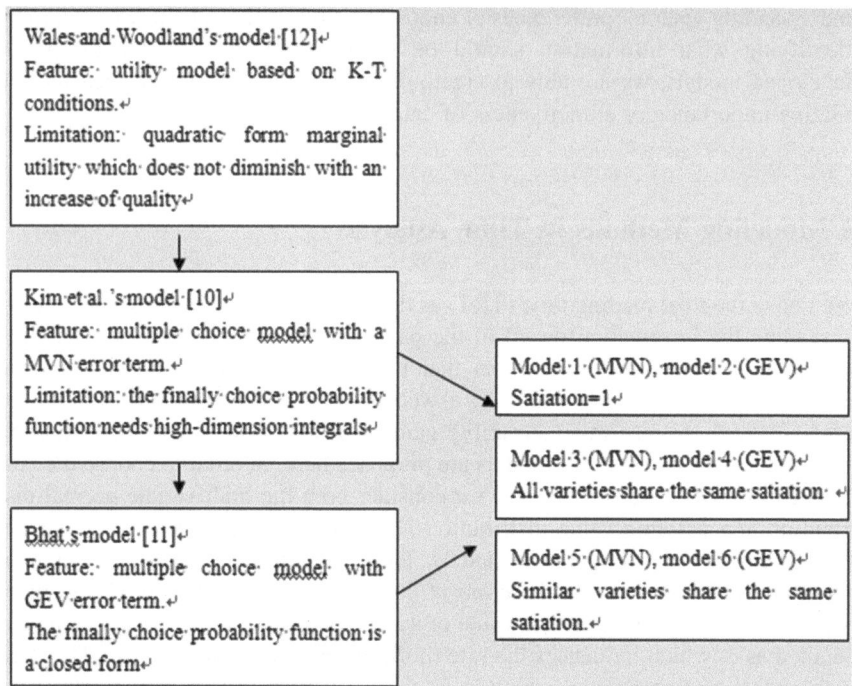

Fig. 1 Development process of utility models

3 Web Log File and Data Description

The data used in this study are from a web log file of a website of a university in Hong Kong, collected from 1 October 2009 to 15 May 2010. During this period, more than 100,000 individuals visited the website. The web log file records second-by-second visitors' clicking behavior, including type and duration of web pages visited. We identify an individual user by using "CFID + CFTOKEN"—a combination of two addresses that are unique to every visitor to the website. In addition, a user session is labeled by "Session ID", which indicates one particular session as users could visit the website on several occasions. A "click" on a link of the website generates an observation. One session can include many observations; a single user with the same Session ID might have only one, or more than one observation. We delete such users with only one observation since their durations on a webpage cannot be calculated correctly, and also users with only one session, because there is a high possibility that these users are not interested in the website. In other words, valid users should have more than one session ID, and each session ID should include more than one observation. We also exclude those visitors who had spent longer than 1,800 s on any single page. After data selection, we have 118,562 visitors who are considered as valid users for our study.

The website contains more than 100 web pages that visitors can request to view. For the purpose of developing our models, we group these pages into six categories according to their functions as follows:

- Category 1: Detailed information about all programs at the University;
- Category 2: Regulations and types of undergraduate programs;
- Category 3: Frequently asked questions;
- Category 4: Information for international, exchange, and visiting students;
- Category 5: Application procedures and online application forms;
- Category 6: All other pages.

4 Use of Time Models for Web Log Data

In general, there are two types of visitors to the website of the university: *browsers*, who are interested in the university and would like to know more about the programs that it offers, and *applicants*, who intend to study at the university and would like to obtain detailed information about specific programs, and may even apply on-line. In this section, we develop the use of time models for these two groups of visitors. For the browsers, a sample of 873 visitors is selected randomly from the web log file; they have the TRT between 15 and 20 min. For the applicants, we select 510 visitors, whose TRT are between 117 and 134 min in the website. The maximum likelihood estimation (MLE) method is adopted to estimate the parameters in the models.

4.1 Six Models for Browsers

The six models are first applied to the data of browsers. In these models, only 5 categories are used, as category 6 contains mixed and unrelated pages. The likelihood is derived by assuming that, on each visit to the website, a browser maximizes the utility of the form $U(x)$, subject to the constraint that $\sum_{i=1}^{5} t_i \leq T$, where T represents the TRT on that visit. Table 1 shows the results of these models.

Although ψ_1 is fixed as a baseline value, it is observed that the value of ψ_1 is the biggest among the five estimated ψs, and ψ_3 has the smallest value in each of the six models. It indicates that pages of category 1 attract the most visitors who were interested in detailed information about the programs offered by the university and, hence, spent more time on these pages. On the other hand, category 3 contains mainly pages related to "frequently asked questions". In general, if a visitor has some problems or wants to learn more about the content of the website, the possibility of viewing such pages in category 3 is high. As a result, category 3 was not frequently visited by the browsers. Similarly, category 4 is not a popular category as it contains information about international visiting and exchange

Table 1 Estimates of six models for browsers

Utility function 1 $U(t) = \sum_{i=1}^{5} \psi_i \ln(t_i + 1)$

	Objective function	ψ_1	ψ_2	ψ_3	ψ_4	ψ_5
MVN	5561.887	40 (fixed as baseline value)	10.6694 (0.0179)	1.7906 (0.0025)	1.9384 (0.0014)	15.3266 (0.0582)
GEV	4954.673	40 (fixed as baseline value)	8.8080 (0.5046)	0.8888 (0.0942)	0.8916 (0.0937)	10.1405 (0.6172)

Utility function 2 $U(t) = \sum_{i=1}^{5} \psi_i(t_i + 1)^{\alpha}$

	Objective function	ψ_1	ψ_2	ψ_3	ψ_4	ψ_5	α
MVN	5103.025	40 (fixed as baseline value)	16.5514 (0.0454)	3.3455 (0.0085)	3.4769 (0.0201)	20.1752 (0.0487)	0.404 (0.0006)
GEV	4930.388	40 (fixed as baseline value)	10.4836 (0.6398)	1.1253 (0.1244)	1.1318 (0.1242)	11.9568 (0.7572)	0.1403 (0.0192)

Utility function 3 $U(t) = \sum_{i=1}^{5} \psi_i(t_i + 1)^{\alpha_i}$, $\alpha_1 = \alpha_2 = \alpha_5 = \alpha_1'$, $\alpha_3 = \alpha_4 = \alpha_2'$

	Objective function	ψ_1	ψ_2	ψ_3	ψ_4	ψ_5	α_1'	α_2'
MVN	5083.119	40 (fixed)	18.2869 (0.3673)	3.0359 (0.0057)	3.2276 (0.0117)	23.0429 (0.2630)	0.4524 (0.0004)	0.5477 (0.0004)
GEV	4927.807	40 (fixed)	10.2813 (0.6341)	0.4797 (0.1569)	0.4835 (0.1577)	11.7409 (0.7506)	0.1246 (0.0206)	0.2816 (0.0617)

(Figures in the parentheses are standard errors, *MVN* means the model with the error term of multivariate normal distribution, *GEV* represents the model with the error term of generalized extreme value distribution)

students. It is also interesting to note that the estimated value of ψ_4 is larger than that of ψ_3 in each model in this browser group. One possible reason fir this could be that most visitors in this group simply scanned types of web pages without any specific aim. The content about the activities of international, exchange, and visiting students appears to be more attractive than frequently asked questions. The estimated value of ψ_2 is much bigger thanf ψ_3 and ψ_4, because the content of category 2 is about the types of undergraduate programs, which is important information for anyone who is interested in attending the university.

In the table, the objective function is $f = -\ln L$, where L represents the likelihood function. We expect to find the minimum of f for the simple reason that the smaller the value of f, the better the likelihood function. It is interesting to note that, in terms of the objective function, models with GEV error terms outperform models with MVN error terms in all three versions of the utility functions. This is an indication that the extreme value distribution used in the Bhat model is perhaps a better choice for the error term, as compared to the multivariate normal distribution used in the Kim et al.'s model.

Models using utility function 2 have a similar structure to that of the Kim et al.'s model, except we set here $\alpha_1 = \alpha_2 = \alpha_3 = \alpha_4 = \alpha_5 = \alpha$ in order to reduce the number of parameters and the interaction among parameters, as well as to employ it as a baseline model. The utility function 2, when applied to the browsers' data, appears to perform better than the models using the previous utility function because the objective functions of utility function 2 are better (smaller) than those in the previous models.

Utility function 3 relaxes the restriction on the value of α and allows it to be estimated from the data. We cannot allow each category to take on different values of α due to its confounding effect with the parameter ψ and assume $\alpha_1 = \alpha_2 = \alpha_5 = \alpha_1'$, $\alpha_3 = \alpha_4 = \alpha_2'$ according to the similarity and degree of attractiveness of each category as observed from previous baseline models. Based on the objective function, models of utility function 3 outperform all previous models. We also observe that satiation parameters $\alpha_1' < \alpha_2'$ in both models, indicating again that categories 3 and 4 are less popular than categories 1, 2, and 5.

4.2 Six Models for Applicants

Another six models are developed for the data set of applicants. The results of these models are presented in Table 2.

The values of the objective functions in Table 2 are larger than those in Table 1, mainly due to the fact that applicants spent much longer times (117–134 min) than browsers (15–20 min) in the website. The second interesting difference between Tables 1 and 2 is that, in Table 1, which is for browsers, the estimated values of ψ_3 are smaller than those of ψ_4 in all models for both error distributions; whereas in Table 2, which is for applicants, the opposite is the case. This is probably due to the fact that applicants are more concerned with the details of the programs and have many questions in mind. As such, they would spend more time on category 3 that contains pages about frequently asked questions than category 4 for some specific information related to international visiting and exchange students.

Once again, based on the values of the objective function, except for one case, models with GEV error terms outperform the models with MVN error terms. However, it is worth noting that the differences between the values of objective functions of the models with two different error terms in Table 2 are smaller than the corresponding differences in Table 1.

The estimates for the parameters, ψ_2, ψ_5, α, α_1', α_2', in Table 2 are similar in magnitude to those presented in Table 1. In particular, we also observe that $\alpha_1' < \alpha_2'$.

Again, based on the values of the objective function, the models using utility function 3 are the best. This time, however, it is the model with the MVN error term that has the smallest value for the objective function. We will choose this one for future analysis.

Table 2 Estimates of six models for applicants

Utility function 1 $U(t) = \sum_{i=1}^{5} \psi_i \ln(t_i + 1)$

	Obj	ψ_1	ψ_2	ψ_3	ψ_4	ψ_5
MVN	5919.146	40	7.4093	2.5550	0.3410	25.5950
			(0.0130)	(0.0039)	(0.0002)	(0.1655)
GEV	5554.244	40	3.5308	0.5912	0.1089	16.5048
			(0.2549)	(0.0517)	(0.0151)	(1.2138)

Utility function 2 $U(t) = \sum_{i=1}^{5} \psi_i(t_i + 1)^{\alpha}$

	Obj	ψ_1	ψ_2	ψ_3	ψ_4	ψ_5	α
MVN	5561.587	40	9.1667	2.6383	0.9599	28.1801	0.3435
			(0.0910)	(0.0038)	(0.0039)	(0.2302)	(0.0006)
GEV	5528.2730	40	5.1352	1.0014	0.1930	18.8173	0.1403
			(0.4414)	(0.1115)	(0.0307)	(1.3790)	(0.0199)

Utility function 3 $U(t) = \sum_{i=1}^{5} \psi_i(t_i + 1)^{\alpha_i}$, $\alpha_1 = \alpha_2 = \alpha_5 = \alpha'_1$, $\alpha_3 = \alpha_4 = \alpha'_2$

	Obj	ψ_1	ψ_2	ψ_3	ψ_4	ψ_5	α'_1	α'_2
MVN	5501.17	40	7.5511	0.7872	0.2897	21.7022	0.2684	0.5487
			(0.0814)	(0.0120)	(0.0098)	(0.8894)	(0.0015)	(0.0005)
GEV	5510.399	40	4.3814	0.1691	0.0351	17.7921	0.0884	0.3779
			(0.4011)	(0.0649)	(0.0138)	(1.3286)	(0.0232)	(0.0385)

(Figures in the parentheses are standard errors)

5 Applications to the Design of a Website Homepage

When visitors access a website, the homepage is usually the first page that appears, and it contains rich information about the contents of this website. Using icons or brief introductory messages shown on the homepage, visitors can discern the allocation of information. On the other hand, if a category of pages does not have a link on the homepage, this would negatively affect the utilization rate of this category of pages as searching time may increase, and visitors may give up and leave the website. Therefore, it is crucial to decide which information should be presented on the homepage.

The use of time models developed in the previous section can provide a quantitative measure to help to make this decision. Only a subset of all categories of pages can have their links on the homepage, due to its limited space. The loss of one or more categories of pages results in visitors' utility loss, and visitors who cannot locate the information that they need may become dissatisfied, and their total utility of visiting the website will be reduced. The time models can be used to calculate the utility loss to determine which categories of web pages can be removed from the homepage, and rank the items according to their utility loss.

5.1 Utility Loss

We first define the utility of a website for a visitor who has spent TRT units of time on the website as the maximum utility that can be obtained by the visitor by optimally allocating his or her time according to the use of the time model. The utility loss is defined as the reduction in utility when a specific category of web pages is removed from the website. Take the university website example, suppose that one of the five categories in the website has to be removed. The utility loss is calculated using the following algorithm:

(1) Collect a visitor's TRT from the web-log file of the website.
(2) Define total utilities before and after removing one category as U_5 and U_4 respectively;
(3) Set all categories receiving zero seconds at the start;
(4) For each additional unit of time (seconds), the marginal utility for each category is determined by using the time model. Assign the unit of time to the category with the largest marginal utility;
(5) Repeat (4) until all units of TRT of the visitor are assigned. Then, the time spent on each category can be obtained, and the total utility U_5 can be calculated;
(6) Suppose that a specific category is removed, but assume that each visitor's TRT is unchanged. Repeat steps (3) (4) and (5) for the remaining four categories. U_4 can be obtained;
(7) The difference between U_5 and U_4 is the utility loss due to the removal of the specific category: Utility loss $= U_5 - U_4$.

Since the TRTs are different across visitors, the utility losses of visitors for each category are different in the sample. Therefore, the average utility loss over the whole sample is computed to represent the utility loss of removing one specific category. Tables 3 and 4 report the utility loss for removing each of the five categories for browsers and applicants, respectively.

Table 3 shows that the utility loss is the largest when category 1 is removed, reducing the total utility gained from the five categories by 63.2 %. Removing either category 3 or 4 produces the least effect on reducing visitors' utility. The standard errors of the utility loss are very small, indicating that the effects are quite homogeneous over the population.

Table 4 shows similar results for the sample of applicants. It is interesting to note that although the percentage loss in utility due to the removal of category 1 for browsers and applicants is similar, the corresponding values for categories 2 and 5 are quite different. Percentage loss in utility when category 2 is removed decreases from 13.3 for browsers to 5.1 for applicants, while the corresponding values when category 5 is removed are 15.4 and 21.6, respectively. This may be due to the fact that category 2 contains general information about undergraduate programs, such as types or regulations, which should be more useful to browsers;

Table 3 Average utility loss of each category for browsers

	Utility loss	Percentage (%)
Category 1	51.4207 (1.3599)	63.2
Category 2	10.7997 (0.1341)	13.3
Category 3	0.4699 (0.0036)	0.6
Category 4	0.4739 (0.0035)	0.6
Category 5	12.4989 (0.1801)	15.4

(Figures in the parentheses are standard errors, and percentages do not necessarily sum to 100)

Table 4 Average utility loss of each category for applicants

	Utility loss	Percentage (%)
Category 1	107.0217 (2.2943)	53.4
Category 2	10.2237 (0.1875)	5.1
Category 3	0.7803 (0.0009)	0.4
Category 4	0.2825 (0.0008)	0.1
Category 5	43.2753 (0.9123)	21.6

(Figures in the parentheses are standard errors, and percentages do not necessary sum to 100)

whereas category 5 contains application procedures and on-line application information, which are more relevant to potential applicants.

Utility loss may result in a loss of visitors for the simple reason that if a visitor cannot locate the information that he or she needs from the website, he or she will be dissatisfied and utility will decrease. With our example of the 5 categories, it is obvious that one should consider removing category 4 or even category 3 first if web page space is limited.

6 Conclusion

Using utility structures and random-utility theory in studying visitors' web page choice behavior is a new and worthwhile research direction. As far as we know, no previous studies have investigated the maximization of the utility of visiting a variety of web pages from the visitors' perspective. The Kim et al.'s model is particularly suitable in this situation, as it explicitly considers the competing and satiation effects. As a result, a demand variety model, based on a translated additive utility structure, is selected. Three different versions of utility functions are proposed in this paper. Two different error term distributions, a multivariate normal distribution, and an extreme value distribution, are used in the three different versions of utility functions in order to select the best model for website design.

We adopt real data from a university website to investigate how visitors allocate their time to five categories of web pages. We make the first attempt to combine web log file data with a utility model, which is proved to be successful for the reasons that: (1) estimates of the parameters are consistent among six models; and (2) results are reasonable and as expected. Therefore, the simultaneous demand utility model that is often applied in economics is shown to be useful in studying the behavior of website visitors.

For solving the content arrangement problem of web pages under limited space, we define a metric to study the effect of removing a category of web pages. "Utility loss" is defined as the difference in maximum utilities obtained by a visitor before and after the removal of a category, if the TRT remains the same. We prove the usefulness of this metric by applying it to a website home-page design problem. The metric can also be applied to the design of search engines and other types of web sites.

References

1. Aaker, D.: Managing Brand Equity: Capitalising on the Value of a Brand Name. Free Press, New York (1991)
2. Chen, S.C., Dhillon, G.S.: Interpreting dimensions of consumer trust in e-commerce. Inf. Manage. Technol. **4**, 303–318 (2002)
3. Jaeki, S., Fatemeh, Z.: A theoretical approach to web design in e-commerce: a belief reinforcement model. Manage. Sci. **51**(8), 1219–1235 (2005)
4. Chen, C.M., Lee, H.M., Chang, Y.J.: Two novel feature selection approaches for web page classification. Expert Syst. Appl. **36**, 260–272 (2009)
5. Wang, Y.E., Lee, A.J.T.: Mining web navigation patterns with a path traversal graph. Expert Syst. Appl. **38**, 7112–7122 (2011)
6. Zhao, L., Zhang, S.Z., Fan, X.F.: Web browsing feature mining of an anonymous user. J. Comput. Res. Dev. **39**(12), 1759–1763 (2002)
7. Erdem, T., Keane, M.P., Sun, B.: A dynamic model of brand choice when price and advertising signal product quality. Mark. Sci. **27**(6), 1111–1125 (2008)
8. Bhat, C.R.: The multiple discrete-continuous extreme value (MDCEV) model: role of utility function parameters, identification considerations, and model extensions. Transp. Res. Part B **42**, 274–303 (2008)
9. Niedrich, R.W., Weathers, D., Hill, R.C., Bell, D.R.: Specifying price judgments with range-frequency theory in models of brand choice. J. Mark. Res. **46**(5), 693–702 (2009)
10. Kim, J.H., Allenby, G.M., Rossi, P.E.: Modeling consumer demand for variety. Mark. Sci. **21**(3), 229–250 (2002)
11. Bhat, C.R.: A multiple discrete-continuous extreme value model: formulation and application to discretionary time-use decisions. Transp. Res. Part B **39**, 679–707 (2005)

Socio-Technical Toolbox for Business Analysis in Practice

Peter Bednar, Moufida Sadok and Vasilena Shiderova

Abstract Socio-technical methods advocate a human-focus analysis that reflects on social and technical factors in the design of organizational systems. The aim of this paper is to report on the experiences of a ST toolbox use in practice by 36 companies. Our findings show that the use of ST toolbox improves companies' understanding of their job practices and enhance their learning about their business sustainability. These experiences of improvements are not dependent on the sector or the size of the visited companies and confirm the perceived usefulness and relevance of ST analysis in practice.

Keywords Socio-technical analysis · Contextual inquiry · Systems practice · Organizational change · Socio-technical toolbox · Systems heuristics

1 Introduction

In this paper we describe some results of use of a particular socio-technical (ST) toolbox by 36 companies. The toolbox, which consists of 27 different analytical tools for organization analysis, was used over a period of six months. The companies ranged from very small shops with only two employees to business entities with more than 200 employees which are part of large franchises.

P. Bednar (✉)
School of Computing, University of Portsmouth, Portsmouth, UK
e-mail: peter.bednar@port.ac.uk

M. Sadok
Higher Institute of Technological Studies in Communications in Tunis,
Tunis, Tunisia
e-mail: moufida.sadok@gmail.com

V. Shiderova
Technical University of Sofia, Sofia, Bulgaria
e-mail: vasilena.shiderova@gmail.com

L. Caporarello et al. (eds.), *Smart Organizations and Smart Artifacts*,
Lecture Notes in Information Systems and Organisation 7,
DOI: 10.1007/978-3-319-07040-7_21,
© Springer International Publishing Switzerland 2014

The activities of these companies cover a large variety of sectors such as manufacturing industry, restaurants, consultancy, education and retail. The involvement and commitment to the ST practice varied from an average of one session per month for some companies to almost weekly sessions for some others. Mostly sessions would be between one and two hours. In many cases, additional to these sessions a number of observations have been conducted in order to understand the business practices as well as a number of interviews and questionnaires have been used. Overall, the companies' experiences of contemporary ST practice provide valuable contribution to our research related this area.

In Mumford [27], more than 50-year history of the ST practices is depicted by discussing its evolution, related theories, practices and international development. ST methods advocate a human-focus analysis that reflects on social and technical factors in the design of organizational systems. The underlying principle of ST practices lies in the active participation of stakeholders, the co-creation, the co-development [4, 11, 18, 25, 27, 29] and promotes a system analysis according to a first person perspective [16]. Consequently, the implementation of ST principals is expected to create the conditions for job enrichment, to support development of good will from the different communities of practices through constructive conversation and interaction between different stakeholders giving the opportunity to develop high level of efficiency and performance.

Anderson [1] argues that in a complex and dynamic work world the teaching of ST approaches support constructive learning and develop critical analysis skills of the students who will be future systems analysts or designers. However, the use of ST methods in professional practice continues to pose a number of challenges [3] and is not always adequately supported.

The aim of this paper is to explore two main related questions. First, what do the companies think about the use of ST practice? And what is the contribution, if any, of ST practice to their business? To explore these questions, the remainder of this paper has been organized into three sections. The Sect. 1 reviews and comments some issues related to the most renowned ST approaches. The Sect. 2 introduces the socio-technical toolbox that has been used by 36 companies for business analysis. The Sect. 3 reports the feedback drawn up on the experiences of ST practices.

2 Background

A wide range of ST methods have been developed and implemented [2]. In Effective Technical and Human Implementation of Computer supported Systems (ETHICS) [24–27] analysts have support mechanisms and descriptions with advice, comments and examples for over twenty different but related analyses. In Soft Systems Methodology (SSM) [9–11] there are also numerous supports for complex analysis with the promotion of a multitude of concepts and techniques (such as CATWOE, PRQ and Rich Pictures). In Client Led Design [29] different methods and techniques from SSM expanded upon and new ones added such as PEARL. In Object Oriented Analysis and Design [20] several techniques from methodologies such as ETHICS and SSM are transformed, changed and incorporated with an object oriented focus (with tools such as the FACTOR analysis for example). The Social Practice Design approach [15] provides support for development of common understanding overcoming communication difficulties. Ward and Daniel [30] address an apparent lack of effective metrics to assess expectations and claims of the contribution of ST practice. The Strategic Systemic Thinking framework by Bednar [4, 6, 7] includes several techniques and modelling support for analysis especially aimed at inquiries into uncertain and complex problems spaces (incorporating para-consistent logic, techniques for structuring uncertainty from multiple systemic perspectives and including techniques for modelling diversity networks etc.). Additionally these methodologies include critically informed discussions support-ing the problematization of the analytical process and enquiry.

In the field of information systems (IS) contextual adaptation is recognized as necessary to dynamic organizational practices in complex environments. It has been acknowledged for example that it is beneficial to conceptualize IS as a Human Activity System, which according to Checkland is a very different problem arena from viewing IS as a data processing system [9–11]. In fact, since the first area of the IS history [14] questions in multidisciplinary contexts—such as sys-tems thinking, structuring uncertainty, defining and managing wicked problem spaces, socio-technical systems, human activity systems, inquiry systems [8, 12, 17, 18, 21, 22] have been addressed. Moreover, the IS universe is more and more characterized by the growth in number of stakeholders, the quality and the quantity of the different users influencing the design and implementation of IS projects as well as the successes and failures of such projects [13].

Holistic IS methodologies support analysis into any relevant aspect of IS analysis and development. Methodologies such as SSM and ETHICS deal with complex organizational issues. Software engineers are recommended [28] to engage with such methodologies when dealing with complex organisational problems (as opposed to stick to their normal formal techniques used for artefact design and project man-agement). IS development is characterized as an emergent socio-technical change process conducted through sense making and negotiations among stakeholders [19].

3 Socio-Technical Toolbox Themes

The ST toolbox used in this study was originally based on a combination of methods and techniques from a collection of a number of contemporary ST methodologies. It has been developed and used in practice in many different types of organizations over a period of approximately ten years. Over the years previous versions of the ST toolbox has been used to support analysis of many business processes such as in warehouses belonging to 10 supermarkets in 2007, 60 doctor practices in 2008, 80 pharmacies in 2009 and 50 news agencies in 2010.

The ST toolbox deals with 8 themes (with heuristics and methods) supporting the application of ST tools for systems analysis in practice. They are:

3.1 Problem Space Definition

In this theme the analyst (or the design group) considers the problems of existing system, future needs and potential benefits of a new system using nine ST methods. Questions about the reasons of change, system sustainability and boundaries are addressed as well as holistic multi-criteria benefit analysis, vertical analysis and context analysis are achieved.

3.2 System Structure Definition

This theme consists of four methods, which deal with the identification of keys objectives, keys tasks and information needs.

3.3 System Purpose

This theme addresses the diagnosis with five ST methods and a questionnaire in order to specify efficiency and job satisfaction needs. It takes into consideration ST aspects such as knowledge, psychological, support and control contracts. This also includes logical aspects such as error categorisation and diagnosis, identification and clarification of problem resolution.

3.4 System Perspectives

In this theme, the analyst assesses future changes (e.g. technological, regulatory, economic, social, and organisational) likely to affect the system within the next five years. This assessment is based on one method consisting of five facets of future analysis.

3.5 System Priorities

In this theme the analyst specifies efficiency and job satisfaction needs and social objectives. This specification is supported by three ST methods.

3.6 Desirable System

This consists of development of organizational and technical design of the new system assisted by two ST methods.

3.7 System Action

This consists of preparation of a detailed work design for the chosen organisational and technical option.

3.8 System for Evaluation and Engagement

This theme is supported by four ST methods and includes the implementation diagnosis, the realization of benefit management analysis and the evaluation and self-reflective element in terms of improved efficiency and job satisfaction.

4 Strategy for Addressing Potential Problems

Despite the positive impact of ST methods in terms of improving working practices and increasing human knowledge [25, 27], Baxter and Summerville [3] provide a summary of potential problems related to the use of ST design approaches. The potential problems have been addressed in the following way:

- **Inconsistent terminology:** this is due to the difficulty to have an agreement about the social and technical factors that need to be considered and analysed in the system development. The ST toolbox supports participatory and user engagement such as Client Led Design.
- **Abstraction:** this is dependent on the difficulty of defining problem space including determining the system boundaries and is related to the use of terminology. The ST toolbox is drawing on the natural and professional language already used by the stakeholders which help them to overcome potential problems of abstraction.
- **Conflicting value systems including difficulties with communication and coordination:** this is a potential result from the multidisciplinarity of the team involved in the ST practice. This can also occur as employees and managers apply different values (humanistic and managerial). The ST toolbox includes methods and tools for organized systemic dialogue and clarification of differences in values and so supports constructive collaboration and problem resolution.
- **Evaluation of benefits and lack of problem solutions:** the former problem is a result of apparent lack of effective metrics to assess the application results of ST

practices. The latter problem is dependent on the difficulty to move from problems space analysis to suggestion and design of appropriate change. The ST toolbox includes specific tools and techniques that help stakeholders to develop problem resolution. In addition, the ST toolbox includes methods for benefit management in order to clarify and describe system expectations in such a way that they can be managed and implemented through actions which are identifiable and can be pursued in the real world.

- **Perceived anachronism and identification of stakeholders:** the first problem is associated to the marginal role attributed to ST practice in organizational changes and innovation in ways of working. The second problem is associated with the lack of pragmatic use of stakeholder analysis. The ST toolbox incorporates several stakeholder analyses, which engages and involves stakeholders in their own definition of desirable change practices and system boundaries.

In the next section, we summarize the generic experiences of ST toolbox use within 36 different companies. This time the use of the toolbox was introduced and supervised in each participating company by a student trainee analyst. All participating companies were voluntary and they committed to engage in a minimum of six workshops. The majority of companies however choose to engage and involve themselves much more than initially agreed upon in the ST practice.

5 Experiences of Socio-Technical Toolbox Use

In this section, an overview of some of the experiences of the participating companies is given. The Tables 1 and 2 provide data about characteristics of companies involved in this study. Furthermore 26 out of 36 participating companies gave additional and explicit evaluation about their experience of their ST toolbox use. Below some examples of companies comments are reported.

> This system analysis is important in every business. It made me realize how many things I can look at to make the system to behave better. For example the problems identified at the possibilities maybe needed good effort.
>   I have been very impressed with the work that has been put into this project, and we have actually implemented a few of the ideas that were set out in the project. These are currently going ok, and we are open to looking in ways of improving our processes after looking at the work that has been done.
>   Very useful to see staff feedback and have an independent outside view of the company.
>   The project had helped look at the issues that were otherwise overlooked.
>   Very useful, helpful and beneficial.
>   We value the comments and observations that have been provided to us whilst visiting the department and applying the practices of the toolbox. A number of the ideas are of great interest and will be used to improve the performance of the department.

The feedback given clearly shows that involved companies recognise the potential value of the use of the ST toolbox. Specifically, they point out that the analysis is contributing to a significantly better understanding of their own

Table 1 Classification of companies according to their activity sector

Activity sector	Number of companies
Commerce	16
Restaurants and cafes	8
Others	12
Total	36

Table 2 Classification of companies by number of employees

Number of employees	Number of companies
≤ 5	12
$5 < X \leq 10$	14
$10 < X \leq 40$	8
>200	2
Total	36

business and practices. They highlight examples such as problem solving capabilities improvements and organizational changes facilitation both at operational and strategic levels. The feedback was consistent not only when companies appreciated the involvement of the trainee analyst but also when they were unsatisfied with the work of the trainee analyst. Overall, every manager that gave feedback explicitly stated their satisfaction with ST toolbox and would recommend its application both in their own and other companies.

6 Conclusion

All method applications are by definition applied by analysts and stakeholders so the outcome would always depend on the specific human actors involved. Any outcome would not be determined by the choice of method, as methods do not apply themselves independently of human involvement and subjective interpretation. The study presented in this paper support the findings of previous research by Mumford [24, 25, 27] and Checkland [10, 11] among others. However, our research further supports the conclusion that ST practice is still today both relevant and useful for any kind of organization in a contemporary fast changing and dynamic environment. The benefits of such use in practice are not reliant on the sector or the size of the organizations.

References

1. Anderson, T.D.: Teaching the socio-technical practices of tomorrow today. In: Whitworth, B., De Moor, A. (eds.) Handbook of Research on Socio-Technical Design and Social Networking Systems. Hershey, PA (2009)

2. Avison, D., Fitzgerald, G.: Information Systems Development: Methodologies, Techniques and Tools, 4th edn. McGraw-Hill, Maidenhead (2006)
3. Baxter, G., Sommerville, I.: Socio-technical systems: from design methods to systems engineering. Interact. Comput. **23**, 4–17 (2011)
4. Bednar, P.M.: A contextual integration of individual and organizational learning perspectives as part of IS analysis. Inf. Sci. J. **3**(3), 145–156 (2000)
5. Bednar, P., Welch, C.: IS, process, organizational change and their relationship with contextual dependencies. In: Proceedings of 13th European Conference on Information Systems: Information Systems in a Rapidly Changing Economy, ECIS 2005, Regensburg (2005)
6. Bednar, P.M.: Contextual analysis. A multiperspective inquiry into emergence of complex socio-cultural systems. In: Minati, G., Abram, M., Pessa, E. (eds.) Processes of Emergence of Systems and Systemic Properties: Towards a General Theory of Emergence, pp. 299–312. Singapore, World Scientific (2009)
7. Bednar, P.M.: Individual emergence in contextual analysis. problems of individual emergence. Special issue of systemica, J. Systeemgroep Nederland (deuch systems Group) **14**(1–6), 23–48 (2007)
8. Checkland, P.: Towards a systems-based methodology for real-world problem-solving. J. Appl. Sys. Eng. **3**(2), 87–116 (1972)
9. Checkland, P.: Systems Thinking, Systems Practice. Wiley, Chichester (1981)
10. Checkland, P., Holwell, S.: Information, Systems and Information Systems. Wiley, Chichester (1998)
11. Checkland, P., Poulter, J.: Learning for Action. Wiley, Chichester (2006)
12. Churchman, C.W.: The Design of Inquiring Systems. Basis Books, New York (1971)
13. D'Atri, A., De Marco, M.: Interdisciplinary Aspects of Information Systems Studies. Springer, Heidelberg (2008)
14. Hirschheim, R., Klein, H.K.: A Glorious and not-so-short history of the information systems field. J. Assoc. Inf. Syst. **13**(4), 188–235 (2012)
15. Jacucci, G., Wagnar, I., Tellioglu, H.: Design games as a part of social practice design: a case of employees elaborating on organizational problems. In: Proceedings of ECIS (2008)
16. Kosaka, T.: Theoretical investigation into systems Analysis. In: Proceedings of The Pacific-Asia Conference on Information Systems (2009)
17. Langefors, B.: Theoretical Analysis of Information Systems. Studentlitteratur, Lund (1966)
18. Langefors, B.: Essays on Infology: Summing up and Planning for the Future. Studentlitteratur, Lund (1995)
19. Luna-Reyes, L.F., Zhang, J., Gil-Garcıa, J.R., Cresswell, A.M.: Information system development as emergent socio-technical change: a practice approach. Eur. J. Inf. Syst. **14**, 93–105 (2005)
20. Mathiassen, L., Munk Madsen, A., Nielsen, P.A., Stage, J.: Object Oriented Analysis and Design. Aalborg, Marko (2000)
21. Mumford, E.: Computer systems and work design: problems of philosophy and vision. Pers. Rev. **3**(2), 40–49 (1974)
22. Mumford, E., Henshall, D.: A Participative Approach to the Design of Computer Systems. Associated Business Press, London (1978)
23. Mumford, E.: Participative systems design: structure and method. Syst. Objectives Solutions **1**(1), 5–19 (1981)
24. Mumford, E.: Designing Human Systems: The ETHICS Method. Manchester Business School Press, Manchester (1983)
25. Mumford, E.: Redesigning Human Systems. IRM Press, London (2003)
26. Mumford, E., Hirschheim, R., Fitzgerald, G., Wood Harper, T. (Eds.) Research Methods in Information Systems. North Holland Publishers, New York (1985)
27. Mumford, E.: The story of socio-technical design: reflections in its successes, failures and potential. Inf. Syst. J. **16**, 317–342 (2006)
28. Sommerville, I.: Software Engineering, 8th edn. Pearson Education, Harlow (2007)

29. Stowell, F., West, D.: Client Led Design: A Systemic Approach to Information Systems Definition. McGraw Hill, London (1994)
30. Ward, J., Daniel, E.: Benefits Management: How to Increase the Business Value of Your IT Projects. Wiley, UK (2012)

Guidelines for User Driven Service and E-Service Innovations

Ada Scupola

Abstract The purpose of this article is to provide a set of guidelines consisting of tools and steps to be used to design service innovations by involving the users. The guidelines are based on an understanding of the service development process as a linear stage process as described by Alam [5] and user roles as described by Nambisan [15]. The tools and steps are illustrated through the way they have been applied to develop and design service and e-service innovations in the case of Roskilde University Library.

Keywords Services · E-services · Design · Innovation · User involvement

1 Introduction

Service innovation and design is becoming a very popular subject both in academia and in the business world, especially in consulting companies. Bitner et al. [1] state that organizations that are most successful in providing new services "prepare and move systematically (and often iteratively) through a set of planned stages from the establishment of clear objectives, to idea generation, to concept development, service design, prototyping, service launch, and customer feedback" [1, p. 4]. In the earliest contributions on service design [2, 3], the activity of service designing was considered as part of the domain of marketing and management disciplines. Shostack [2] for instance proposed the integrated design of material components (products) and immaterial components (services). This design process, according to Shostack [2, 3] can be documented and codified using a "service blueprint" to map the sequence of events in a service and its essential functions in

A. Scupola (✉)
Department of Communication, Business and Information Technologies, Roskilde University, Hus 44.3, 4000 Roskilde, Denmark
e-mail: ada@ruc.dk

L. Caporarello et al. (eds.), *Smart Organizations and Smart Artifacts*,
Lecture Notes in Information Systems and Organisation 7,
DOI: 10.1007/978-3-319-07040-7_22,
© Springer International Publishing Switzerland 2014

an objective and explicit manner. Similarly, previous literature on service innovation (e.g. [4–7]) suggests that service innovation has to be anchored in the organization's strategy in order to succeed [1]. A new trend within service innovation and service design is the direct or indirect involvement of the users in such processes (e.g. [4, 8–10]). User involvement may contribute to service innovations that are more in line with the user needs and wants and may result in increased customer satisfaction, services with less point of failures and at the very end an increased competitive advantage of the company. Given this background, the purpose of this article is to develop and provide a set of guidelines that can be used to involve the user in the service innovation or design process.

The article is structured as follows. The introduction presents the background of the article. The Sect. 2 briefly presents the theoretical background including conceptual definitions of services and e-services, user involvement in the service innovation and design process as well as the tools that can be used in such a process. The Sect. 3 illustrates how the tools were used in Roskilde University library to involve users in the innovation of the services offered by the library and on this base develop some guidelines for user involvement. Finally, the last section presents some concluding remarks.

2 Theoretical Background

2.1 Understanding Face to Face and E-Services

According to Bitner et al. [1], one of the most distinctive characteristics of services is their *process* nature. Unlike physical goods, services are dynamic and unfold over a period of time through a sequence or constellation of events and steps. The service process can be viewed as a chain or constellation of activities that allow the service to function effectively [2, 3]. In contrast to goods, which can be separated from the immediate producers and sold on an anonymous market, services are not anonymous and are produced and consumed simultaneously [1]. Therefore, services require face-to-face contact between the producers and the consumers in the production/consumption phase. This may not always hold entirely true, but the consumption will at least start right after the end of production—as in the case of repair work [11].

In the last 2 decades or so, the advent of information and communication technology (ICT) and especially the World Wide Web have affected services in several ways and research has flourished on the subject of technology–based services, Internet-based services or e-services [11, 12]. Especially in the case of information and knowledge services (informational services), it is the service itself which is affected. With ICTs, it is possible to enter data, information and knowledge (to the extent it can be codified) on digital media and use communication networks for transportation [13]. This means that data, information or knowledge services increasingly can be separated from the immediate producers and sold on anonymous markets. It could therefore be claimed that there is a degree of convergence between goods and services enabled by the use of digital communications and that services in a sense become goods [11].

2.2 The Service Innovation and Design Process

One main characteristic of services is that the customer is essential in the service provision process, whether this process is face to face or Internet-based. However, while a lot of literature especially within the service marketing field has addressed customer involvement in the final act of service providing by focusing for example on the moment of truth, customer experience, or service co-creation, the concept of user involvement in the service innovation process and design is not a well-defined concept despite the fact that much has been written about it [8].

A broad applied way to understand service innovation is to analyze the different phases or steps of the innovation process [14]. In order to do so, this paper draws on the service innovation model developed by Alam and Perry [4] characterized by 10 steps: (1) Strategic planning; (2) Idea generation; (3) Idea screening; (4) Business analysis; (5) Formation of cross-functional team; (6) Service and process design; (7) Personnel training; (8) Service testing and pilot run; (9) Test marketing; (10) Commercialization. This model takes into account the core element in user involvement in new service development highlighting the objective/purpose of involvement, the stages of involvement in the organizational innovation process, the intensity of involvement and the modes of involvement.

2.3 The User Roles

Nambisan [15] has developed three roles that customers can have in new product development: "customer as a resource", "customer as co-creator" and "customer as user". More recently Scupola and Nicolajsen [7] and Nicolajsen and Scupola [16] have showed that the roles developed by Nambisan [15] in the context of New Product Development, can also be applied in the context of new service development. The role of the customer as a resource in the phases of generating new product ideas has been extensively investigated by the marketing and innovation literature. According to Nambisan [15], the contribution of customers as a resource varies with the maturity of the technology and the alignment of the product line with the customer base. In the case of continuous innovations, customers are generally passive and firms have to find out about the customers opinion through market surveys or focus groups. Previous literature [9] also argue that there are a number of challenges related to using customers as a resource in idea generation including selection of customers, creation of incentives to foster customer participation and capture of customer knowledge.

Customers may also play a key role as co-creators of new products or services. As co-creators, customers can participate in a number of activities varying from design activities to development activities. According to Nambisan [15, p. 396] customer-firms interactions tend to be much more intense and frequent during co-creation, and mechanisms to support such interactions are costly and technology intensive. Similarly, Alam [5, 6] found that the stages where customers' involvement was valuable were much more expensive, time-consuming, more cumbersome and risky in terms of return on investment. The last role that Nambisan [15] has identified is the customer as a user. In such a role customers can provide value in two ways in the service process: service testing and support. For example in the software industry many firms have used their customers in beta product testing, thus enabling those firms to reduce their investments in internal product testing units. For example, the involvement of users in product testing can be used to identify problems early on in the development phase, thus minimizing the costs of redesign and re-development.

2.4 Tools for User Driven Service Innovation and Design

Previous literature has identified a number of tools to involve users in the service innovation or design process [17]. In this chapter such tools are distinguished into two main categories: face to face and ICT-based tools. An example where ICT-based tools were used to directly involve customers in the design process is the use of e-forums to involve customers to contribute to the innovation process by Lego, where customers have been recruited to engage in software code development for LEGO mind storm. In addition, the distinction is made here between tools that require direct and pro-active involvement and participation from the participants and tools where the participants are central but have just a passive role in the sense that they are investigated or observed in order to gain insights into the service process. The first are here called "direct tools", while the latter are called "indirect" tools. One of the most used "direct" face-to-face tools in service design and innovation is workshop. An example of "indirect" tool is the use of ethnographic studies to understand problems with current service offerings or visiting online communities. Based on the classification above, a taxonomy of design tools for user-driven service innovation is proposed in Table 1.

Table 1 A taxonomy of design tools for user-driven service innovation

Categories of service innovation and design tools	Face-to-face	ICT-based
"Direct"	Workshops (e.g. future workshops) interviews focus groups	Online idea competitions blogs facebook e-forums
"Indirect"	Ethnographic studies paper based surveys complaint box	Online discussion groups virtual communities online surveys log data

3 User-Driven Service Innovation in Practice: The Case of Roskilde University Library

In order to illustrate how such tools have been applied and can be applied in practice to involve users in the service innovation process, here an action research study of Roskilde University Library is presented [18]. The process employed in this study consists of three phases: (1) Uncovering current service innovation practices with focus on user involvement and tools for involvement; (2) Using ICT-based tools for direct user involvement in the service innovation process; (3) Using future workshops to generate ideas from employees, users and users-employees combined.

3.1 First Phase: Uncovering Current Service Innovation Practices

In the first phase, an exploratory study investigating current service innovation processes and sources of innovation with focus on user involvement at Roskilde University Library was conducted to get an understanding of the innovation processes at the library and especially to understand whether and how library users were involved in such a process. Semi-structured qualitative interviews as well as a number of meetings and workshops lasting between 1 and 2 h with top managers, middle managers, and 'front-line' librarians were the main data collection tools used in the study. In this phase, the researchers acting as "external facilitators" had been the main agents collecting and analyzing the data and writing a report to the library management on the library current practices for service innovations and for user involvement in such innovation processes as well the strategic need for new service innovations or service improvements.

The results of this phase show that the library's traditional approach to innovation is mainly based on the use of 'internal development plans' where most ideas come from top management, collaboration with external partners and competitors but also, even though to a lesser extent, from employees. The study shows that traditionally at RUB the users had mainly taken on the "role as a resource" in the service innovation process and been involved mainly with indirect tools such as surveys and customer complaints box. In addition, users have been indirectly represented through the employees understanding of the users' wants and wishes, likes and dislikes. This understanding is mainly gained through face-to-face interactions in the provisions of services like courses on how to use the library resources, library consultation services and other services. These users' inputs often result in small changes in the practices of the employees, or sometimes the ideas may be sent to top management for evaluation and further action. Such service encounters, traditional user satisfaction surveys and complaint/satisfaction boxes have been the main ways for the library to collect opinions and wishes from the users. Web-based interactive tools in the form of online chat had just recently been adopted at RUB on an experimental basis to establish contact with users. This type of customer contact was just a virtual version of the face-to-face encounter and at the time of the study still limitedly used.

3.2 Second Phase: Using ICT-Based Tools to Directly Involve Users in the Idea Generation Process of Service Innovations

Given the results of the first phase indicating very limited customer involvement in the service innovation process, a decision was made by the library together with the team of researchers acting as facilitators to use ICT-based tools and face-to-face tools to directly involve the users in the process and hear their voices. It was agreed that in the second phase of the process, ICT-based tools had to be used to directly involve the users in a dialogue with the library and generate ideas from the users concerning library service innovations. After some considerations and discussions, a decision was made to implement a blog to collect ideas directly from the library users. This choice was due to the library's previous experience with a blog that had been used for internal organizational purposes. This process was initiated by the researchers, but it was run completely by the library and the ideas generated at the end of the process were analysed, ranked and selected for implementation by the library employees and management. It can be said that the decision of using the blog is the result of the situadness of this process as this choice was made due to RUB's previous organizational experience with using a blog for internal organizational and communication purposes.

After having agreed to use a blog in the idea generation stage of the service innovation process, a small team was established to design and implement the blog. The team comprised four employees from different library departments as well as two researchers that functioned as external facilitators. The team met on an ongoing basis for 6 months. In this period the blog was designed and set up and a pre-test was conducted by a group of computer mediated communication experts.

Different blog names and layouts were discussed inspired by other blogs regarding content, tone etc. After some discussions and meetings, a decision was made to formulate four themes within which innovative ideas were sought. These themes were formulated by the library based on their innovation needs, therefore making the results of this action "situated" in relation to the library' actual needs at the moment of the study.

The themes were formulated as questions and aimed at getting ideas on the overall library services, the library's face to face services, the library e-services as well as the library physical settings. In addition to the questions a small piece of text giving examples of the kind of input looked for was put on the first page of the blog.

The blog initiative was advertised in several ways both online on the library's web page and at Roskilde university campus. For example book markers with the blog address were handed out to the library users when they loaned books.

To motivate library users to contribute ideas on the blog two gift vouchers were promised at the end of the idea generation period to two randomly drawn contributors. This was written on the main page of the blog. The idea generation period lasted for 3 months, during which the library employees commented and responded to the users' postings, since the idea was that the blog should function as a web-based interactive platform between the library users and the employees. At the end of the 3 months period, the ideas generated through the blog were analysed and discussed by library management for their relevance and implementation potential at a management meeting and the selected ideas were implemented in the following year.

3.3 Third Phase: Using Future Workshops

The third phase of the service innovation process consisted of 3 parallel future workshops organized by the researchers/facilitators aiming at involving users with face-to-face design tools in the idea generation and design process. The main purpose of this phase was to complement the ideas generated by the ICT-based tools with new ideas generated through face-to-face complementary tools, thus generating ideas, conceptualizing service innovations and, to the extent possible, designing service innovations that the library could use and implement to improve its service offerings, service satisfaction and position itself as an innovative library. One workshop was organized with only library employees in order to find out what the library employees believed was needed concerning service innovations, one was organized with only library users and a third one was organized with mixed participants, users and library employees. The workshops took place simultaneously at the library premises and were facilitated by three researchers/facilitators. An announcement was put in the library looking for potential participants to the workshops. There were six participants in each workshop. A ticket to a movie theater was given to the workshop participants to increase motivation to participate. The workshops consisted of 3 phases: a first phase in which the participants had to criticize the current library services; a creative phase where the participants had to come up with new service concepts/ideas and an implementation phase where the ideas had to be concretized into specific service designs. The researchers/facilitators recorded the ideas generated on post it and discussion in the three different workshops and different phases of the workshops in a spreadsheet. The ideas were then ranked for relevance, selected for implementation and finally implemented by the library.

4 Towards Some Guidelines for User-Driven Service Innovations

Based on the description of the phases and actions described in the above case, a design methodology for user-driven service innovations is proposed here as follows and briefly summarized in Table 2:

1. Uncover current organizational practices and needs concerning service innovations and design. This can be done using for example tools such as interviews, workshops, focus groups with key organizational employees. This phase should be conducted by a neutral process facilitator and if possible by someone external to the organization. This phase should identify specific areas to focus later actions and service innovation efforts on. Go to 2 or 3. Possibly conduct both phase 2 and 3.
2. Identify a suitable form of ICT-based tool to generate ideas from the organization's users and to the extent possible from external partners on service innovations. Go to 4 and possibly 3.
3. Organize (future) workshops to elicit further ideas for service innovations and design involving users, but also employees. It is suggested that the optimal would be to organize at least three different workshops:

    a. A workshop where the participants are only employees.
    b. A workshop where the participants are only users or customers of the services.
    c. A workshop where both customers/users and organizational employees participate in a mixed way. Go to 4 and 2 if it has not been conducted yet.

4. Have organizational meetings to evaluate the ideas generated in step 2 and 3. Go to 5.
5. Implement the service innovations found important in step 4. Go to 6.
6. Communicate to the stakeholders involved in the process (users, employees and, eventually, other partners) which service innovations/changes were implemented and why.

Table 2 Summary of steps of the design guidelines for user driven service innovation

Steps of the design guidelines	Actions
Step 1	Uncover current service innovations practices and needs in the organization
Step 2	Use ICT-based tools to generate ideas for service innovations with user involvement
Step 3	Use face-to-face tools to generate ideas for service innovations with user involvement
Step 4	Evaluation of the collected ideas
Step 5	Implementation of the ideas
Step 6	Provide feedback to the involved stakeholders in the process about the results of the service innovation process

5 Conclusions

By taking the starting point on the concept of services, service design and service innovations, the article provides a set of guidelines for user driven service innovations that can be used to develop service innovations that are conceptualized and designed with the involvement of the customer/user. These guidelines draw on the new service development process developed by Alam and Perry [4] and the roles that the customers can take on in new service development developed by Nambisan [15] to identify how users/customers can be involved in the service innovation process. In addition, the guidelines draw on a taxonomy of tools, categorized as face-to-face and ICT-based tools that can be used to involve the customer in the service innovation and design process. Examples of face-to-face tools include workshops, interviews and focus groups. Examples of ICT-based tools include e-forums, online idea competitions, blogs and virtual communities.

The design guidelines are derived from and illustrated with an in depth case study of Roskilde University Library. The case presents 3 phases where both face-to-face and ICT-based tools were applied in order to design library service innovations.

The first phase uncovers the library's current organizational needs and practices concerning service innovations and design. In this phase interviews, documentary material and workshops were the tools used to collect the necessary data. The second phase utilizes a blog to solicit and collect ideas from the library users regarding four pre-defined themes. This phase includes also screening and evaluation of the ideas by the library management. The third phase includes the conduction of three parallel workshops, respectively composed of only users, only employees and users-employees respectively. Also in this phase the service innovation ideas and designs generated in the workshops have been evaluated by the library top management for suitability and potential for implementation.

The guidelines presented in this article are important first of all because they can be used to get a comprehensive understanding of the service innovation and design process and the tools that can be used for user involvement in such a process. User involvement has, in fact, recently been determined as being key to successful service innovations. In addition this methodology is important because it is constituted of a series of actions clearly specifying what to do in order to design service innovations with the involvement of the customer or user. Such actions guide the design process and are the basis for the choice of the tools to be used in each step of such process.

The service marketing literature has showed that services are heterogeneous and each service process depends on the service and the organizational context under consideration. Consequently the output of such actions and tools unfold during and with the design process, being such actions and choices of the tools situated in the specific service and organizational context under consideration. The guidelines presented in this article can be conceptualized as a situated plan for action. That is, they function as a set of guiding actions to develop service innovation and design, but thye do not determine the course of actions. The outcome of the course of actions depends on the specific service and organizational context in question as well as the specific users that get involved in such a design process. The results and applications also depend on the specific goals of the design process.

5.1 Implications and Limitations

This article provides a set of guidelines to develop service innovations and design with the involvement of the users or customers of the services. Being the methodology very comprehensive, it is not expected to be able to follow all the steps in a project. However the methodology is constructed in such a way that depending on the project, only one or more steps can be conducted in order to design service innovations and one or more of the proposed tools can be used to develop user driven service innovations. For example by following the model of Alam and Perry [5], it is possible to focus on one or more phases of the innovation process. Similarly it is possible to focus on one or more roles of the customers and finally it is possible to apply one or more of the tools suggested for idea generation and design of service innovations. Such combinations lead to many potential ways the methodology and related tools can be used and applied.

References

1. Bitner, M.J., Ostrom, A.L., Morgan, F.N.: Service blueprinting: a practical technique for service innovation. Calif. Manag. Rev. **50**(3), 66–94 (2008)
2. Shostack, G.L.: How to design a service. Eur. J. Mark. **16**(1), 49–63 (1982)
3. Shostack, G.L.: Service positioning through structural change. J. Mark. **51**(1), 34–43 (1984)

4. Alam, I., Perry, C.: A customer-oriented new service development process. J. Serv. Mark. **16**(6), 515–534 (2002)
5. Alam, I.: An exploratory investigation of user involvement in new service development. J. Acad. Mark. Sci. **30**(3), 250–261 (2002)
6. Alam, I.: Removing the fuzziness form the fuzzy front-end of service innovations through customer interactions. Ind. Mark. Manage. **35**, 468–480 (2006)
7. Scupola, A., Nicolajsen, H.W.: Service innovation in academic libraries: is there a place for the customers? Libr. Manag., **31**(4/5), 304–318 (2010)
8. Magnusson, P., Matthing, J., Kristensson, P.: Managing user involvement in service innovation. J. Serv. Res. **6**(2), 111–124 (2003)
9. Matthing, J., Sandén, B., Edvardsson, B.: New service development: learning from and with customers. Int. J. Serv. Ind. Manag. **15**(5), 479–498 (2004)
10. Scupola, A., Nicolajsen, H.W.: Blogs and user involvement in the service innovation process: challenges and pitfalls. Int. J. E-Bus. Res. **9**(3), 27–37 (2013)
11. Scupola, A., Henten, A., Nicolajsen, Westh, H.: E-services: characteristics, scope and conceptual strengths. Int. J. E-Serv. Mob. Appl. **1**(3), 1–16 (2009)
12. Bitner, M.J., Brown, S.W., Meuter, M.L.: Technology infusion in service encounter. J. Acad. Mark. Sci. **28**(1), 138–149 (2000)
13. Hofacker, C.F., Goldsmith, R.E., Bridges, E., Swilley, E.: E-Services: a synthesis and research agenda. J. Value Chain Manag. **1**(1/2), 13–34 (2007)
14. Cooper, R., Edgett, G., Scott, J., Kleinschmidt, E.J.: Organizing the stage-gate process: what best-practice companies do. Res. Technol. Manag. **45**(6), 43–50 (2002)
15. Nambisan, S.: Designing virtual customer environments for new product development: toward a theory. Acad. Manag. Rev. **27**(33), 392–413 (2002)
16. Nicolajsen Westh, H., Scupola, A.: Investigating issues and challenges for customer involvement in business services innovation. J. Bus. Ind. Mark. **26**(5), 368–376 (2011)
17. Prandelli, E., Sawhney, M., Verona, G.: Collaborating with Customers to Innovate. Edward Elgar, UK (2008)
18. Yin, R.K.: Case Study Research Design and Methodology, vol. 5, 2nd edn. Sage Publications, London (1994)

Engaging "New Users" into Design Activities: The TERENCE Experience with Children

Tania Di Mascio, Rosella Gennari, Alessandra Melonio
and Laura Tarantino

Abstract The diffusion of digital technology is bringing new types of users "into the market", like children, elderly people, or technology illiterate people. Designers and researchers have to face new design challenges having at disposal a lighter and less structured body of knowledge about characteristics and demands of these users, and even consolidated design methods may prove to be inefficient. With respect to these issues, and more specifically with focus on data gathering techniques, in this paper we discuss the experience of the TERENCE project, aimed at developing a technology enhanced learning system for improving text comprehension in children 7–11 years old. In particular, our experience suggests extending the repertoire of inquiry techniques with methods shaped and informed by gamefulness phenomena.

Keywords User centered design · Data gathering methods · Children

1 Introduction

The growing diffusion of innovative digital technology in everyday life is extending the population of users both in number and in typology, bringing into the realm of technological products people traditionally not served by ICT.

T. Di Mascio · L. Tarantino (✉)
Università degli Studi dell'Aquila, L'Aquila, Italy
e-mail: laura.tarantino@univaq.it

T. Di Mascio
e-mail: tania.dimascio@univaq.it

R. Gennari · A. Melonio
Libera Università di Bolzano, Bolzano, Italy
e-mail: gennari@inf.unibz.it

A. Melonio
e-mail: alessandra.melonio@unibz.it

L. Caporarello et al. (eds.), *Smart Organizations and Smart Artifacts*,
Lecture Notes in Information Systems and Organisation 7,
DOI: 10.1007/978-3-319-07040-7_23,
© Springer International Publishing Switzerland 2014

Elderly, young people, people with special needs, technology-reluctant and/or technology-illiterate people are just a few examples of not traditional ICT users with novel demands and novel expectations on interactive artifacts, which translate into novel design and research issues.

Technology is successful when it is well contextualized and it is based on a clear understanding of needs, cultural constraints, and behaviors of the persons using it. A rigorous design approach requires that the design solution is iteratively created/developed using state-of-the-art knowledge both from existing theories and successful design solutions and design practices, referring to both the characteristics of the desired product (e.g., interaction techniques, visual elements, gestures) and the design process itself (e.g., methods and grounding theories). In case of new users' typologies, not only designers and researchers rely on a less heavy and often less structured body of knowledge, but even consolidated techniques and methods may turn out to be less efficient, sometimes exactly when and where they become even more crucial than in more traditional application domains. It is desirable that the design is conducted according to methodologies that actively involve users in the design process, like User Centered Design (UCD) or participatory design, which have the positive side effect of favoring the integration of designed artifacts into organizations sometimes new to digital innovations (e.g., schools and hospices). But, if it is reasonable to expect that extensive contextual studies are conducted *with users* to elicit insights on their demands, characteristics, tasks and behavior, it is legitimate to ask whether existing methods for the analysis of the context of use are really adequate for interacting, e.g., with children or elderly or people with special needs.

According to Information System (IS) design science (see, e.g., [9]), theories play a dual role in the design process: they constitute the ground of an artifact construction, and can be the outcome of the design process. Knowledge and understanding of a problem domain and its solution can be achieved by the building and the application of the desired artifact. It is then desirable that the growing interest around new users, and the consequent production of novel ad hoc innovative interactive technology, be characterized by the twofold purpose of building artifacts and enriching related state-of-the-art knowledge. While for an extensive discussion on how HCI and IS design science research may cooperate we refer to [15], we here recall that, e.g., in the case of the so called "second paradigm" in the HCI discourse [8], design and evaluation of artifacts and processes for creating new knowledge are well represented by Hevner's three cycle view [10]: in this view an iterative process bridges the design science activities (the *Design Cycle*) with the contextual environment on the one side (the *Relevance Cycle*) and the knowledge base of scientific foundations, experience and expertise on the other side (the *Rigor Cycle*), as sketched in Fig. 1. Particularly in the case of new user types, it is hence expected (1) a considerable work in the Relevance Cycle and (2) additions and extensions of original theories and methods in the knowledge base, gained from performing the research and from testing the artifact in the application environment.

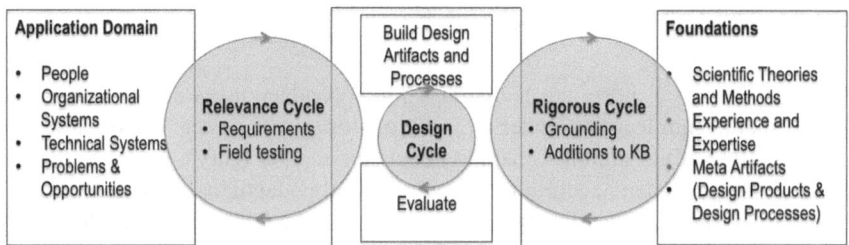

Fig. 1 Hevner's three cycle view of design science research

According to this view, in this paper we report the experience gained within the TERENCE project, a European FP7 ICT multidisciplinary project that is developing an Adaptive Learning System (ALS) for supporting "poor comprehenders" and their educators (parents and teachers). Poor text comprehenders are about 10 % of young children; they are proficient in word decoding and other low-level cognitive skills, but show problems in deep text comprehension. Experiments show that inference-making questions centered on a number of identified skills, together with adequate visual aids, are pedagogically effective in fostering deep comprehension of stories [2]. However finding stories and educational material appropriate for poor comprehenders is a challenge and the few systems promoting reading interventions are based on high school or university textbooks. TERENCE main objective is to face and solve such issues by developing the first ad hoc ALS, in Italian and in English, for improving the reading comprehension of 7–10 years old poor comprehenders, building upon effective paper-and pencil reading strategies, and framing them into a playful and stimulating pedagogy-driven environment.

The project is now in its final phases and we are able to draw conclusions on the achieved results and on the design experience as a whole. While previous papers focused on specific aspects of the system (like system functionality and architecture [3], models underlying the learning material [1], and usability evaluation [4]), here we focus on the analysis of the context of use by presenting methods and techniques used to classify users—especially the learners—and to elicit requirements (Relevance Cycle) with the twofold objective of (1) turning these considerations into a new inquiry method to enrich the body of knowledge (Rigor Cycle), and (2) discussing how and to which extent their adoption contributed to the successful of the system. In particular we will discuss how the recourse to innovative game-based field studies allowed us both to overcome flaws and limit of existing techniques and to comply with constraints posed by the involved organizations and by project resources and budget.

The remainder of the paper is structured as follows. After reporting in Sect. 2 we report on the two rounds of field studies in TERENCE, in Sect. 3 the game-based user investigation is presented in a structured way. Finally, in Sect. 4, conclusions are drawn.

2 The Field Study in TERENCE

Primary TERENCE users are learners, while secondary users are educators and experts that design learning material, made of stories and games: smart games are used for stimulating inference-making about stories, and relaxing games are used for motivating learners, according to a stimulation pedagogical plan identified by experts. To support the diverse users' tasks TERENCE include modules and interfaces designed according to a UCD approach. The overall design process proceeded iteratively, by applying the following steps for each of the four generations of prototypes/system: (1) analysis of Context of Use and Users' Requirements (CUUR); (2) design of learning material, tasks and GUI prototypes, and (3) evaluation.

CUUR was conducted through a preparatory study followed by two rounds of field studies, in the UK and Italy. The preparatory study and the 1st round of field study of CUUR (May 2010–January 2011) have been the base for the first prototypes. The *preparatory field study* was conducted by brainstorming with about 30 domain experts of text comprehension and HCI, with the main aim of understanding how children are assessed by psychologists as poor comprehenders [14]. The *1st round of CUUR* was based on a combination of traditional user-based and expert-based data gathering methods and involved about 70 educators and 100 learners. It focused on *users*, *tasks* (mainly reading comprehension), and *environment* (physical, instructional, devices), for determining organizational and ethical constraints, main requirements of learning material, and a first cognitive characterization of learners [14].

The main goal of the *2nd round of CUUR* (February 2011–June 2011) was to redefine types of users into classes of users—and defining associated personas— according to requirements relevant for the adaptive engine of the ALS, and its output was the base for the second and the third releases of the system. At this stage some kind of direct interaction with learners was crucial to gather high quality data; furthermore to ensure pedagogical effectiveness of the system, a large-scale study was mandatory. The studies hence involved 2 schools in UK and 5 in Italy, for a total of about 550 learners, aged 7–11, and were run as part of regular school activities.

As experts recommend, data gathering methods cannot be used with children "as is": e.g., children might become anxious at the thought of taking a test and tests may conjure up thoughts of school [7]. Druin suggests using indirect methods [5] and proposes methods that allow working with children as partners according to a co-design approach [6]. There are also examples of co-design at school: e.g., in [16] authors explore the application of co-design methods with children 7–9 aged. However, when situated at school and within school activities co-design has some limitations if it is done with many learners and organizational constraints: for example, in TERENCE, schools imposed that all children of a class had to be involved at the same time and that the timing of data gathering activities had to be below one hour.

On the other hand, theoretical and empirical studies show that learners are more motivated to participate in school-class activities if they are shaped like games (e.g., [11, 12]). In [13] authors overview research findings about the correlations between the appeal of games and the psychological need satisfaction they provide, and propose a motivational model that shows that, besides the basic elements of *move* of the player and *outcomes* showing progresses, at least three factors determine engagement: *autonomy*, amounting to a sense of choice and psychological freedom (e.g., players may choose the level to play or the avatar), *competence*, realized by carefully balancing the game challenges to the players' skill, and *relatedness needs*, i.e., the sense of communion with others, attained by stimulating collaboration or competition.

All this considered, we decided to base on games not only the ALS stimulation plan but also the field study. We designed and experimented an innovative children-oriented data gathering approach based on gameful activities designed according to motivational models. The protocol of game-based activities was checked and assessed with schoolteachers (e.g., if a challenge was deemed too difficult or too boring for a school class, it was revised according to teachers' feedback). Data gathering was organized as 6 different games, each of which structured as an independent game aimed at gathering information on a topic to be investigated (identified during the 1st round of CUUR). There were 2 collaborative games, involving all class learners at the same time, and 4 single-player games. At the start of each game, investigators explained goal and moves for advancing through the game. Autonomy, competence and relatedness needs were pursued across the various games. *Autonomy* was elicited by allowing learners to choose among several options for tackling a challenge or to take the decision to skip it. *Competence* was pursued by stimulating diverse skills across games (e.g., some games required mainly verbal skills whereas others mainly drawing skills). The presence of a investigator working as guidance helped to satisfy *relatedness* needs; in two games these were achieved by stimulating the school class to work together. A framework was created for each game specifying the goals and moves of the game, and how autonomy, competence and relatedness needs are pursued. In Fig. 2 we provide an example of instantiation of the framework for a game associated to a specific topic to be investigated, while in Sects. 3 and 4 we provide a structured description of the method and a discussion on its impact on the success of the project, respectively.

3 Game-Based User Investigation

To formally describe the method we propose, we adopt a presentation structure inspired by the one used by usability.net. Furthermore, for all the techniques cited in the following and we refer to http://www.usabilitynet.org/tools/methods.htm.

Summary The *game-based user investigation* is a children-oriented data gathering method, based on game administration, for discovering facts, opinions

Investigation topic	Gather information about the learners' favorite game characters (useful for designing avatars of TERENCE stimulation plan games).	
Game description	**Goal**. The goal of the challenge is to describe popular video game characters. **Moves**. Each learner has to choose a card from the container. A card depicts a character of a popular console game. The entire class then discusses what they like or dislike about that character.	
Autonomy	Each learner can choose whether to extract the card and participate, or not, in the game; each learner can choose what to tell about the selected character.	
Competence	Each learner can express his own verbal skills.	
Relatedness needs	Each learner can feel part of the class by talking about characters or listening to others' preferences.	

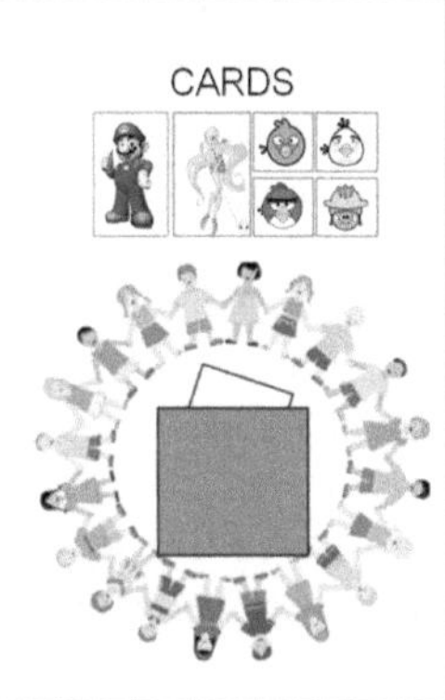

Fig. 2 An example framework instantiation

and behaviors of potential users of the system being designed. Depending on the selected setting (laboratory or real context) it may or may not produce field data. It is preferably done by at least two investigators interacting with individual users or group of users (min 2–max 30 ca.) per session, depending on whether work group is an aspect to be evaluated for the system being designed. During a session, investigators play with users, observe them as they play, take notes on the activities that take place, and possibly record audio/video data. Investigation involves a *direct observation* by investigators actually present during game administration and an *indirect observation* on collected materials (e.g., game results, notes, audio/video recording) by teams including also other investigator. The aim is to gather as much genuine and reliable data as possible.

Benefits This method embodies characteristics from other traditional investigation techniques: as *questionnaires* it allows to gather a high quantity of data in relatively short sessions, as *interviews* it allows a direct interaction with users, as *user observation/field study* it allows to view users in their real context. Anyhow, differently from any other technique, it is based on the administration of specifically designed game-based activities, which introduces a *new kind of interaction with users* in the repertoire of data gathering methods. Due to this specificity, the new method succeeds in offering benefits typical of the above mentioned investigation techniques while overcoming their limitations: compared with questionnaires, it guarantees high quality of data; compared with interviews, it guarantees high quantity of data in short time, compared with user observation/field study, it prevents obtrusiveness since investigators do not interfere with routine activities but rather propose new ones. Furthermore, this method allows investigators to collect a high quantity of structured user-produced data (game results), to be archived for later (statistical) analysis.

Method As in more traditional data gathering techniques, the application of the method requires a sequence of three stages: *planning*, *running*, and *reporting* (see Fig. 3), described in the following subsections.

Fig. 3 The overall structure
of the method

Fig. 4 Focusing on the
running stage

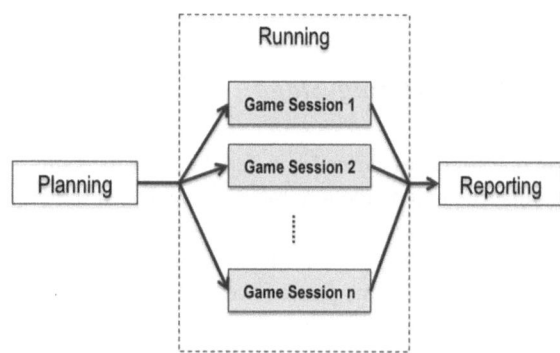

3.1 The Planning Stage

The *planning* stage is mainly devoted to designing/realizing the "investigator kit",
based on the outcome of a preliminary study necessary to acquire in-depth
knowledge on topics/subtopics to be investigated, appropriate language and way of
approaching, context constraints. The kit includes games, game materials, customary notes templates, and a database to be populated by data gathered during the
running stage. Depending on the established schedule, the running stage may
consist of a number of independent game sessions, each based on the same
"investigator kit" (see Fig. 4).

The *investigator kit* is designed according to the following requirements:

- there must be a specific game for each specific topic to be investigated;
- the overall set of games has to include games with different cognitive load so
  that a game session can mirror customary warm-up, peak, and relaxing interview
  phases;
- topics (and associated games) have to be prioritized according to their relevance
  to the project in order to be able to shape the individual game session on the fly at
  running time while maintaining the warm-up/peak/relaxing structure (necessary
  to adjust the session depending on interrupts and other unpredictable events);
- the estimated duration of a game session should not exceed 45/60 min.
- Design of individual games has to consider a number of factors:
- each specific game must cover all subtopics of the topic it is associated to; these
  subtopics are the primary inspiration for the creation of the game that, in any
  case, has to be shaped according to consolidated game frameworks [13];
- mandatory characteristics of individual games are: playfulness, child personal
  enrichment, compliance with ethical issues;

- each specific game must include a rewarding mechanism, designed so to stimulate the production of genuine data from each child;
- individual games should produce children-generated collectable results (e.g., conceptual maps).

3.2 The Running Stage

As previously discussed and depicted in Fig. 4, the *running* stage may consist of a number of independent game sessions based on the same "investigator kit". Each session includes the four phases of *nurturing*, *motivation*, *body*, and *closing*, according to the structure depicted in Fig. 5.

Nurturing In this phase investigators introduce themselves, explain the aim of the session, and establish a playful atmosphere. It is essential to make clear that the participation to games is free and to be sure that children do not see investigators in negative terms.

Motivation In this phase, techniques from motivational theory [13] are used to ensure a sense of responsibility in the children, essential to get reliable data.

Body In this phase investigators administer games and observe children. Games are selected at run-time from the "investigator kit" according to a flexible plan that takes into account: estimated duration of the games, remaining time, topic coverage, topic priorities, warm-up/peak/relaxing cognitive curve, number of involved children. Each administered game requires the four steps of *energizing*, *playing*, *rewarding* and *reorganizing* giving rise to the overall iterative structure of the body phase in Fig. 6:

- *Energizing* In this step goals, moves, and rewards are introduced and excitement is provoked.
- *Playing* In this step the main *direct observation* takes place: the specific game is administered and investigators keep focus on how children carry on game activities, while stimulating children in maintaining interest and supporting their requests. Investigators try to be aware of influences affecting children, take notes of each behavior interesting for later analysis, and may take photos, audio and video recording of the game areas. If the setting is a real context, field data about operation areas are recorded as well, as a reminder of the environmental context.
- *Rewarding* At the end of the specific game, investigators officially close the game, declare winners for group games (if planned), and deliver prizes.
- *Reorganizing* In this step investigators collect and organize produced material.

Closing For ethical and motivational reasons, at the end of the game session it is important to make sure that each child gets a reward. Furthermore, in this phase investigators reorder collected material and write down first impressions about the experience before the analysis. It is also a good idea to spend some time with secondary stakeholders that attended the game sessions to clarify and solve any doubt.

Fig. 5 The structure of a session

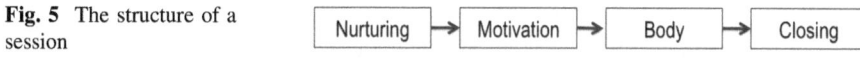

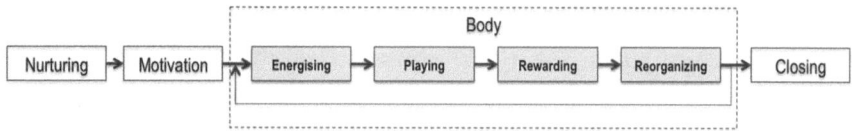

Fig. 6 Focusing on the body structure

3.3 The Reporting Stage

Since the method produces vast amount of high quality data, it is important to analyze them by an *indirect observation*: investigators use collected data to populate the database designed in the planning stage, and conduct statistical analysis to produce user classification, personas design, and requirements specification.

4 Discussion and Conclusions

We discussed some aspects of the design experiences acquired within the TERENCE project that is developing an ALS for supporting poor comprehenders and their educators. We focused on data gathering issues, which, in the case of children, make flaws and limits of traditional methods emerge (e.g., difficulties in involving and motivating users, coping with organizational constraints). The age of learners, along with literature studies on children involvement in school activities, suggested us to explore a game-based approach as primary data gathering method.

The data we gathered were qualitatively genuine (a child could express his/her true self) and dependable for creating fine-grained profiles of learners and their preferences. The reliability of data is supported by evidence from teachers and parents of the involved children (gathered via contextual inquiries). The new approach proved to be definitely engaging for children and teachers, to the point that the involved schools became so interested in the project that volunteered to participate in the prosecution of TERENCE activities (this allowed us to carry on a large scale evaluation with about 900 learners in two countries). The chosen approach also allowed us to conduct an extensive study with many users within time limit and organizational constraints.

On the other hand it has be said that game design and game material constructions require considerable human resources, and that the semi-structuredness of collected data may make their analysis expensive. Notwithstanding these drawbacks, the attained results and their contribution to the success of the project make it reasonable to study if and how a game based approach can fit in the body of knowledge of UCD contextual studies, since its goals and effects may outbalance some flaws of traditional techniques not only for the new types of users that are entering the realm of technological artifacts, but also for more traditional users.

References

1. Alrifai, M., Gennari, R., Tifrea, O., Vittorini, P.: The domain and user model of the TERENCE adaptive learning system. In: 1st International Workshop of Evidence-Based Technology Enhanced Learning (ebTEL 2012), pp. 83–90. Soft Computing, Springer (2012)
2. Cain, K., Oakhill, J.V.: Comprehension Problems in Oral and Written Language. Guildford Press, New York (2007)
3. Cofini, V., de la Prieta, P., Di Mascio, T., Gennari, R., Vittorini, P.: Design smart games with context, generate them with a click, and revise them with a GUI. J. Adv. Distrib. Comput. Artif. Intell. 1, 59–68 (2012)
4. Di Mascio, T., Tarantino, L., Vittorini, P., Caputo, M.: Design choices: affected by user feedback? affected by system performances? lessons learned from the TERENCE project. In: 10th Biannual Conference of the Italian SIGCHI Chapter (CHItaly 2013), pp. 24–33. ACM, New York (NY), USA (2013)
5. Druin, A.: The role of children in the design of new technology. J. Behav. Inf. Technol. 21, 1–25 (2002)
6. Guha, M.L., Druin, A., Chipman, G., Fails, J.A., Simms, S., Farber, A.: Working with young children as technology design partners. Commun. ACM 48(1), 30–42 (2005)
7. Hanna, L., Risden, K., Alexander, K.: Guidelines for usability testing with children. J. Interact. 4(5), 9–14 (1997)
8. Harrison, S., Sengers, P., Tatar, D.: The three paradigms of HCI. In: International Conference of Computer Human Interaction (CHI2000) (2007)
9. Hevner, A.R., March, S.T., Park, J., Ram, S.: Design science in information systems research. J. MIS Q. 28(1), 75–105 (2004)
10. Hevner, A.: A three cycle view of design science research. Scand. J. Inf. Syst. 19(2), 87–92 (2007)
11. Jong, M.S., Lee, J., Shang, J.: Educational use of computer games: where we are, and what's next. In: Huang, R., Spector, J.M. (eds.) Reshaping Learning, New Frontiers of Educational Research, pp. 299–320. Springer, Berlin (2013)
12. Prensky, M.: Digital game-based learning. J. Comput. Entertain. 1(1), 21–31 (2003)
13. Przybylski, A.K., Rigby, C.S., Ryan, R.M.: A motivational model of video game engagement. Rev. Gen. Psychol. 14(2), 154–166 (2010)
14. Slegers, K., Gennari, R.: State of the art of methods for user analysis and context of use. Technical Report, TERENCE project, deliverable D1.1 (2011)
15. Tarantino, L., Spagnoletti, P.: Can design science research bridge computer human interaction and information systems? In: Spagnoletti, P. (eds.) Organizational Change and Information Systems, pp. 409–418. Springer, Heidelberg (2013)
16. Vaajakallio, K., Lee, J., Mattelmaki, T.: "It has to be a group work!": Co-design with children. In: 8th Conference on Interaction Design and Children, (IDC'09), pp. 246–249. ACM, New York (NY), USA (2009)

User-Centered Design of a Web-Based Platform for the Sustainable Development of Tourism Services in a Living Lab Context

Andreja Pucihar, Ana Malešič, Gregor Lenart
and Mirjana Kljajić Borštnar

Abstract The tourism sector in the Gorenjska region, where outstanding natural, historical and geographical potentials are supported by national and regional policies, still faces many challenges in terms of attracting more tourists for longer periods. We address this problem with an open innovation approach, bringing together tourism service providers, end-users (tourists), information and communication technology providers and policy makers; and with the establishing of a regional tourism living lab, which is a real life environment in which researchers, developers and users are co-creating new products or services. We describe the process and experiences of the user-centered design of the web-based platform for sustainable development of tourism services in a living lab context. The phases of the co-design process of web platform development are described, from idea formation through prototype development, testing, and gathering user feedback through several workshops. The final outcome, the "GoGorenjska" web platform, is presented, and further research is outlined. Based on the feedback from tourism service providers and tourists, we can conclude that the platform itself has vast open innovation potential, providing a critical mass of users in the phase of full production on the market.

Keywords Living lab · User-centered design · Services · Tourism

A. Pucihar (✉) · A. Malešič · G. Lenart · M. K. Borštnar
Faculty of Organizational Sciences, University of Maribor, Kidričeva cesta 55a,
4000 Kranj, Slovenia
e-mail: andreja.pucihar@fov.uni-mb.si
URL: http://www.fov.uni-mb.si

A. Malešič
e-mail: ana.malesic@fov.uni-mb.si

G. Lenart
e-mail: gregor.lenart@fov.uni-mb.si

M. K. Borštnar
e-mail: mirjana.kljajic@fov.uni-mb.si

L. Caporarello et al. (eds.), *Smart Organizations and Smart Artifacts*,
Lecture Notes in Information Systems and Organisation 7,
DOI: 10.1007/978-3-319-07040-7_24,
© Springer International Publishing Switzerland 2014

1 Introduction

Slovenia lies in the heart of Europe, where the Alps meet the Mediterranean, and the Pannonian Plain meets the Karst. Slovenia is a small, green country, with wonderful nature, offering mountains, seaside, forests, lakes, rivers, caves and more; all which is on only 20,273 km^2. Slovenia is divided into 12 regions. One of the most attractive regions for tourists is the Gorenjska region, which is located in the northern part of Slovenia. Tourists can, for example, visit Lake Bled and Lake Bohinj, go hiking in Julian Alps and the Kamnik-Savinja Alps, visit Triglav National Park (Triglav is the highest mountain in Slovenia with a peak of 2,864 m a.s.l.), engage in a wide range of outdoor activities in resorts. such as Kranjska Gora (mostly recognized as a skiing resort, organizing also the men's FIS Alpine Skiing World Cup race every year) and explore the history of old towns such as Kranj and Škofja Loka [1].

Because of the diversity of natural resources, tourism offers enormous economic potential and represents one of the key industries in Slovenia. Further and more intense development of the tourism industry is one of the key priorities for Slovenia and is defined in Slovenia's 2014–2020 development strategy [2].

Despite the many abovementioned natural potentials, a strong orientation to the sustainable development of green and eco-tourism services, and even formal recognition of its importance on the national level, the tourism industry in Slovenia is still facing many challenges in attracting more tourists and convincing them to stay longer in the country.

The initial idea to address current challenges in the tourism industry in Gorenjska region came from CentraLab project, which uses the living lab approach and co-design process with end users with the aim of innovatively fostering regional development. The overall goal is to transform Central Europe into a wide-reaching laboratory for innovation and competitiveness, and to establish a new policy framework for innovation and competitiveness. Altogether, 10 partners from eight countries participate in the project. Each partner had to set up a living lab into the most challenging industry in their region. Having this in mind, we have chosen tourism as a priority industry in our region. We have established living lab for addressing the abovementioned challenges with key stakeholders in the region.

The challenges have been discussed with seven essential stakeholders in Gorenjska region. It has been expressed that main challenges and problems are reflected in a weak collaboration and participation of tourist service providers in the development of new innovative services, low responsiveness to changes in tourism demand, and the insufficient entry of small and medium-sized providers and especially small, local providers in the tourism market [3].

With the wide use of Internet and Web 2.0 technologies, the tourism industry has been dramatically transformed. Tourists are able not just to extensively search for information on the web but also share their own experiences on various tourist portals and social networks [4, 5, 6]. User-generated content (from customer reviews, to blogs, comments, posts of trip information on various portals, and social networks) represents an increasingly valuable and reliable source for tourists planning their trips and vacations; significantly, such information is freely available on the web.

Furthermore, tourist service providers are also trying to exploit opportunities of Internet, Web 2.0 technologies and social networks. Mainly, they use the above-mentioned technologies as a marketing channel to reach as many (potential) customers as possible [7]. Feedback information gained from their customers (evaluation of their services and facilities) is another important added value. In addition, many new types of tourism cyber-intermediaries have been created [5, 6] such as Tripadvisor, VirtualTourist, booking.com and many others.

Despite the wide availability of novel technologies, the exploitation of their full potential remains a challenge. Tourist service providers are exploring opportunities of how to use all the information to generate and provide innovative, value added services for different customer segments (family, sport, seniors, etc.).

A tourism living lab has been established with the following stakeholders: two local tourist organizations, a regional tourist organization (also in a role of policy maker), a national park, a tourist farm, a leading regional hotel provider, a regional cultural institute, a university, the Geodetic Institute of Slovenia, and a web-design company.

The goal of the tourism living lab is to foster collaboration between tourist service providers in the region and beyond; a parallel goal is to explore the opportunities of tourists' engagement in the process of the co-creation of new, innovative tourism services. Having in mind the potential benefits of Internet and Web 2.0 technologies, it has been decided to develop a web-based platform that will enable collaboration between tourist service providers, sharing their current offers, and tourists sharing information about experiences from their trips. We intend to investigate the potential impact of tourists on the creation of new, innovative tourism services [8].

In this paper, we present one of the phases of the tourism living lab operations in the Gorenjska region, which was established under the CentraLab project (Central European Living Lab for Territorial Innovation), implemented through the Central Europe Programme, co-financed by the European Regional Development Fund (ERDF). We describe the process and experiences from the user-centered design of the web-based platform for sustainable development of tourism services in a living lab context.

2 Literature Review

Two methodologies have been used to address the abovementioned problems and challenges in the tourism industry in Gorenjska region: a living lab approach to form a network of stakeholders for problem solving (policy makers, tourism industry representatives from the region, university representatives/researchers, Geodetic Institute representatives, web-design company, end-users), and user-centered design for web-based platform development, which will enable collaboration between tourist service providers and tourists.

There are many different definitions of living labs. In a broader sense, a living lab is a technologically socio-economic approach, which is used as a strategy for the development of products, services, innovation, and adaptation [9, 10]. Følstad [11] and Gričar [12] define a living lab as an environment in which researchers, developers and users are working together to develop innovative product, service or solution, in accordance to users' needs, in the shortest time possible, and test it in a real environment.

A living lab approach engages end users in development and innovation processes as co-creators of new products, services or solutions [13]. Such an open ecosystem for research and innovation must use the tools, processes and methodologies that enable end-users to participate, co-create products, services or solutions, and to test the results [14, 15]. This is a customer-focused approach whose goal is to develop innovative products or services that are consistent with the needs of end-users. It is also user-oriented research methodology aimed at refining existing solutions [12, 16, 17].

Living labs can operate for different purposes in different research domains and industries. In the context of IT systems development, Ståhlbröst [18] defines a living lab as a human-centric research and development approach in which IT systems are co-created, tested, and evaluated in the users' own private context [18].

To summarize, living labs provide structure for user participation [19]. Important elements are the multi-methodological research approach and the multi-stakeholder aspect [20]. In addition, living labs can differ from more traditional methods of innovation creation by incorporating the following key elements: user involvement from the very early beginning of development, and experimentation in everyday contexts [20]. In addition, living labs can be defined as user-centric environments for open innovation. The main characteristic of such environments is the early involvement of end-users in the process of creating innovations. Rapid prototyping, in which users drive the innovation process and closely work together with developers and other stakeholders is also an extremely important role of the innovation development cycle [10]. The process of conveying the needs to the developer is a complex, often trial-and-error-like process in which the developer responds with concept models or prototypes to solve the needs until the user is sufficiently satisfied [17].

A prototype is an early sample, model or release of a product or a service built to test a concept or process or to act as a solution to be improved, replicated or learned from. Prototyping or rapid prototyping could result in the technology becoming a means of making not only prototype parts rapidly but also small batches of some production parts (by "production", service production is meant in this context) [21]. Rapid prototyping is a user-centered design approach in which users participate in a rapid, iterative series of tryout and revision cycles during the design of a system, product or a service until an acceptable version is created [22].

"User-centered design" (UCD) has recently become a widely used principle of good practice for the design of interactive systems [23]. Two types of approaches to user-centered design and development can be recognized: product-oriented and process-oriented. The product-oriented approach focuses mainly on the creation of a product. The utilization of the product can be a fixed and well understood idea; meaning that design requirements can be defined in advance. The process-oriented approach requires designers to view their entire process of development in the context of human learning, work, and communication. The main idea is to respond to the changes throughout the entire life cycle of the project [22]. User-centered design can be defined as a design philosophy and approach that places users at the center of the design process, from the stages of planning and designing the system (product, service, solution) requirements to implementing and testing the product.

Another term that is used to define involving of users into design processes is "participatory design", which is defined as a user-centered design approach in which users are actively involved in the design process of a system or product or service or solution that addresses their specific needs [22].

3 User-Centered Design of the Platform in a Living Lab Context

In this chapter, we will introduce user-center design of the web-based platform for sustainable development of tourism services in the living lab context based on a case of the tourism living lab in the Gorenjska region. User-centered design of the platform design has been implemented through the following steps: identification of stakeholders, problem identification and living lab formation, definition of the main user requirements for the platform, user-centered design of the platform, and evaluation of the platform.

3.1 Identification of Stakeholders

The first step was the identification of the key stakeholders in the region: in our case, tourist service providers, policy makers, researchers and developers. After that, the first contacts were made via telephone with an introduction of the project aims and scope, focused to Gorenjska region and to the tourism industry. The main stakeholder in the region is the Bled Regional Tourist Organization, which is also in a position of policy maker. As the Bled Regional Tourist Organization has recognized the potential of collaboration in the project, they also successfully encouraged other industry players to join the initiative.

3.2 Problem Identification and Living Lab Formation

The abovementioned activities resulted in the first workshop, which was organized with seven important stakeholders in the region (one in the position of regional policy maker), and two research and development organizations (R&D): the Faculty of Organizational Sciences, University of Maribor (project partner) and the Geodetic Institute as a provider and developer of innovative solutions based on geographic information systems (invited by project partner). As the living lab project was ensured funding for 36 months of operation, the budget issues were not considered to be limitations for involvement of any partner.

At the first workshop, the project goals were introduced in detail to all participants; the living lab approach and its potential benefits were introduced in detail. Brainstorming about the current status of tourism in Gorenjska region led to the identification of the main challenges and problems of the tourism industry in the region, which are reflected in the weak collaboration and participation of tourist service providers in the development of new innovative services, low responsiveness to changes in tourism demand, and the insufficient entry of small and medium-sized providers and especially small, local providers in the tourism market [3]. All workshop participants agreed that the identified challenges could be better addressed with the collaboration of as many stakeholders as possible. They also recognized the living lab as an appropriate collaborative environment for addressing identified challenges. In addition, they recognized Internet and Web 2.0 technologies as an important tool for setting up the collaboration with tourists as well as with other tourist service providers in the region. After a discussion, all participants agreed to form a living lab. In addition, it was decided that R&D partners Faculty of Organizational Sciences, University of Maribor and Geodetic Institute prepare a presentation of examples of current innovative ICT solutions for tourism and prepare starting points for discussion of possible innovative solution development to address the challenges in Gorenjska region for the next workshop.

Figure 1 is a detailed description of the tourism living lab. It presents stakeholders and their participation intention in the scope of the lab.

3.3 Definition of Solution

The second workshop was intended to present examples of innovative ICT solutions in tourism by R&D partners. The emphasis was on Internet, Web 2.0 and geographic information systems. For that purpose, the R&D partners prepared a web site for presentation of cultural heritage route for famous Slovene poet Dr. France Prešeren. The 8th of February is a Slovene cultural holiday called "Prešeren Day". On that day, numerous cultural events are organized throughout Slovenia. In the municipality of Žirovnica, where the hometown and birth house of Prešeren are located, they organize 8 km long hike along a cultural heritage route consisting of the birth houses of several poets and writers who have lived this region. The website consists of multimedia presentation of all cultural monuments, including photos, movies, 3D animations, and interactive maps. The website also incorporates Web 2.0 functionalities for rating and commenting on the presented contents. Figure 2 presents the website of Prešeren's cultural heritage route.

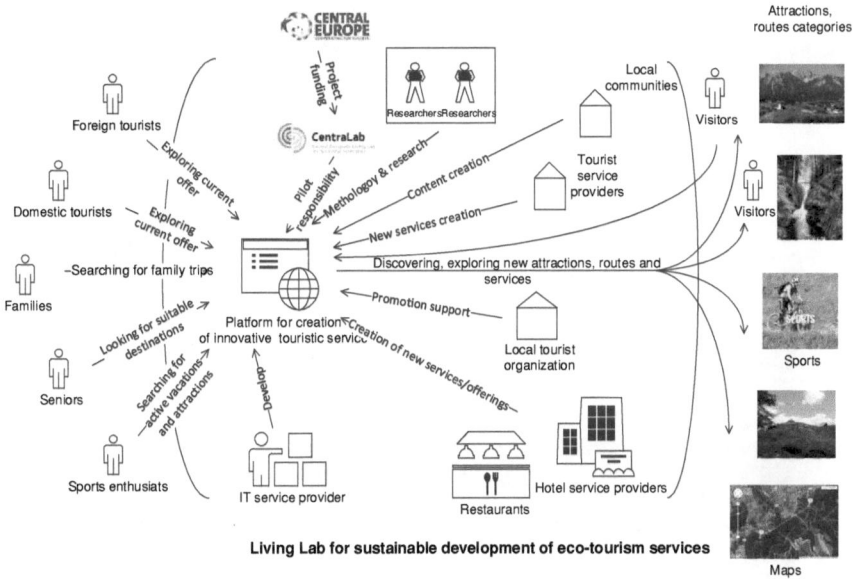

Fig. 1 Living lab for sustainable development of eco-tourism services

The intention of this website was to present the full functionalities of novel ICT solutions to stakeholders.

As the development of such professional materials for website presentation (videos, animations, 3D photographs etc.) incurs high costs, the discussion turned to exploration of the possibilities of gathering information and contents from various existing sources available by tourist providers, as well as the tourists who might have an interest in sharing their content publically, as can already be observed from different existing websites and portals.

The discussion afterwards led to several ideas to foster collaboration with ICT exploitation. As many tourism websites and portals with different business models already exist on the Internet, it was a challenge to find differentiation and innovative elements.

In the end, we came up with an idea to develop a web-based platform that will enable collaboration between tourist service providers and tourists. The main idea was to engage users into a co-design process of new innovative tourism services. The intention of the platform was to enable tourist service providers to present their existing tourism offers and tourists to share their "real-life" experiences of the attractions and routes that they have discovered. The platform will enable the sharing of multimedia content and incorporating Web 2.0 functionalities for commenting, rating and adding additional content. The innovation part differentiating the platform from others available on the market is reflected in the possibilities to re-use existing content (in our case attractions) for the creation of new routes (two or more attractions connected in routes). To our knowledge, the

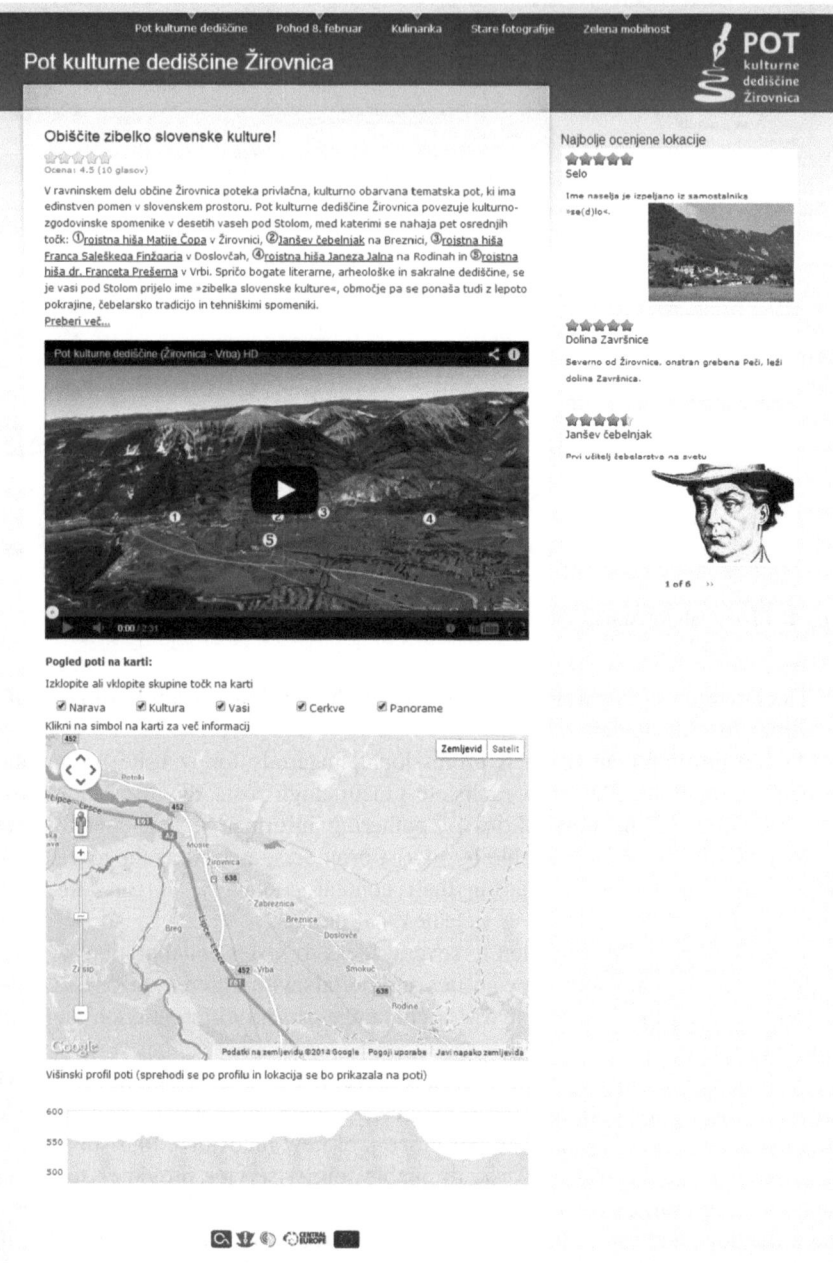

Fig. 2 Prešeren's cultural heritage route website

possibility of content re-use and adding to content existing by tourism service providers and end-users, is new and directly implements the open innovation philosophy. Tourist service providers will obtain insight to what tourists actually want and will have an opportunity to improve and develop new services targeted to different customer segments. The research question that will be addressed later with the wider utilization of the platform on the market is whether user involvement in a co-creation process can lead to the design of new innovative value-added tourism services. Figure 3 presents the innovation functionalities of the platform.

After the idea had been initiated, and main user requirements gathered, the platform's technical and functional specifications had to be designed. This was a task of the R&D partners.

3.4 User-Centered Design the Platform

Based on specifications, the first prototype of the platform was developed by the Geodetic Institute and tested by the University of Maribor, Faculty of Organizational Sciences. There were several iterations of prototype development and its testing based on 70 specification criteria. After all criteria had been successfully fulfilled, the prototype was sufficiently mature to be tested with the real users, i.e. tourist service providers and tourists.

The prototype was tested by all tourism living lab stakeholders (7) and with 52 users in a role of tourists. In our case, they were undergraduate and graduate students. Prototype testing was conducted in several workshops, separately for tourist service providers-stakeholders and tourists. All participants had to prepare in advance photos and descriptions of at least three attractions. At the workshop, they were introduced to the platform and its functionalities for adding the content, e.g. a description of attractions and connecting attractions to the routes.

While working with the platform, some participants were instructed to use the instructions, and others used the platform without consulting the instructions. With that, we wanted to investigate the level of platform simplicity/complexity. After they had finished working with the platform, all the participants were asked to complete a questionnaire, which consisted of 18 questions on the platform ease of use and usefulness, 10 questions about collaboration possibilities and innovation potential of the platform and 7 questions about demographic data. The overall evaluation of questionnaires showed that there were no significant differences between opinions of those users who used instructions and those who did not. Thus, we have concluded that the platform's level of complexity is not too high to prevent regular Internet users to use it. All the questions about ease of use and usefulness were rated higher than 3 on a five-point Likert scale (from 1-strongly disagree to 5-strongly agree). The results suggested that user requirements were successfully implemented through the platform.

With regards to comments, those of the users were mainly related to some unclear steps or a lack of instructions related to the uploading of new content about

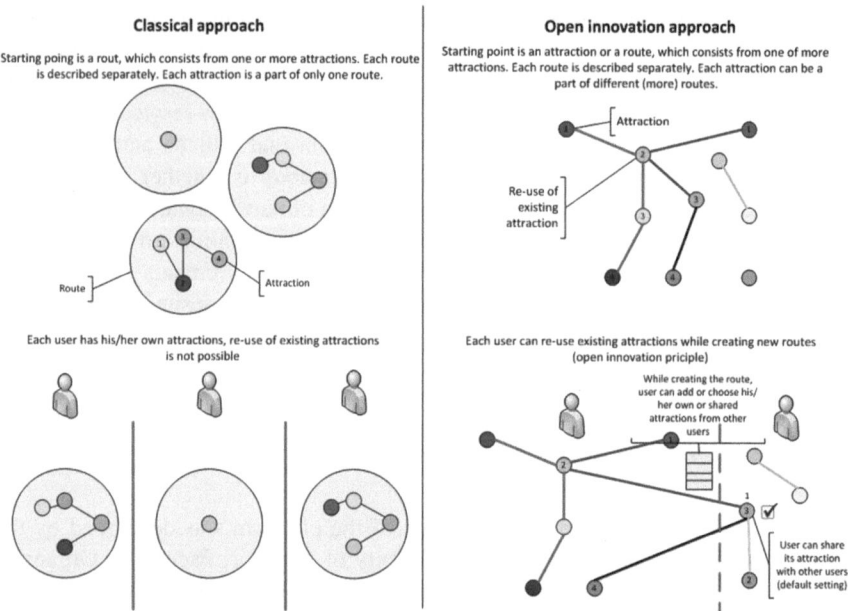

Fig. 3 Innovation functionalities of the platform

attractions, and the connection of existing content in the platform of other users to the new routes. These steps could be simplified and also supported by instructions that would smoothly lead users step by step throughout the whole procedure of uploading and re-using the contents. Furthermore, some errors related to the use of interactive maps integrated in the platform were identified. Users also claimed that the platform would need a modern user interface appearance. This requirement was expected as the aim of the first platform was to test the ease of use and usability of its functionalities. Figure 4 presents the first platform's user interface.

Users' comments were the basis for the development of the new version of the platform.

In this phase, we engaged a professional web design company to develop a second version of the platform, with improved simplicity, functionalities and a modern user interface. Several prototypes were built and tested, first by the R&D partners and later, after the platform satisfied the requirements, by all Tourism Living lab stakeholders (7). Figure 5 presents final user interface of the platform, which was significantly changed and modernized. Moreover, six main categories of attractions and routes were defined and presented in the entering page of the platform: nature, culture, family outings, sports, eco farms, and history. In this phase, a GoGorenjska! logo was designed and the website domain name reserved (http://www.gogorenjska.com).

After the tourism living lab partners had confirmed the new version of the platform, workshops were organized with 55 tourists (undergraduate and graduate

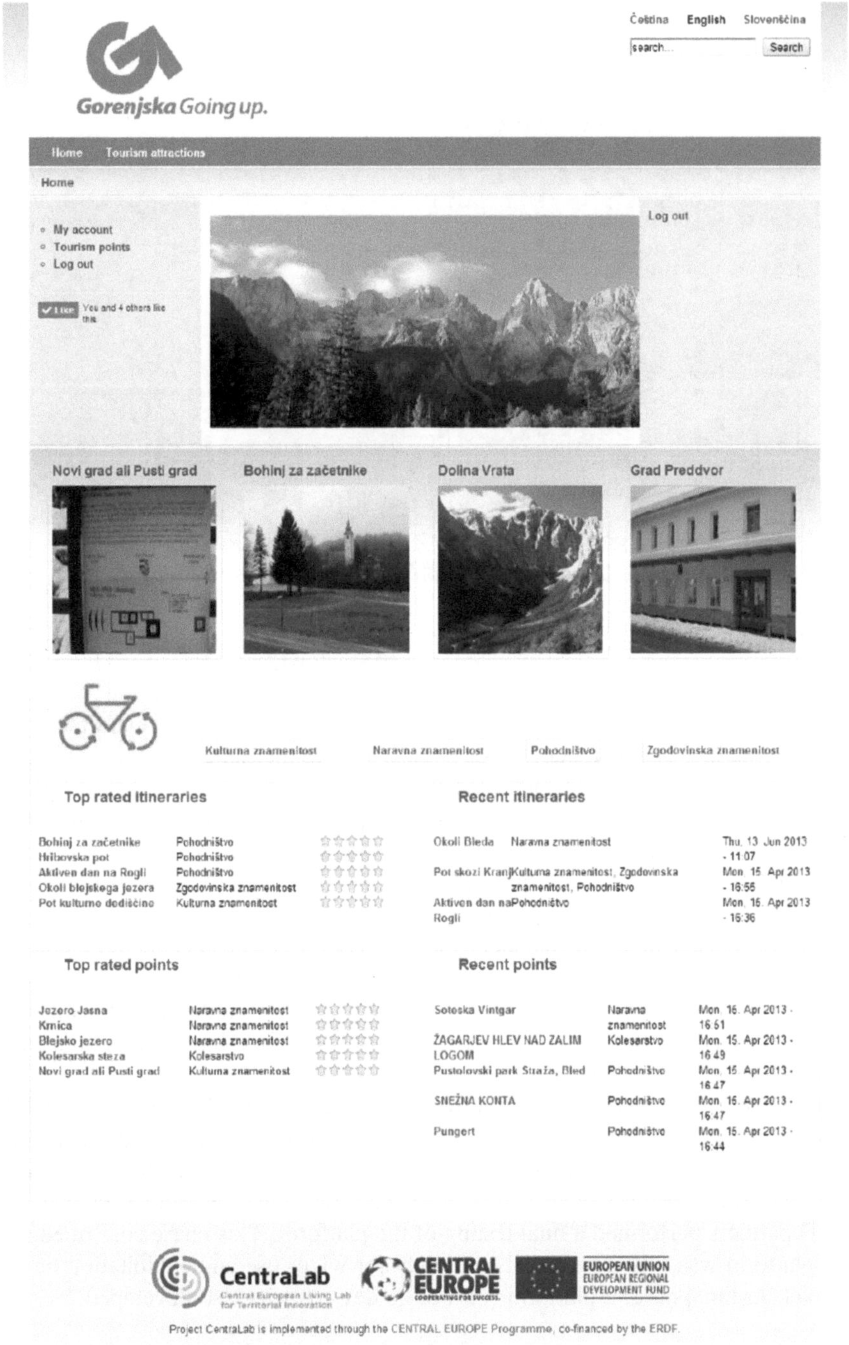

Fig. 4 First platform's user interface

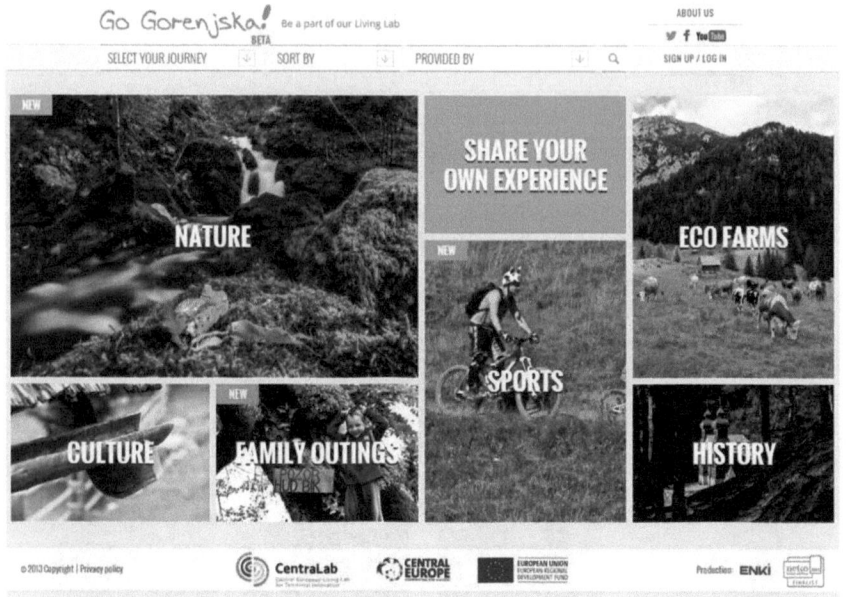

Fig. 5 Final user interface of the platform

students) and five tourist service providers from the region that were not members of the living lab. The methodology of workshops was the same as in the first phase: they were asked to prepare multimedia content for a description of three attractions. At the workshops, they were introduced to the platform and its main functionalities. After they had completed working with the platform, all the participants completed the same questionnaires as prepared and used for the evaluation of the first version of the platform.

Although there were no statistically significant differences between opinions of the users of the first version of the platform and users of the second version of the platform, a deeper investigation of the comments confirmed that functionality has been improved and simplified and that the user interface has been significantly improved.

However, there were still 15 errors identified by workshops' users while working with the platform. These were non-working buttons and fields; the categorizer and search were also not fully functional. The comments were sent to web design company, which incorporated them into the platform. After that, the R&D partners performed a final testing of the platform. This phase confirmed that the platform was fully functional and ready for wider use and exploitation on the market. In this phase, a platform for mobile devices was also developed.

4 Discussion and Conclusions

The aim of this paper was to present the experiences of the user-centered design of the web-based platform for sustainable development of tourism services in the living lab context. We present the case of a tourism living lab, founded in Gorenjska region in the scope of CentraLab project. The main challenges identified in the region were the weak collaboration and participation of tourist service providers in the development of new innovative services, low responsiveness to changes in tourism demand, and the insufficient entry of small and medium-sized providers and especially small, local providers in the tourism market. We addressed these problems and challenges with the formation of a tourism living lab in Gorenjska region. Seven important stakeholders joined the living lab, including two R&D organizations.

The main goal was to explore the potential of Internet and Web 2.0 technologies to foster collaboration between tourist service providers and tourists. The main challenges were to define innovation characteristic of the platform, as many of different websites and portals for tourism already exist on the market and operate with different functionalities and business models.

The R&D partners took responsibility to investigate the most appealing existing solutions and to develop a preliminary idea for the solution. For that purpose, a website for Prešeren's cultural heritage route was developed, which included the rich functionalities of Internet and Web 2.0 technologies. Based on this presentation and further discussion among living lab stakeholders, the idea to develop a web-based platform that will enable collaboration between tourist service providers and tourists on a common platform was initiated. The platform enables the collaboration of tourist service providers that can share their existing offers, and tourists who can share their personal experiences from trips they have made, attractions they have visited. The platform's Web 2.0 functionalities enable the collaboration aspect to all users (commenting, rating, adding the multimedia content, re-using the content, etc.). The innovation characteristic of the platform is in the collaboration aspect of tourist service providers and tourists acting on the same platform, sharing their offers and experiences, commenting, rating, re-using and updating existing contents. With those functionalities, new content is generated in the frame of the open innovation principle. Open innovation is defined as a paradigm that assumes that companies can and should use external ideas in addition to internal ideas, e.g. innovating with partners to explore advances in newest technologies [24, 25].

User-centered design has been used to successfully transfer the defined innovation functionalities into the platform. With that principle, users (living lab stakeholders and then tourists in later stages) were at the center of the design process from the beginning of the platform development. We adapted the approach according to our case and needs.

User requirements were gathered on a workshop with stakeholders and R&D organizations. Both R&D organizations are experts in the field of information technology development, its usage, implementation and exploitation. Furthermore, all stakeholders are advanced users of the Internet and use many of its services in a daily business. The idea was proofed through the first version of the platform that was developed in several prototype iterations and tested first by the R&D partners, and later, when it was fully operational, with stakeholders and then also with potential tourists: in our case, 52 students.

Feedback information from users obtained through the questionnaire presented the basis for the next step of the platform development with improved simplicity, functionalities and contemporary user interface. In this phase, we engaged a professional web development company. Again, several prototypes were developed and tested first with R&D partners. After the platform fulfilled all the requirements, it was tested by stakeholders and later by 55 tourists (students) and with five tourist service providers that were not members of the tourism living lab. During that phase, final comments of the platform were gathered, and a further 15 errors were detected. The report was sent to the web design company, which incorporated them into the final version of the platform. After that, the final testing was done by R&D partners and other stakeholders of the living lab. The results have shown that the platform is fully functional and that it meets all user requirements regarding innovation potential (collaboration of tourist service providers and end-users in content creation, and reuse of content).

With the involvement of the stakeholders and end users in the co-design process from the very beginning, from idea formation to all prototype design phases, we attempted to ensure that platform will fully meet user requirements and exploit the innovation potential of Internet and Web 2.0 technologies on the market. The success of our approach was confirmed by the final version of GoGorenjska portal being nominated as one of the three finalists for the national Netko award in 2013, organized by the Chamber of Commerce of Slovenia, in the category of digital presentation of public services.

The next phase of the tourism living lab will be to release the platform on the market. For this purpose, a business model will have to be defined. Attracting a critical mass of users of the platform is a precondition that would allow us to investigate the possible co-creation value and innovation potential of the platform. More specifically, it is necessary to answer the question of whether tourists, by sharing their own experiences, rating and commenting existing content, adding and re-using the content of tourist service providers, can help create new, innovative tourism services.

References

1. The Official Travel Guide by Slovenian Tourist Board. http://www.slovenia.info/en/Regions/The-Gorenjska-region.htm?_ctg_regije=21&lng=2
2. Republic of Slovenia, Ministry of Economic Development and Technology: Slovenia's Development Strategy 2014–2020. Ministry of Economic Development and Technology, Slovenia (2013)

3. Malešič, A., Pucihar, A., Kljajić Borštnar, M., Lenart, G.: Opportunities for the establishment of cross-border living lab for sustainable development of eco-tourism services. In: Balantič, Z. et al. (eds.) Smart Organization: High Potentials, Lean Organization, Internet of Things. Proceedings of the 32nd International Conference on Organizational Science Development, pp. 565–575. Kranj, Slovenia (2013)
4. Kaewkitipong, L., Rotchankitumnuai, S.: The use of web 2.0 technologies in tourism industry: a conceptual model. In: CONF-IRM 2012 Proceedings, Paper 76. http://aisel.aisnet.org/confirm2012/76 (2012)
5. Sigala, M.: WEB 2.0 in the tourism industry: a new tourism generation and new e-business models. Eco Club **90**, 5–8 (2007)
6. Sigala, M., Christou, E., Gretzel, U.: Social media in travel, tourism and hospitality: theory, practice and cases. J. Tourism Hist. **5**, 99–101 (2013)
7. Noti, E.: Web 2.0 and the its influence in the tourism sector. Eur. Sci. J. **9**(20), 115–123 (2013)
8. Pucihar, A., Lenart, G., Malešič, A., Kljajić Borštnar, M.: Web based solution to co-create innovative eco-tourism services. In: Gornik, T. (ed.) Twenty years later: Proceedings of 20th Conference on Days of Slovenian Informatics, Portorož, 15–17 April 2013. Slovenian Society of Information Technology, Ljubljana (2013)
9. Liedtke, C., Welfens, Maria J., Rohn, H., Nordmann, J.: Living lab: user-driven innovation for sustainability. Int. J. Sustain. High. Educ. **13**(2), 106–118. Emerald Group Publishing Limited, Bingley (2012)
10. Schaffers, H., Budweg, S., Ruland, R., Kristensen, K.: Collaborative environments to support professional communities: a living lab approach. In: Camarinha-Matos, L.M. et al. (eds.) PRO-VE 2009, IFIP AICT, vol. 307, pp. 635–642. Springer, Heidelberg (2009)
11. Følstad, A.: Living labs for innovation and development of information and communication technology: a literature review. Electron. J. Virtual Organ. Netw. **10** (Special Issue on Living Labs), 99–131 (2008)
12. Gričar, J.: The Use of e-Technology to Develop Cross-Border e-Regions, pp. 233–239. Development Challenges in Slovenia, Slovenia (2009)
13. CoreLabs. Building Sustainable Competitiveness—Living Labs Roadmap 2007–2010. Recommendations on networked system for open user-driven research, development and innovation (2007)
14. Chen, T.-Y.: Formulate Service Innovation in Accordance with a Living-Lab Based Service Engineering Architecture. University of Miaoli, Taiwan (2011)
15. van der Walt, S., Buitendag, A.K., Zaaiman, J., Vuuren, J.: Community living lab as a collaborative innovation environment. Issues Inf. Sci. Inf. Technol. ZDA **6**, 421–425 (2009)
16. Bergvall-Kåreborn, B., Holst, M., Ståhlbröst, A.: Concept design with a living lab approach. IEEE (2009)
17. Eriksson, M., Niitamo, V.P., Kulkki, S.: State-of-the-art in utilizing living labs approach to user-centric ICT innovation—a European approach. CDT at Luleå University of Technology, Sweden, Nokia Oy, Centre for Knowledge and Innovation Research at Helsinki School of Economics, Finland (2005)
18. Ståhlbröst, A.: Forming Future IT—The Living Lab Way of User Involvement, pp. 30–40. Luleå University of Technology, Luleå (2008)
19. Almirall, E., Wareham, J.: Living labs and open innovation: roles and applicability. Electron. J. Virtual Organ. Netw. **10**, 21–46 (2008)
20. Schuurman, D., Lievens, B., De Marez, L., Ballon, P.: Innovation from user experience in living labs: revisiting the 'innovation factory'-concept with a panel-based and user-centered approach. The International Society for Professional Innovation Management (ISPIM), United Kingdom (2012)
21. Kochan, A.: Rapid Prototyping Gains Speed, Volume and Precision. Emerald Group Publishing Limited, Bingley (2000)
22. Baek, E.O., Cagiltay, K., Boling, E., Frick, T.: User-centered design and development. In: Spector, M.J. et al. (eds.) Handbook of Research on Educational Communications and

Technology: A Project of the Association for Educational Communications and Technology, pp. 659–670. State University San Bernardino, California (2007)

23. Thimbleby, H.: Understanding user centred design (UCD) for people with special needs. In: Computers Helping People with Special Needs. Lecture Notes in Computer Science, vol. 5105, pp. 1–17 (2008)

24. Chesbrough, H.W.: Open Innovation: The New Imperative for Creating and Profiting from Technology. Harvard Business School Press, Boston (2003)

25. Chesbrough, H.W.: The era of open innovation. MIT Sloan Manage. Rev. **44**(3), 35–41 (2003)